Historic
Canada

SAINT JOHN WEST AND ITS NEIGHBOURS

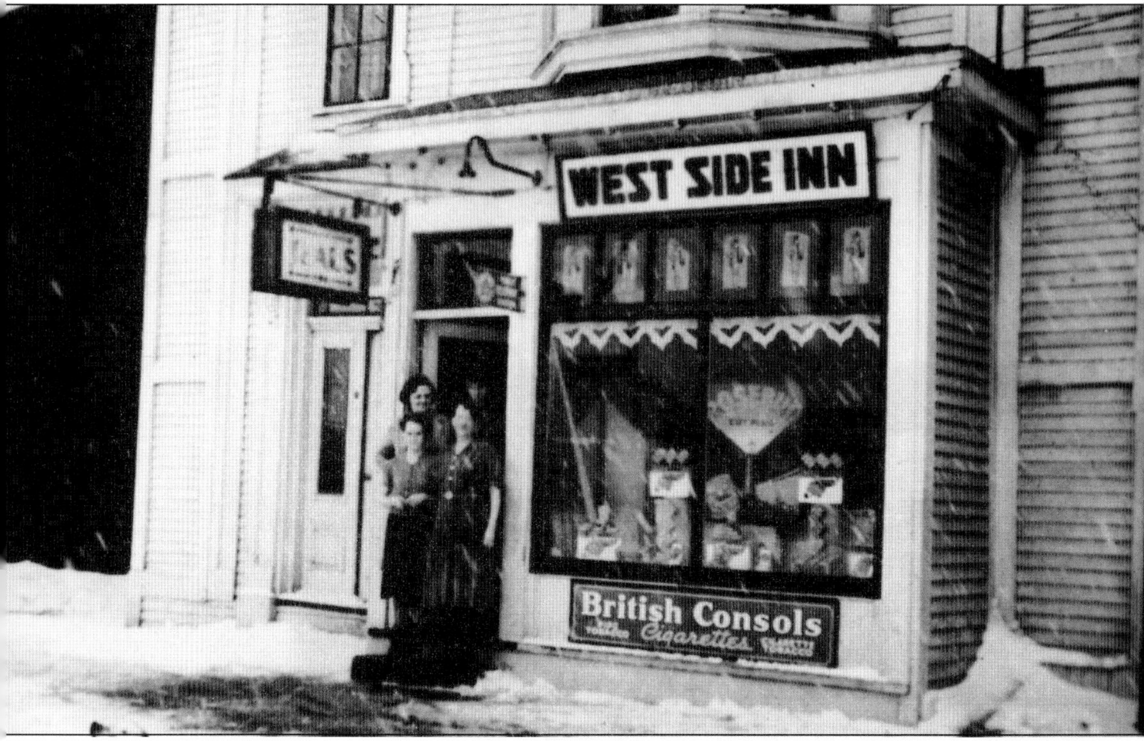

This inn was located on lower King Street in Saint John West and provided room and board and lunches to residents of what was then known as Carleton.

Historic
Canada

SAINT JOHN WEST AND ITS NEIGHBOURS

David Goss and Fred Miller

ARCADIA
PUBLISHING

ISBN 978-0-7385-7269-7

Published by Arcadia Publishing
Charleston SC, Chicago IL, Portsmouth NH, San Francisco CA

Printed in the United States of America

Library of Congress control number: 2009936603

For all general information contact Arcadia Publishing at:
Telephone 843-853-2070
Fax 843-853-0044
E-mail sales@arcadiapublishing.com
For customer service and orders:
Toll-Free 1-888-313-2665

Visit us on the Internet at www.arcadiapublishing.com

Contents

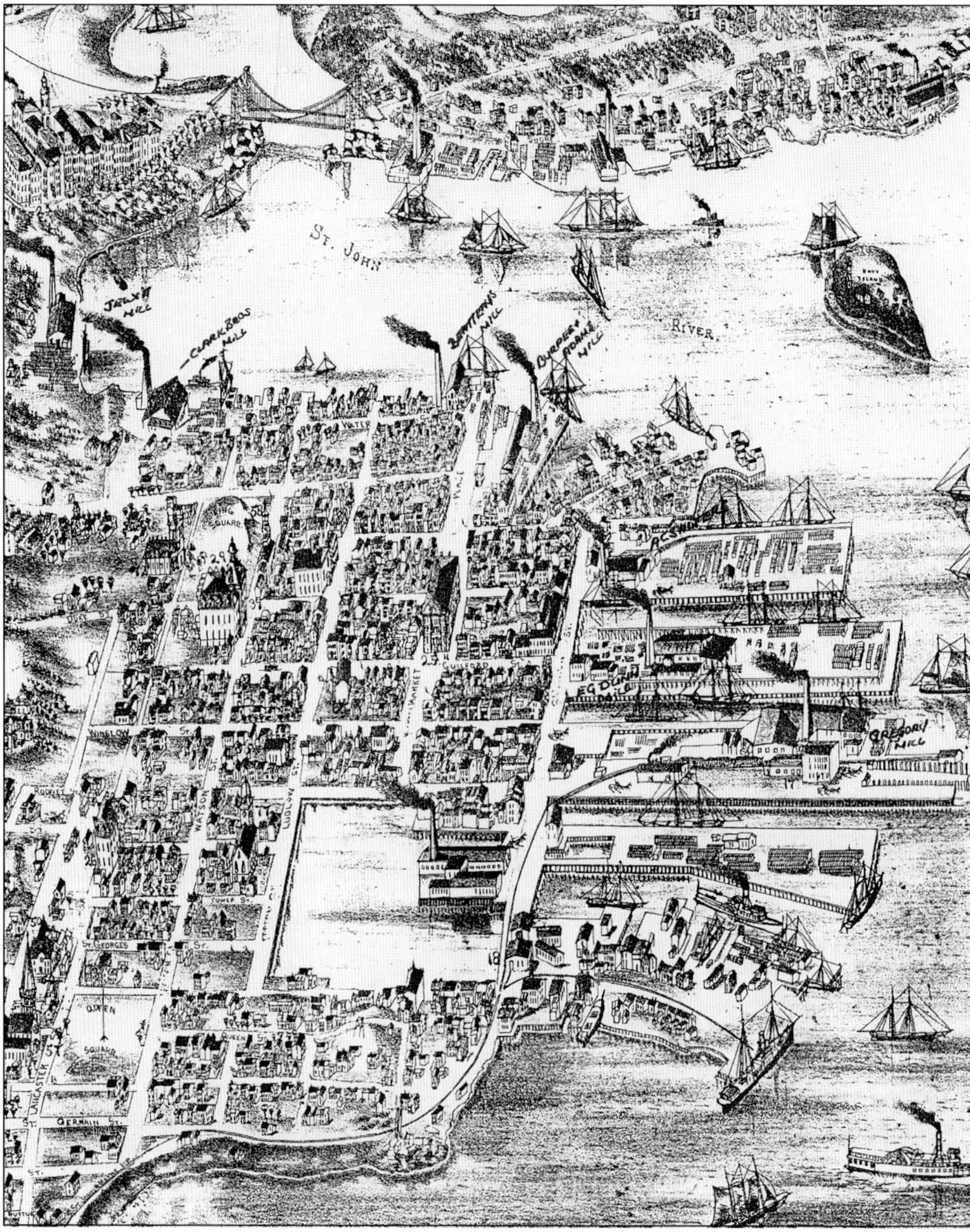

In 1882 Saint John was one of many cities that had an illustrated map made. Advertisers were given space to show their properties in great detail around the border of the maps, but in addition, as every home and business was shown on every street, these sketch maps provide us with birds-eye views of towns and cities. In this instance, only what was then known as Carleton, later as West Saint John, and now as Saint John West, has been excerpted from the larger map that shows the whole of Saint John.

Introduction

The Indians were the first to settle in the area that was to become modern-day Saint John West and that is shown in its later history in this book. These early inhabitants lived on the island in the middle of what was then about a mile of waterway between land that was to become Saint John West and land that would later see the development of the central city. Their name for the area was "Managuashe," which means "Hills and Angry Waters." Of course, this referred to the hills of Carleton—known now as Courtenay Hill and Tower Hill—and, on the opposite side the harbour, what became known as Fort Howe. The angry waters of "Managuashe" were the Reversing Falls, created by the 26-foot tides battling with the power of the 450-mile river that took the Indians inland to their hunting grounds.

It is believed that the first white man to come to the area was Estavan Gomez, who in 1535 identified a river on the coast of North America as Rio de la Buelta, or "River of the Return." This reference leads historians to suspect that what he found was what we now call the Reversing Falls. From then on there were regular visits from Europeans, so Champlain's arrival on Saint John the Baptist Day in 1604 was probably no surprise to the natives. It was this visit that eventually gave the river and the city the name Saint John, though a variation of the original name of the area, "Managuashe," still lives on today in Saint John West as a street name . . . Manawagonish.

Upon its founding in 1783 by settlers driven out of America as a result of the Revolution, Saint John was immediately sectioned into four distinct areas due to the terrain the new settlers found themselves upon. Indeed, one of those settlers from New York, Sarah Frost, wrote in her diary on June 29, 1783: "It is, I think, the roughest land I ever saw . . . but this is to be the city."

And indeed it was to be. With great energy the ten thousand who arrived in that first year set to work creating what became, for a time, the pre-eminent city of eastern Canada, a city that was later compared favourably with Boston and New York.

In 1783, young Sarah Frost saw only swamps and trees, but it did not take long for the landscape to change. The settlers built in Upper Cove, Lower Cove, across the great marsh to the north in Portland, and across the harbour in Conway (which was later known as Carleton (until 1889), and later still as Saint John West). Each of these areas developed as the land dictated, and though technically a part of Saint John, they remained fiercely independent in their views and in the ways they lived and did business.

Being separated from the others by the half-mile span of the tidal harbour, it was only natural that Carleton (which took its name from Sir Guy Carleton, the commander-in-chief of the British forces in North America) would be the most independent of the lot. Technically, Carleton was a combination of the half dozen blocks of Brooks and Guys wards from Sand Point on edge of the harbour to the city line, the parish of Lancaster, and a swath of wilderness, devoid of human activity save for the 1813 Martello Tower perched high on a promontory overlooking the community, built there to guard against any further problem with the country they had left. Over the years the names Carleton, West Saint John, and Saint John West have been used interchangeably, and they will be used in a sense contemporary with that of the photograph or era under discussion throughout this book.

Those who chose to live in what was then known as Carleton found that they could make a living fishing, farming, quarrying, cutting lumber, and building ships. Gradually, they developed wharves in the harbour area, and began servicing ships from around the world that were bringing goods and immigrants to the newly-developing nation. Work was hard, but there was plenty of it, and the community prospered. Churches, schools, and mercantile concerns were built, and as times changed, so did the mix of businesses, with diversification in the form of foundries and factories that grew up to service the steamships and railways that became the main focus of life for most of the workers in the area.

This collection of photographs shows how Saint John West developed, saw its business and residential areas gutted, and grew again, only to suffer through a disastrous fire where most of its men worked. Since World War II national policy has favoured Central Canada, so after achieving a great deal of success the Saint John West area once again went into decline, and today just a few of the industries and only a handful of the jobs so plentiful in its heyday survive.

For the past twenty years, Fred Miller has been collecting photographs from the people who lived through these changes—through the good times and the bad. He has also collected their stories, and the stories they were told by their parents so, in word and picture, we can see back to the earliest days of Carleton. The 204 photographs in this book constitute about half of the collection Mr. Miller has in his possession. Right to the day the manuscript was due to be mailed, folks proud of their connection to Saint John West were still bringing photographs in. You'll see their names under the photographs, and they are the true authors of this book. Fred and I are grateful to each of them.

Fred Miller
David Goss
May 21, 1995

Acknowledgements

We have identified all photographs of which we know the origin in the caption under each photograph and thank those who loaned or gave pictures, or who gave permission for use of pictures in their collection.

We are especially grateful to: Jamie Wilson of Wilson Studio on Prince William Street for the use of copyrighted material from the Erb Collection; to Harold Wright, for use of material that he has procured for various historical projects and publications that he has been involved in over the years; and Mr. Rob Roy of Rob Roy Productions, who was able to make many a faded or cracked photograph useable and who has carefully copied most of the photographs in this collection. We also acknowledge the public agencies once again, especially the cooperation received from: the National Harbours Board; the Province of New Brunswick Provincial Archives; the New Brunswick Museum; and the Saint John Regional Library (particularly for help with the text). The government of Canada is also to be thanked as through the Local Initiative programs and the student summer work project it has funded a number of summer programs that have resulted in photographs and material for Miller's Collection.

If we have missed someone, we are sorry, and will certainly try to correct this oversight. Neither of us are professional historians and putting this book together has been a new experience for both of us, so we hope you enjoy the end result enough to forgive us our trespasses where they occur.

One

Carleton: The Early Days

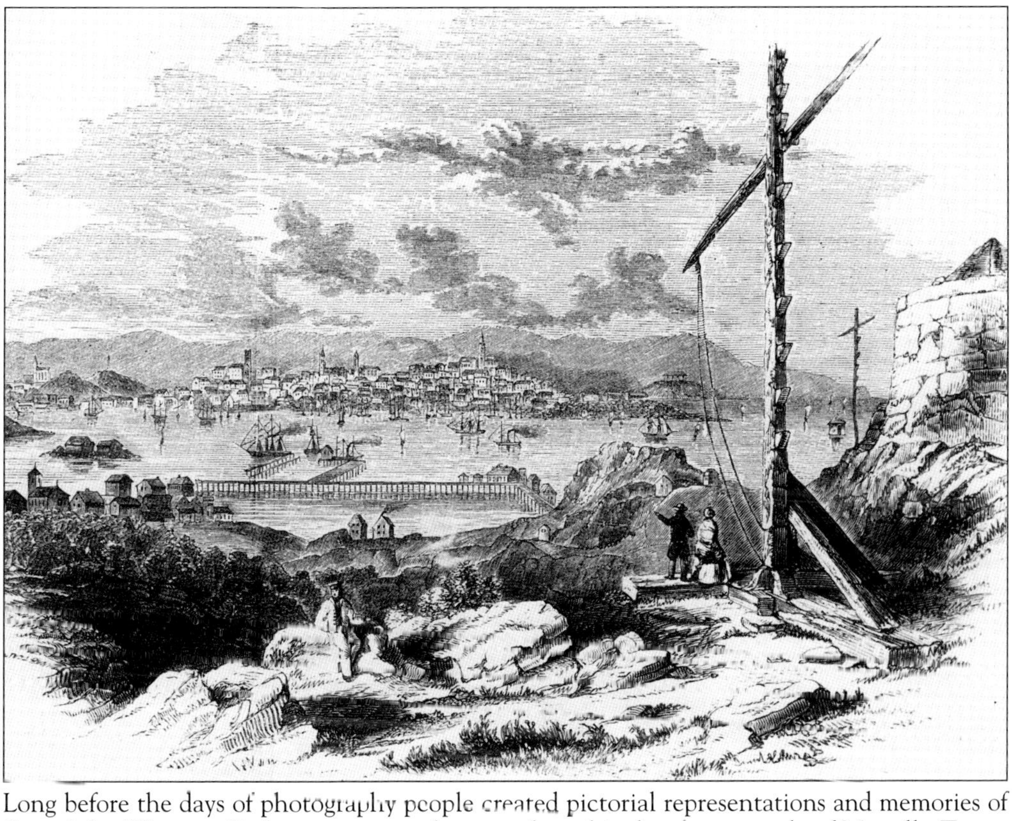

Long before the days of photography people created pictorial representations and memories of Saint John West, or Carleton, as it was known when this sketch was made of Martello Tower under construction. The tower was built between 1813 and 1815 as a defense against American invasion and it overlooked the mouth of the harbour, which is seen in the middle of the picture. Also shown are the millpond and Sand Point wharf on the nearest shore, and Navy Island off to the left in the middle of the channel. On the far horizon can be seen the city of Saint John, which at that time was growing rapidly. (New Brunswick Museum.)

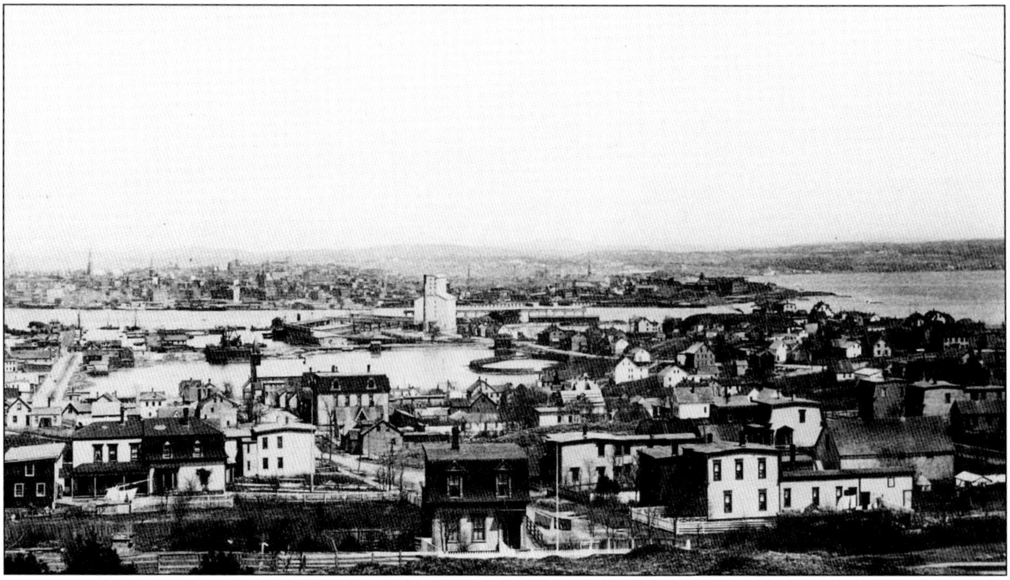

This 1880s photograph, taken from Martello Tower and overlooking the lower part of Saint John West, enables us to see the changes that have taken place since the sketch on the previous page, which was made in the early part of the century. The millpond, which flooded due to the 26-foot tides in the harbour, can be seen in the middle of the picture. Many of the houses that are shown in this early photograph still stand today. (New Brunswick Museum.)

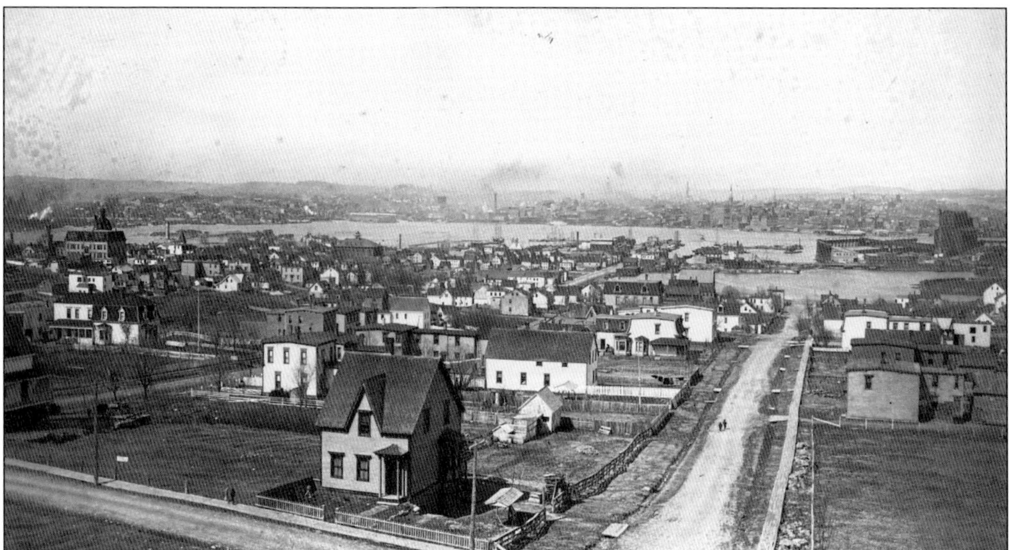

This 1905 photograph shows the dome of the Old Albert School at left, Navy Island in the channel, and the old wooden wharves on the river. Martello Road leads from Martello Hill to the millpond. On the edge of the pond is the circular skating rink that was run by Hilton Belyea. (Provincial Archives and Erb Collection.)

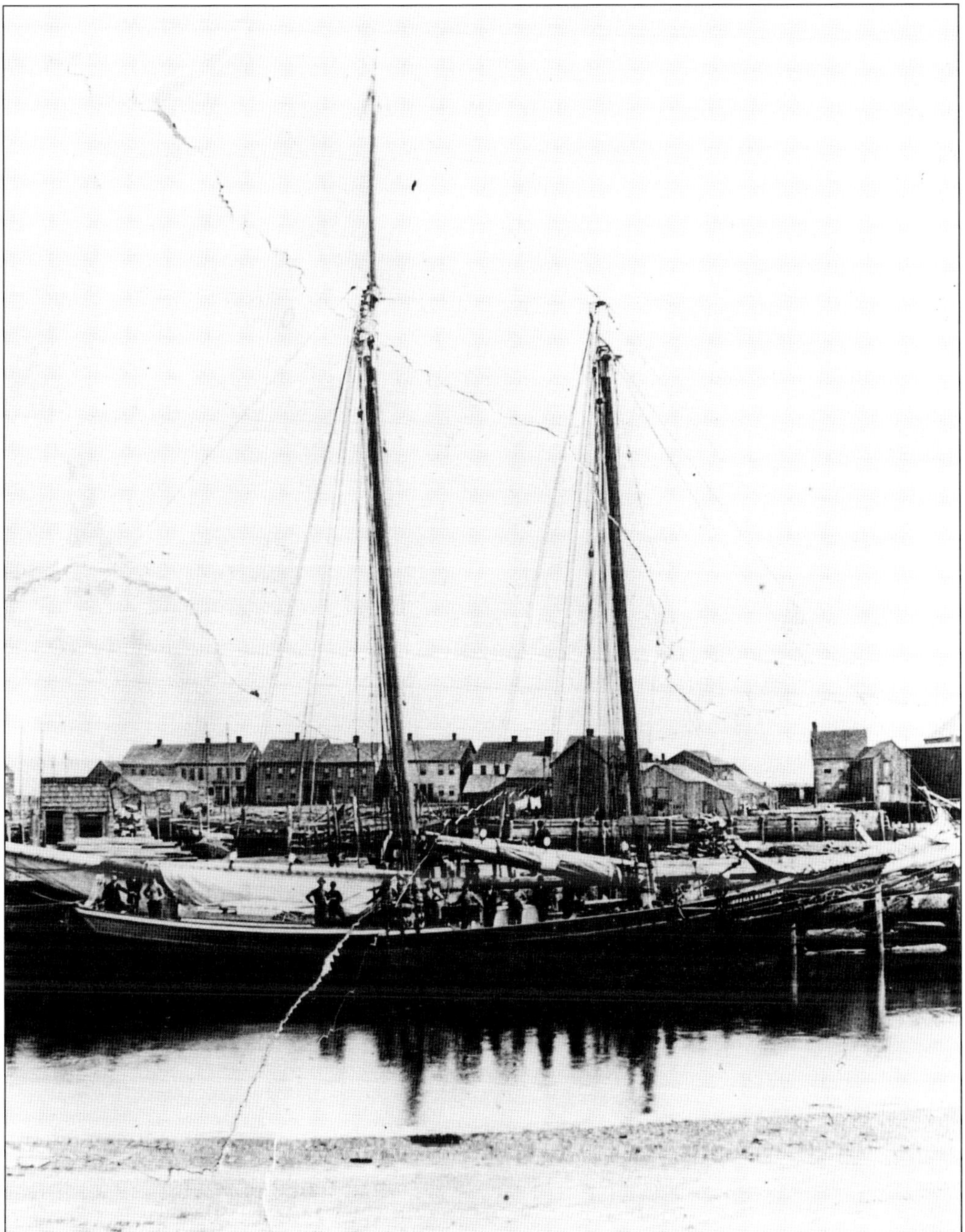

A wooden vessel is tied up at the dock on Protection Street in this 1870 photograph. Saint John West's well-known shipbuilders included the Olive family at Market Place and Old Fort, McLaughlin and Stackhouse at Blue Rock, and the Wellington Brothers at Sand Point, to name just three. Hundreds of men were employed and hundreds of ships built between 1783 and the decline of the shipbuilding industry in the early 1900s. (Provincial Archives.)

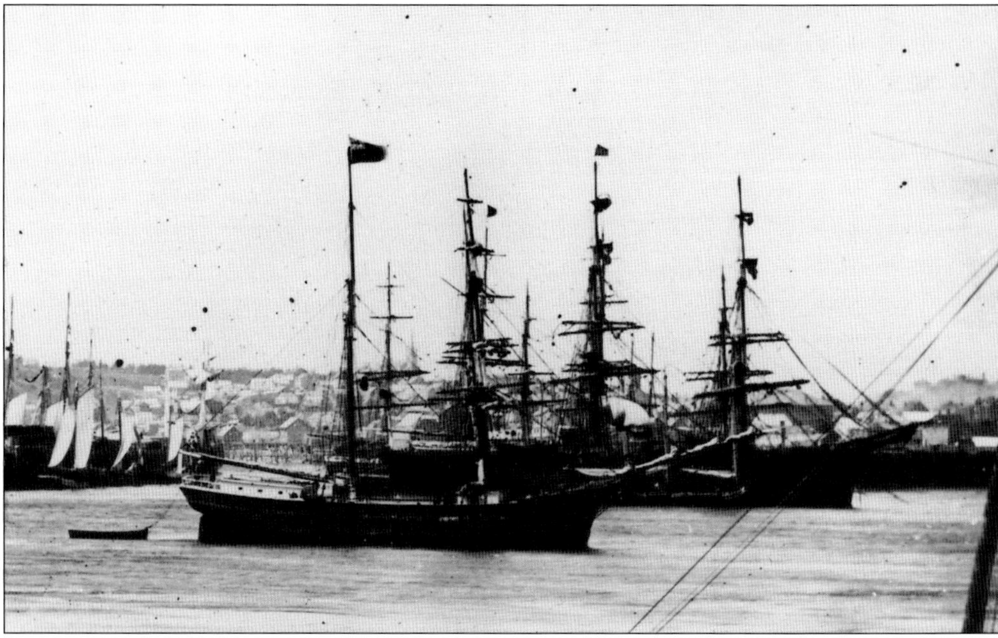

These tall ships are anchored opposite Sand Point awaiting a berth. It is highly likely that some of these ships were built in Saint John, as so many were built here that it was once said it was as easy to buy a ship as to buy a suit in the city. (Provincial Archives.)

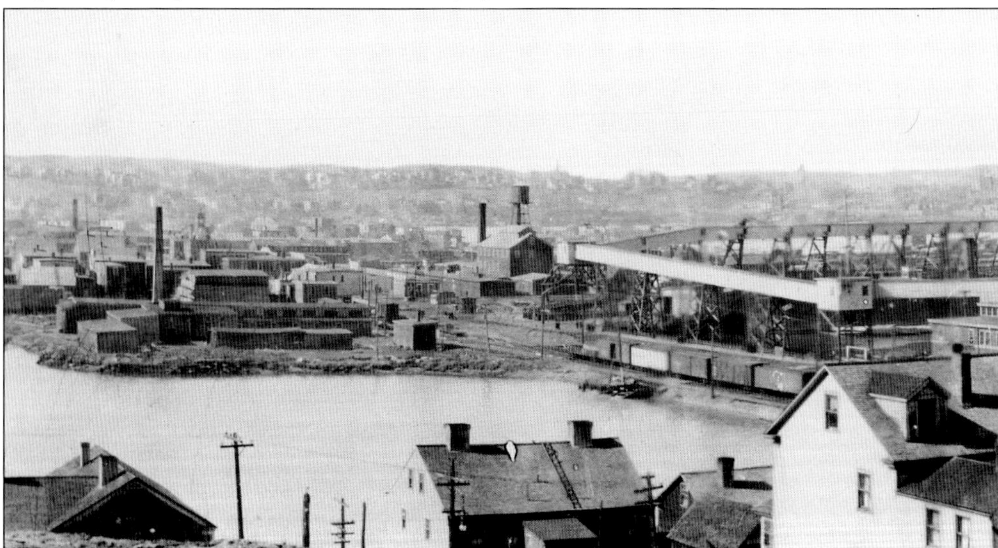

The tidal millpond, around which the first settlers in Saint John West built their homes and around which the first industries and the railway congregated, was gradually filled in as a result of this multiple use and by the turn of the century it finally came to be regarded as little more than a convenient dumping area. Despite the fact that it once boasted a fine oval skating rink on its south shore and was once used as one of the earliest salmon hatcheries, by the late 1920s it became obvious that the millpond was the best place to dump the material scooped from the harbour. When the pond was filled in it became the site of single family housing for soldiers and sailors returning from World War II. (National Harbours Board.)

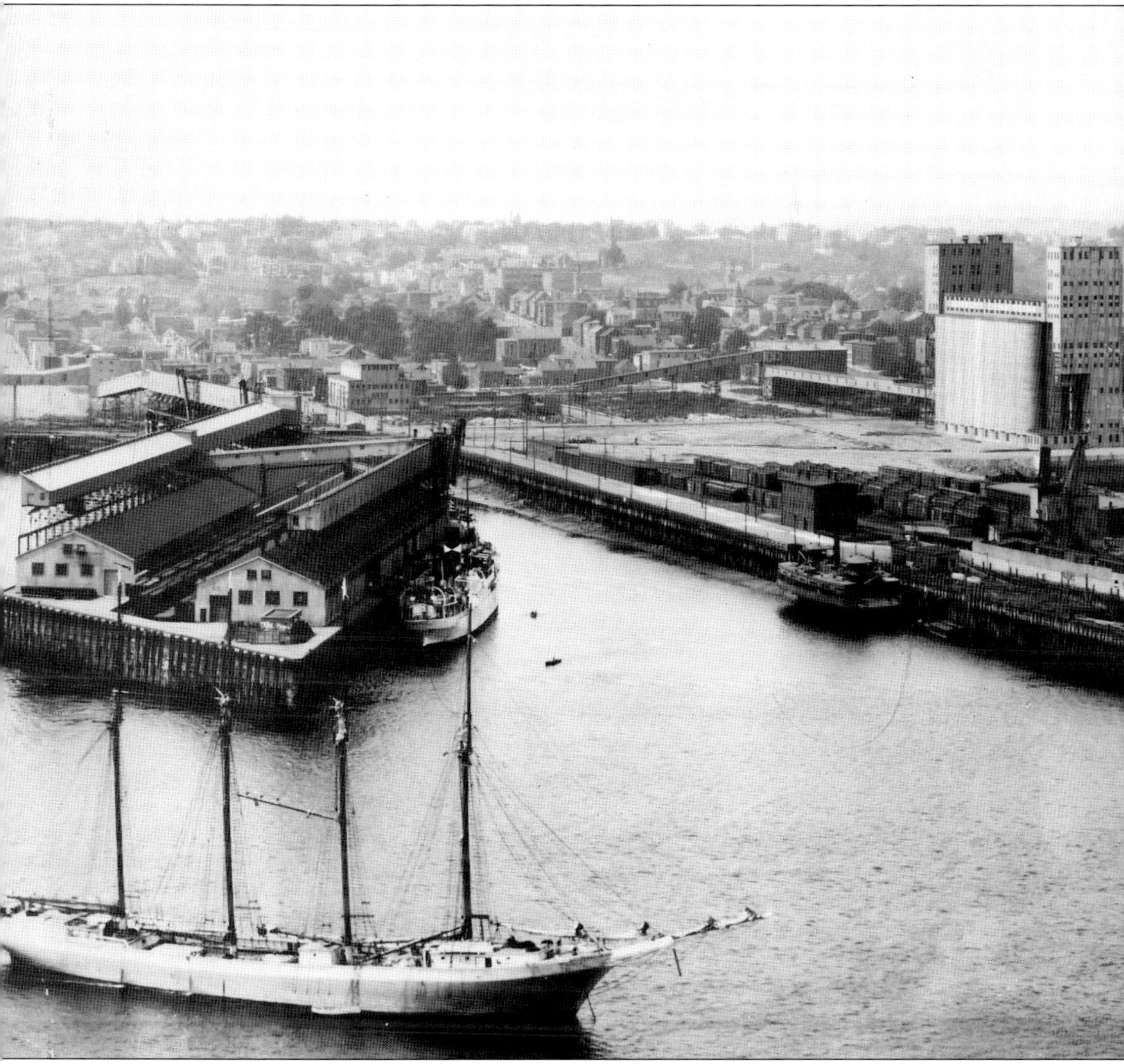

A wooden vessel approaches Rodney Wharf where the ferry that provided service from Carleton to the city centre docked. It's hard to believe it, but this area was used as a bathing beach by the first settlers.

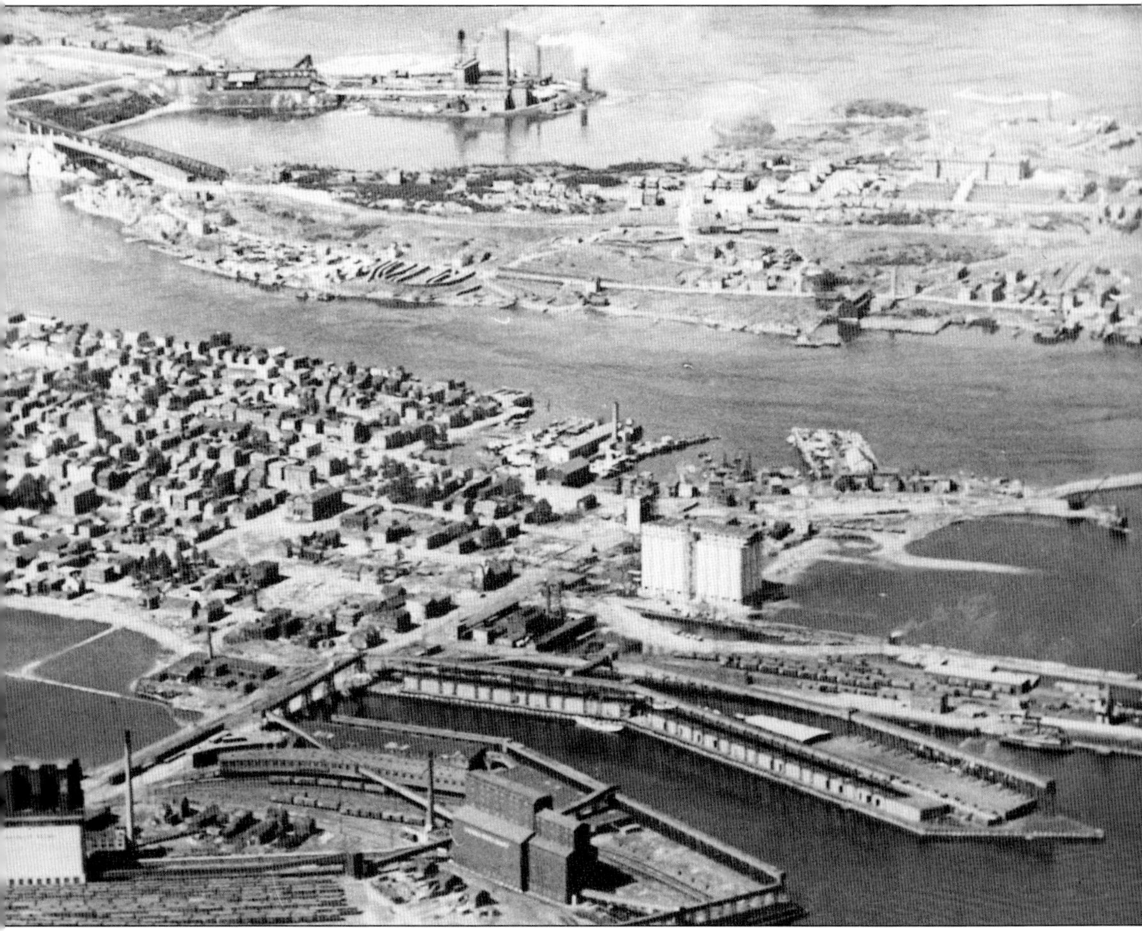

After Saint John was chosen as Canada's winter port in the mid-1890s it became obvious that more berths for modern ships were needed to meet the needs of industrial and commercial shippers. Here a cofferdam (a watertight structure designed to keep water from flowing into the area where construction is taking place) is being built across the channel to divert the river flow so that new wharves can be built. (National Harbours Board.)

Two

Harbour Development

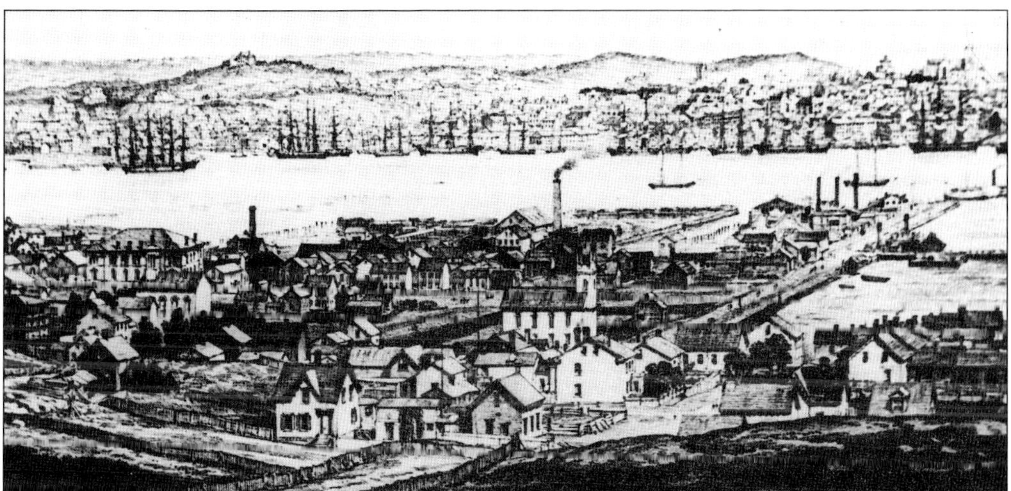

This is a sketch of Saint John West as it would have appeared in the days of wooden ships and iron men when many of the ships built along the coast were rigged out in the harbour before departing for Britain loaded with huge deals cut from the New Brunswick forests. (New Brunswick Museum.)

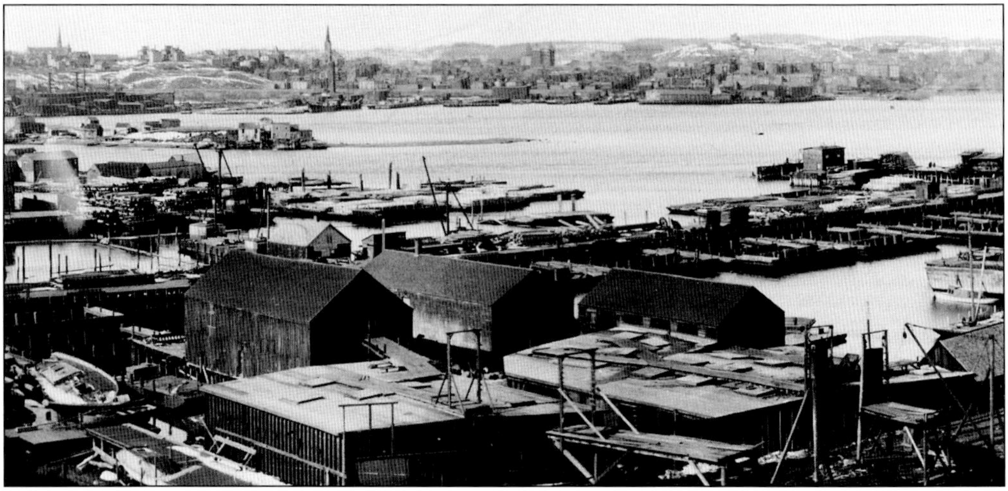

This *c.* 1900 photograph of the lower Carleton area shows Navy Island in the middle of the channel between Saint John West and Saint John North. All of the wharves were built of wood at that time. (National Harbours Board.)

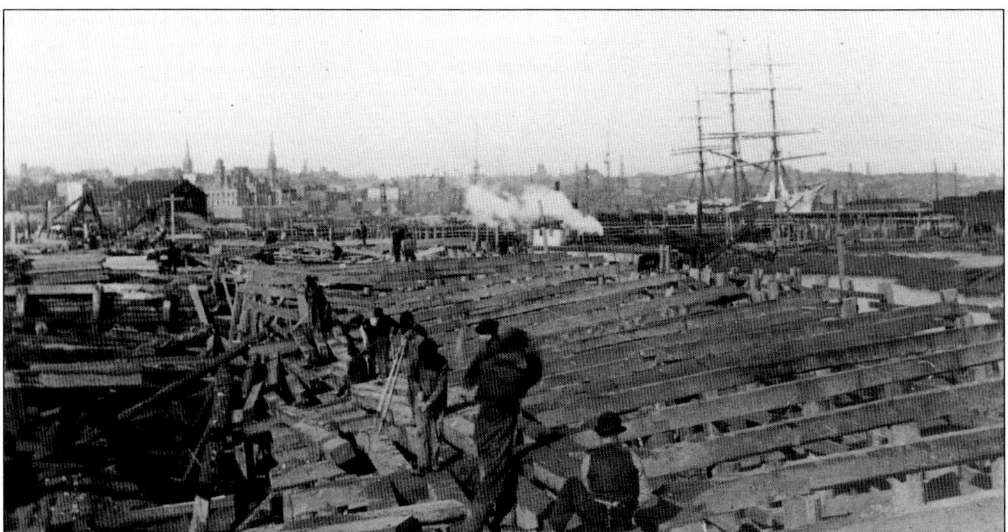

Construction of the West Side docks in 1898, just after Saint John had been designated as the winter port for Canada. It soon became apparent that the docks had to be in better shape than in previous times to handle inland-bound cargo efficiently. (National Harbours Board.)

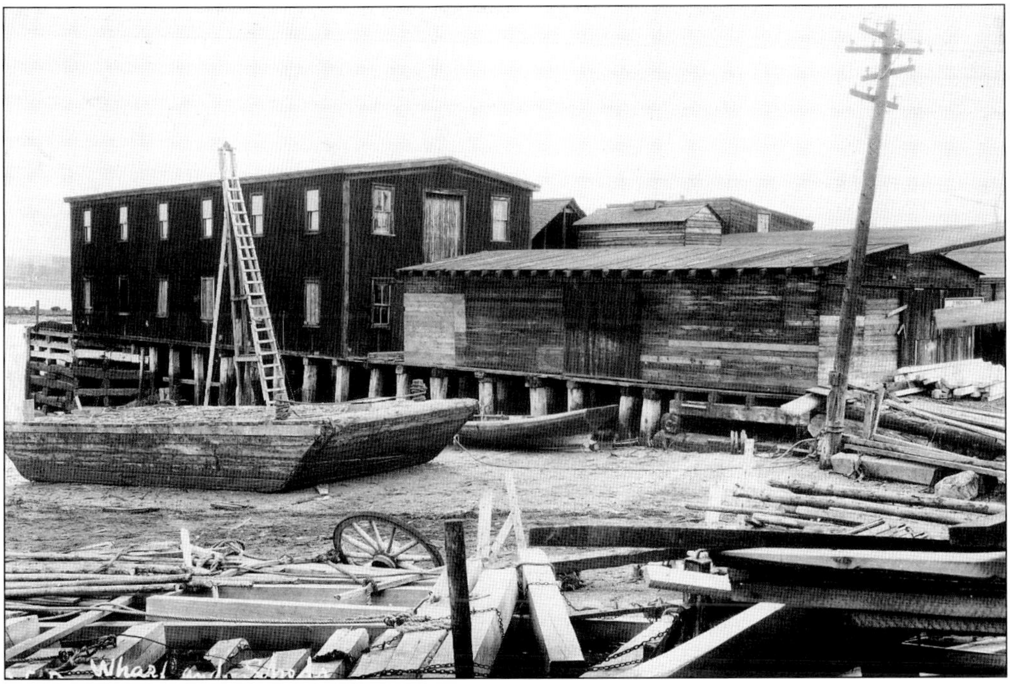

Although this photograph was taken in 1928, it shows the typical wooden slips that were quite adequate for local trade until the mid-nineteenth century. However, as steel ships became the norm, structures such as J. Fred Belyea's Wharf and Smokehouse would no longer do the job, and new construction was vital if the facilities at the docks and yards were to keep up with twentieth-century change. (National Harbours Board.)

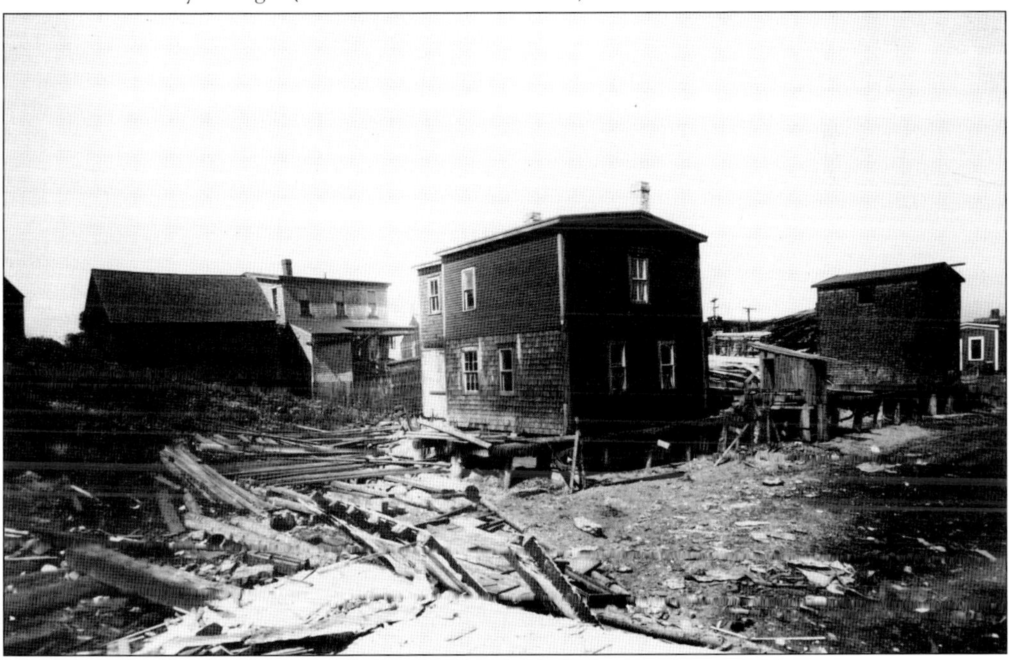

This is another example of the type of wharf and shed that served adequately for local trade but proved inadequate for international freight and grain shipments. (National Harbours Board.)

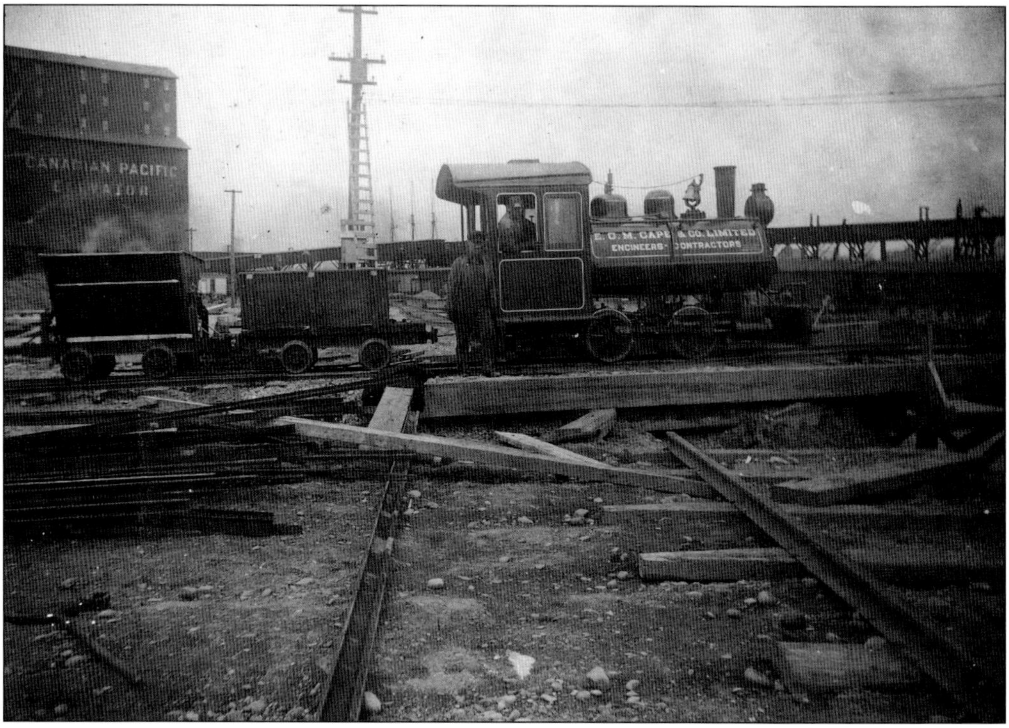

This "donkey car" or small steam engine was used to haul gravel from the cofferdam area to the millpond behind the new piers in order to fill the pond in to make a level backup cargo area. (Don Galbraith Collection.)

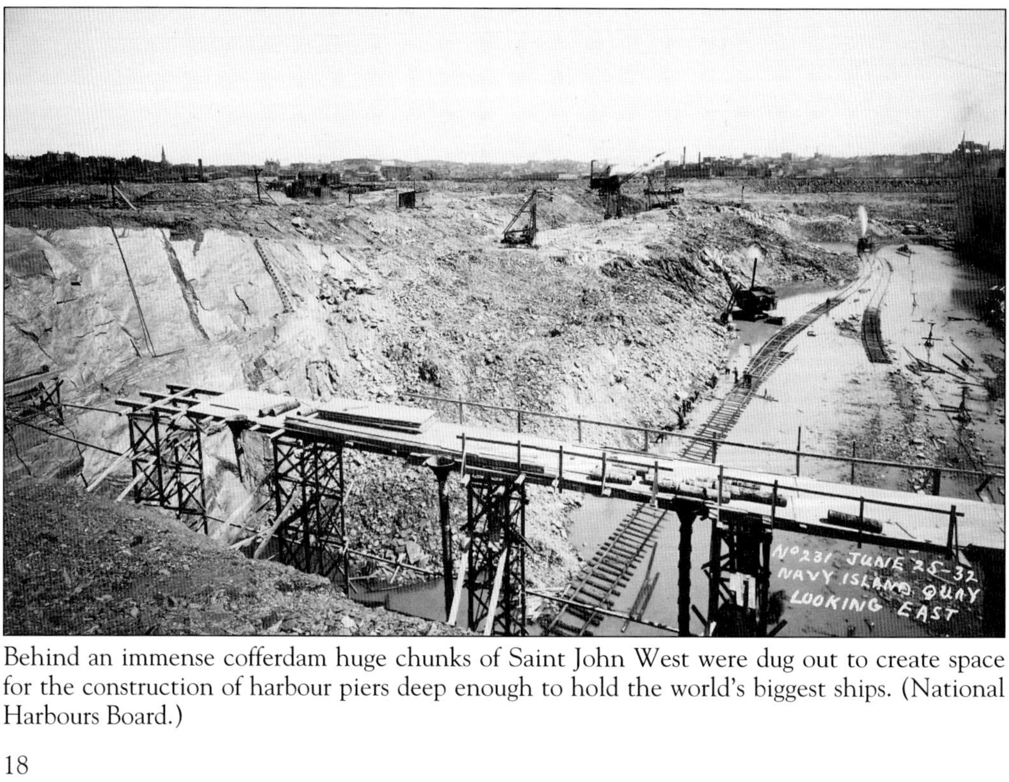

Behind an immense cofferdam huge chunks of Saint John West were dug out to create space for the construction of harbour piers deep enough to hold the world's biggest ships. (National Harbours Board.)

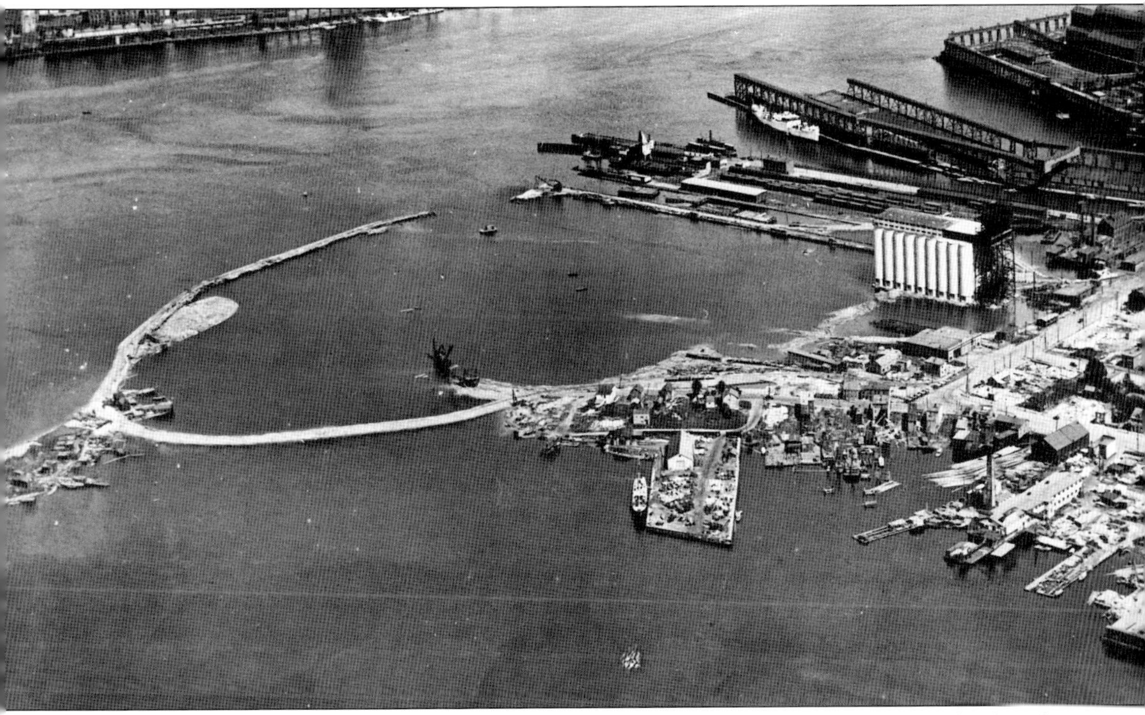

Looking east at the cofferdam which was built out from Saint John West to Navy Island and then swung south across the harbour as the first step in making a protected and dry working area to build new piers. This process took seven years between 1927 and 1934. (National Harbours Board.)

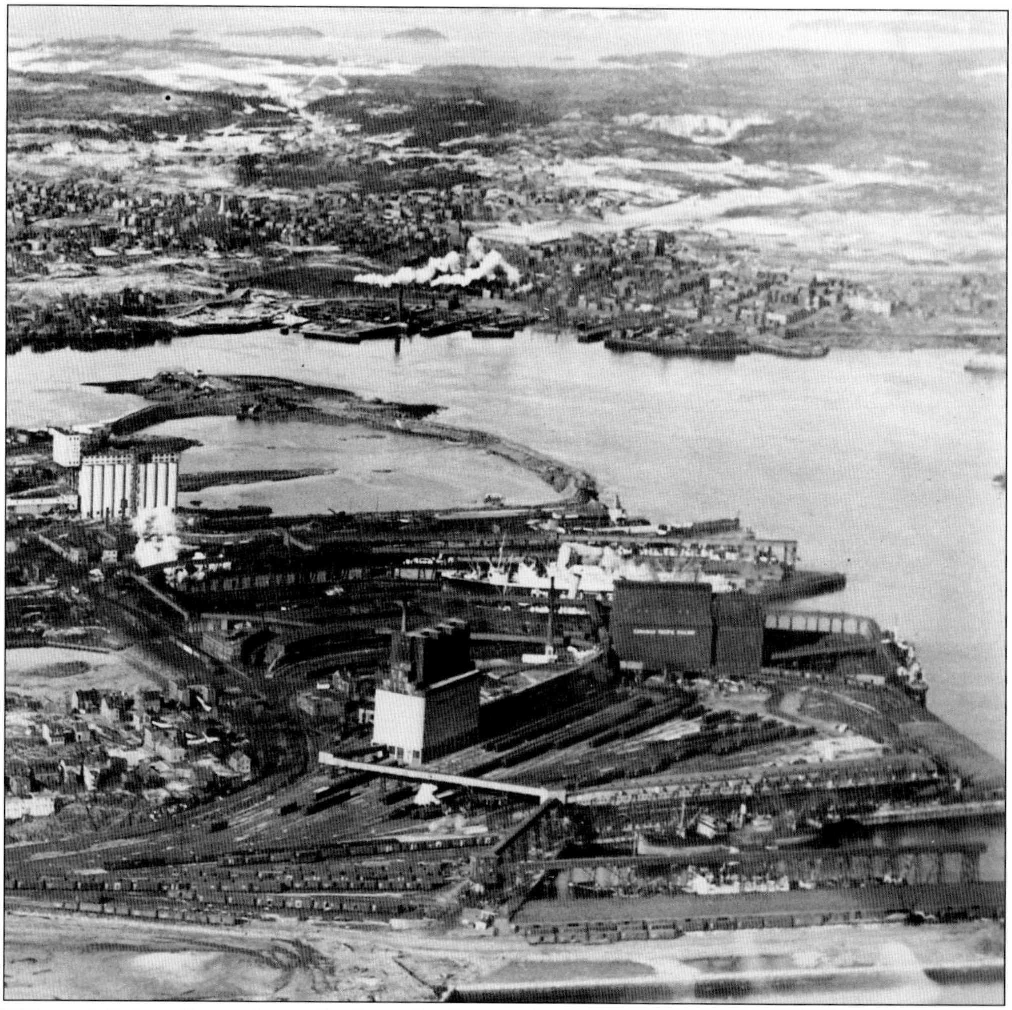

This aerial view shows the cofferdam which completely encircled the pier construction area in the harbour. Once pumped out, the cofferdam held back the highest tides in the world in the Bay of Fundy to create a dry area for construction work. Ships berthed in other piers continued to work as the new construction went on. (National Harbours Board.)

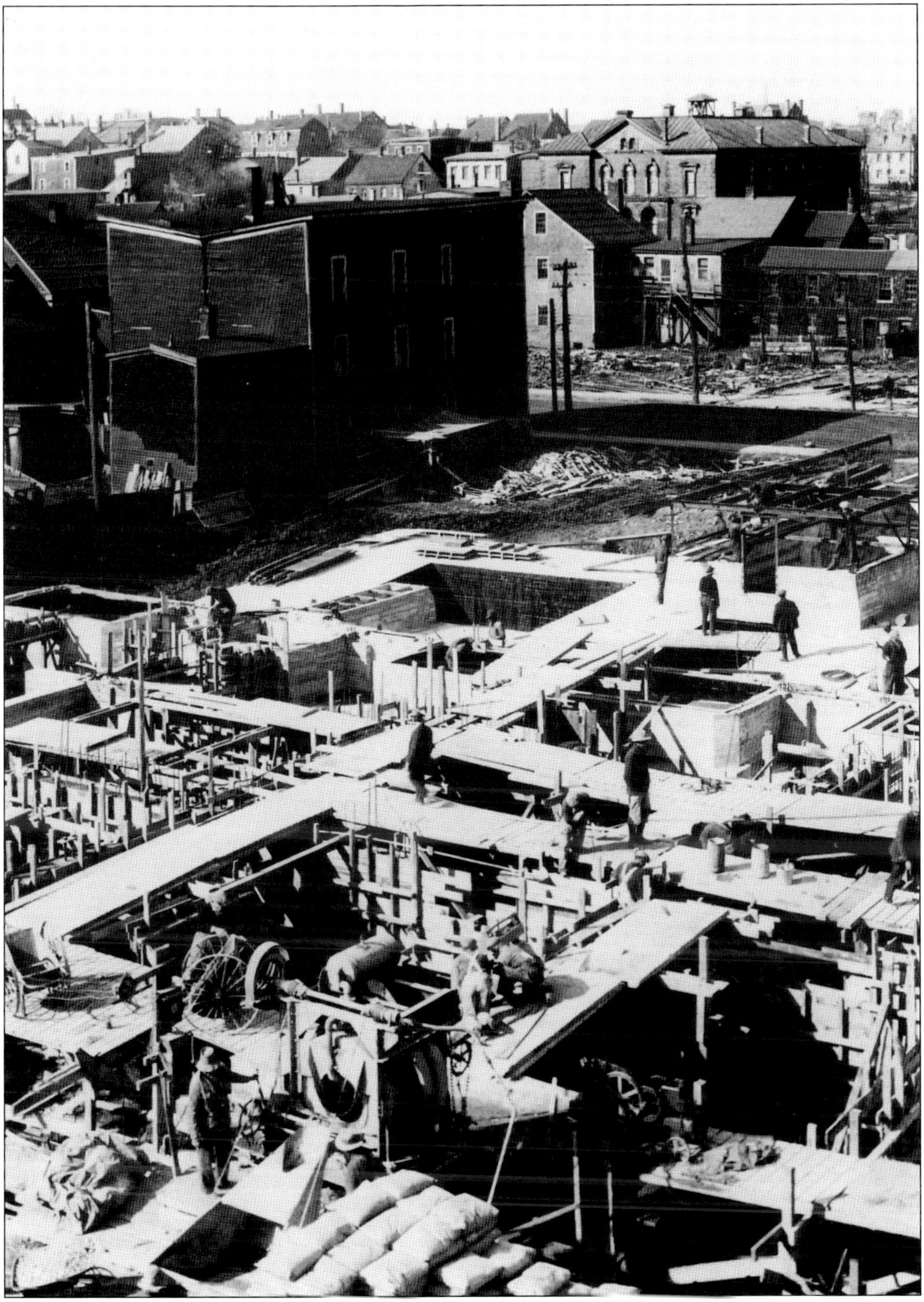

One of the projects undertaken during the rebuilding of the port was the construction of a huge grain elevator and dumper which allowed boxcars to be picked up, loaded, and unloaded quickly—almost as if they were toy cars. (National Harbours Board.)

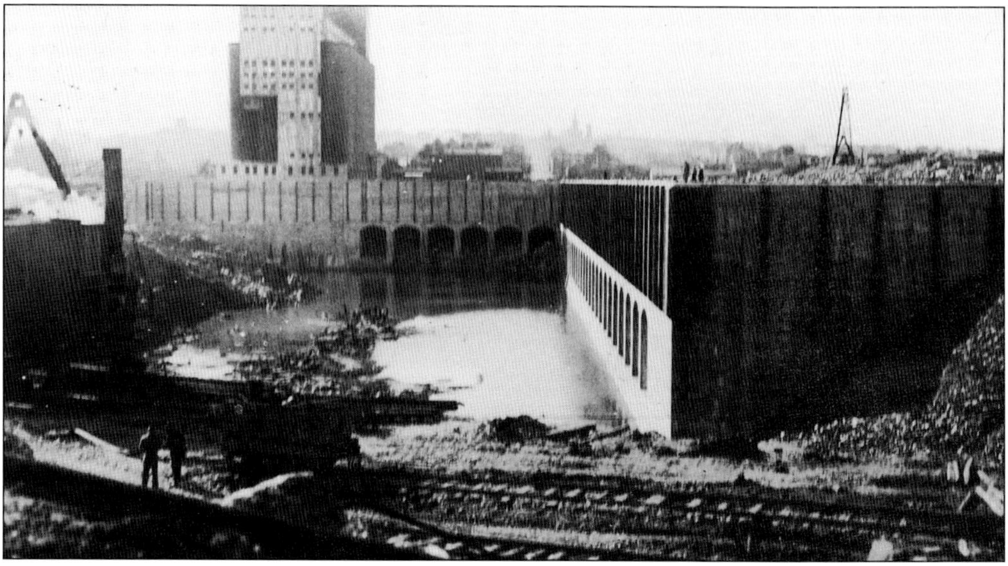

In 1934 an unknown resident of the West Side positioned himself at the cofferdam on the outer edge of the harbour to take this photograph. The shot looks directly in towards the grain elevator and the new wharf construction site.

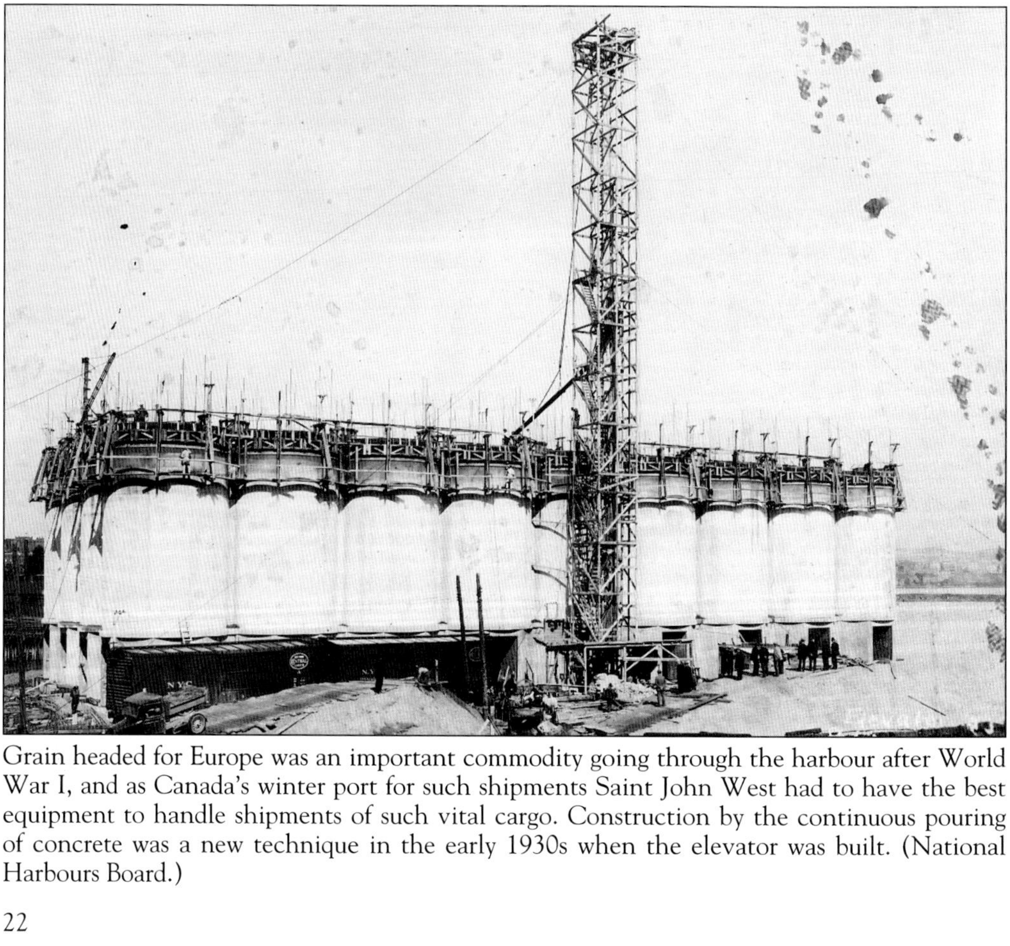

Grain headed for Europe was an important commodity going through the harbour after World War I, and as Canada's winter port for such shipments Saint John West had to have the best equipment to handle shipments of such vital cargo. Construction by the continuous pouring of concrete was a new technique in the early 1930s when the elevator was built. (National Harbours Board.)

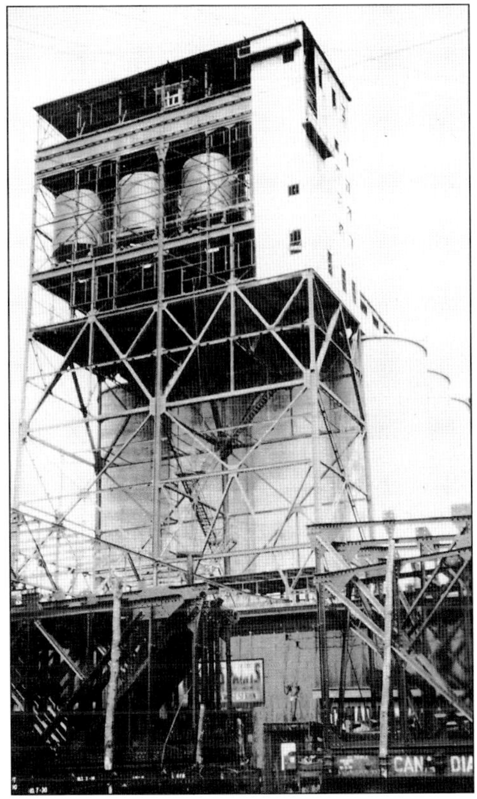

When this photograph was taken the steelwork was almost complete on the huge grain elevator. The elevator was long an important part of the landscape in Saint John West, as it dominated the horizon from the mid-1930s until the late 1980s, when grain shipments ceased going through Saint John. (Allan Family Collection.)

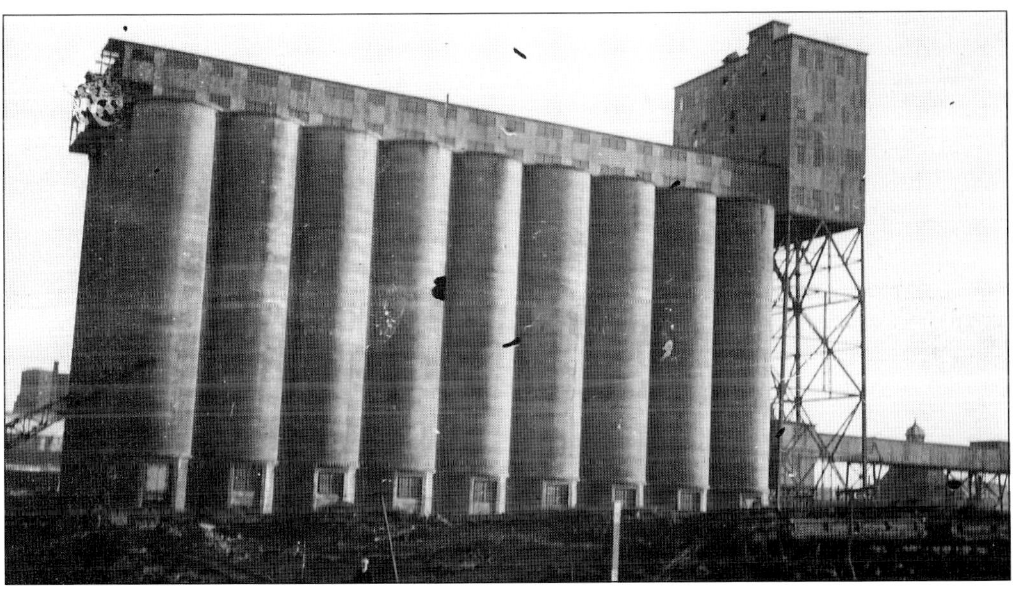

The finished grain elevator in 1932. (Allan Family Collection.)

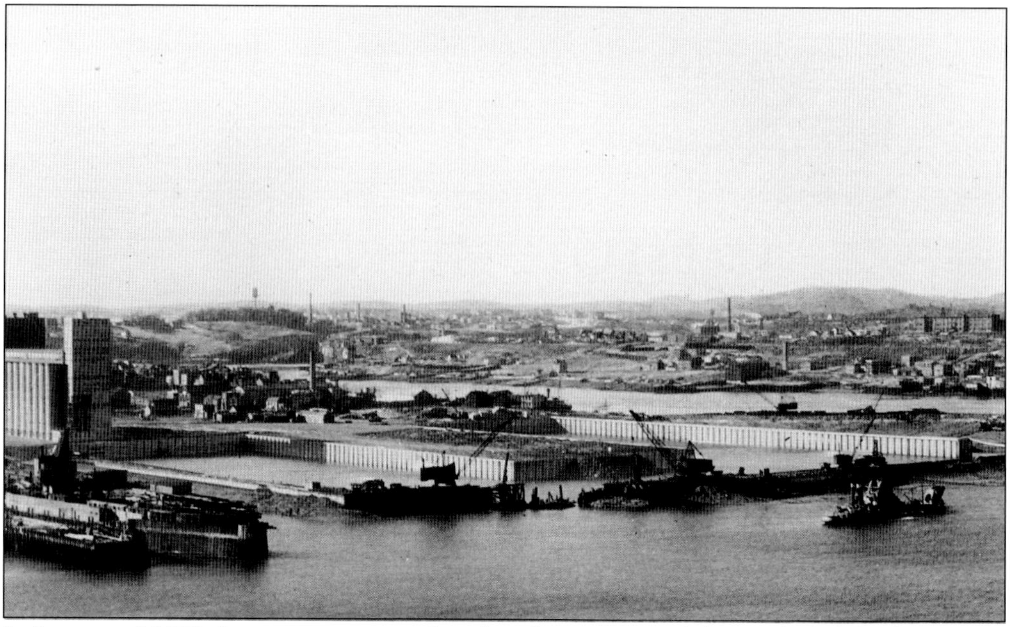

In January of 1933 the piers were complete but the erection of the steel-clad sheds atop the piers had not begun. The cofferdam was being removed bucketful by bucketful and the channel dredged so that ships could start steaming into the berths. (National Harbours Board.)

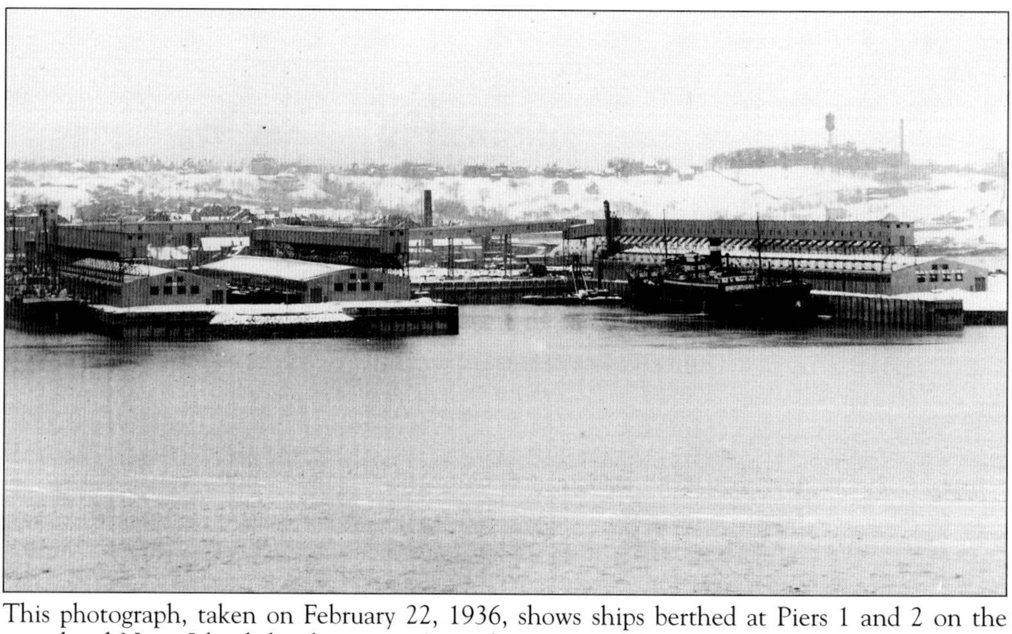

This photograph, taken on February 22, 1936, shows ships berthed at Piers 1 and 2 on the completed Navy Island development. Atop the piers are the connections to the huge grain elevator situated just to the left of this shot. With this new technology shipments of grain could pass from a boxcar to the elevator to the ship without a man's touch. (National Harbours Board.)

Three

Union Street Disappears

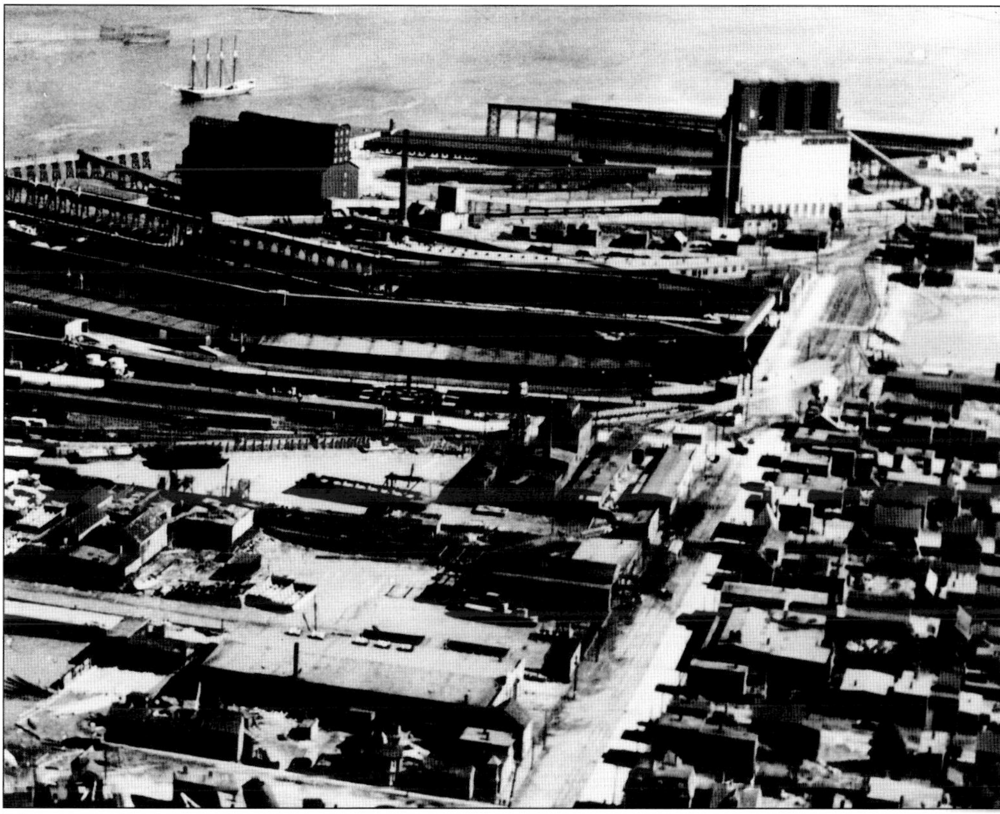

This view looks south and shows Union Street, Middle Street, and lower King Street, which together comprised the business section of Saint John West until the turn of the century. With its new status as Canada's winter port after 1898, Saint John's port facilities expanded dramatically, and this development had great repercussions on the city as a whole. A comparison between this scene and the way the area looks today gives us some insight into the changes that occurred with the modernization of the port. To provide freight storage area and new tracks to hold the railcars of grain, all the houses and businesses that are seen here were torn down. Some moved a few blocks west, and were rebuilt on the upper portion of King Street, some left Saint John West for other areas of the city, while still others just closed their doors and ceased business altogether. (National Harbours Board.)

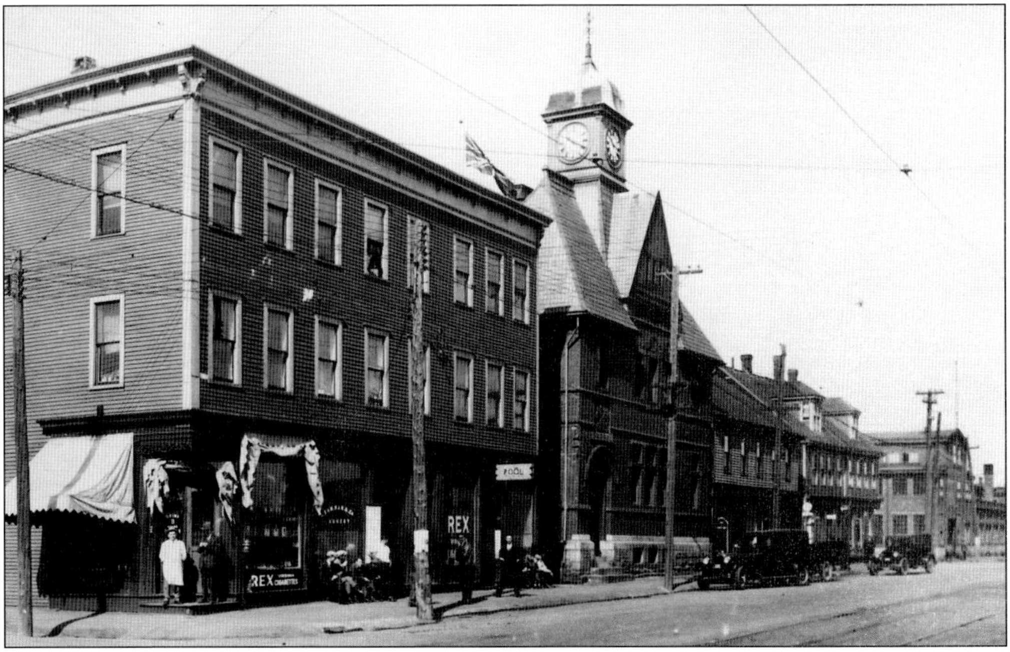

Union Street at the corner of Winslow in 1928. From the corner are: B. Ross, Grocer; Sam Wah's Laundry; Lane's Pool Hall; the post office; Emerson Hardware; Morris Tufts' Grocery; and Union Foundry. All were busy businesses in the Union Street area of Saint John West that were destined to disappear. (National Harbours Board.)

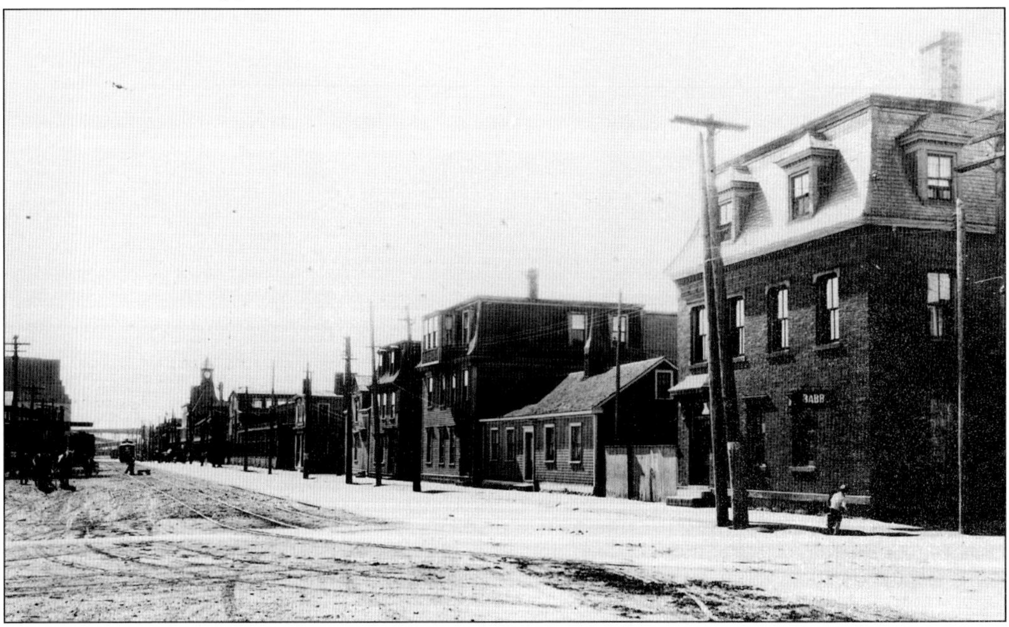

A second view of Union Street looking south from King Street. The Babb building on the nearest corner is a substantial brick structure which stands out from most Saint John West buildings which were of wood frame construction, wood being very cheap. Few buildings in this area had basements because the huge tides seeped through the sandy soil even in areas well inland from the shore. (National Harbours Board.)

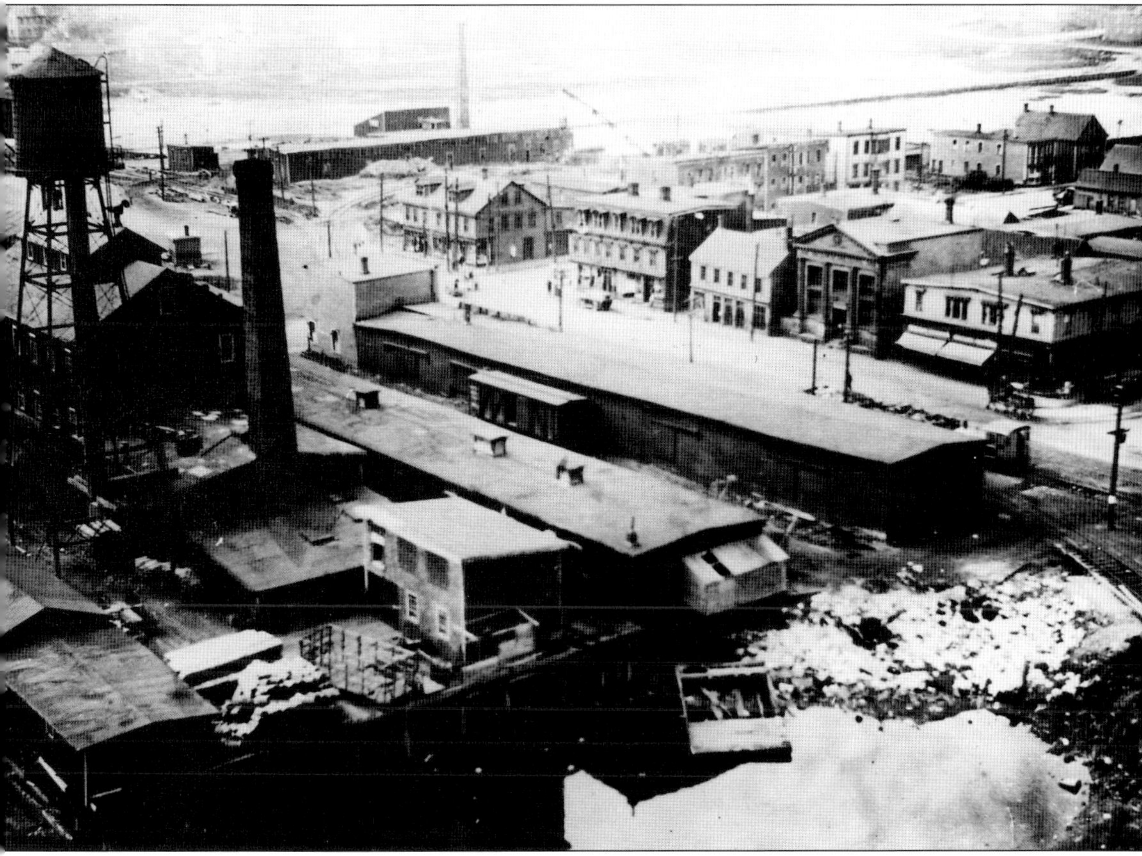

Adjacent to the mercantile businesses, banks, and the post office were mills such as Fowler's Mill to the left with its water tower, and just over the smokestack the Canada Wire and Nail Company. (McMulkin Collection.)

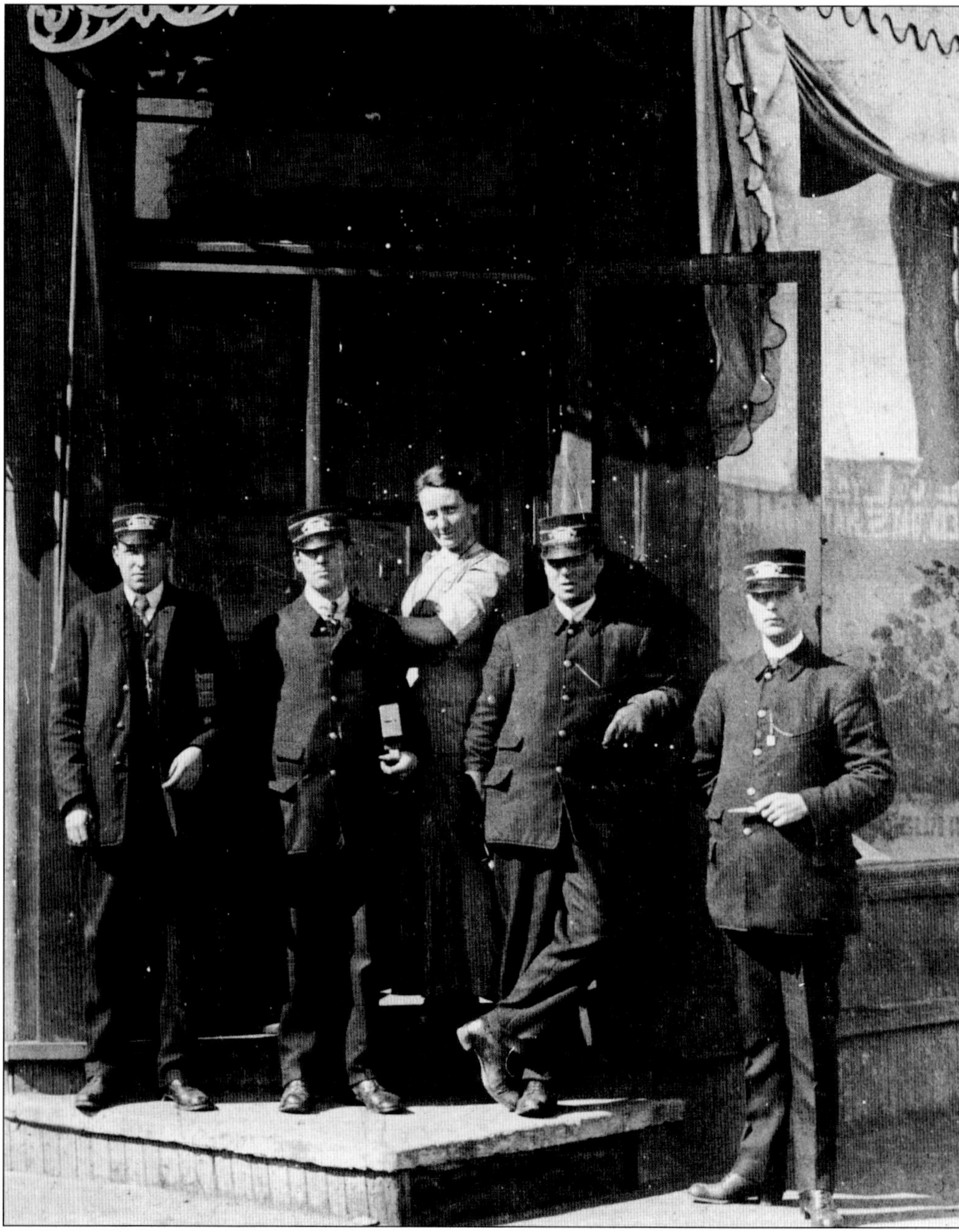

Susie Murphy's Lunch Counter on the corner of Winslow and Union Streets around 1910. This was a popular gathering place for the area streetcar drivers whose car barn was just across the street. The car barn was also destined to disappear when Union Street was torn down—another testimony to the effect of these changes on neighborhood people and places. Second from the left, standing next to Susie Murphy, is John Vincent Kelly. He joined the street railway company in 1910. (Murphy Family Collection.)

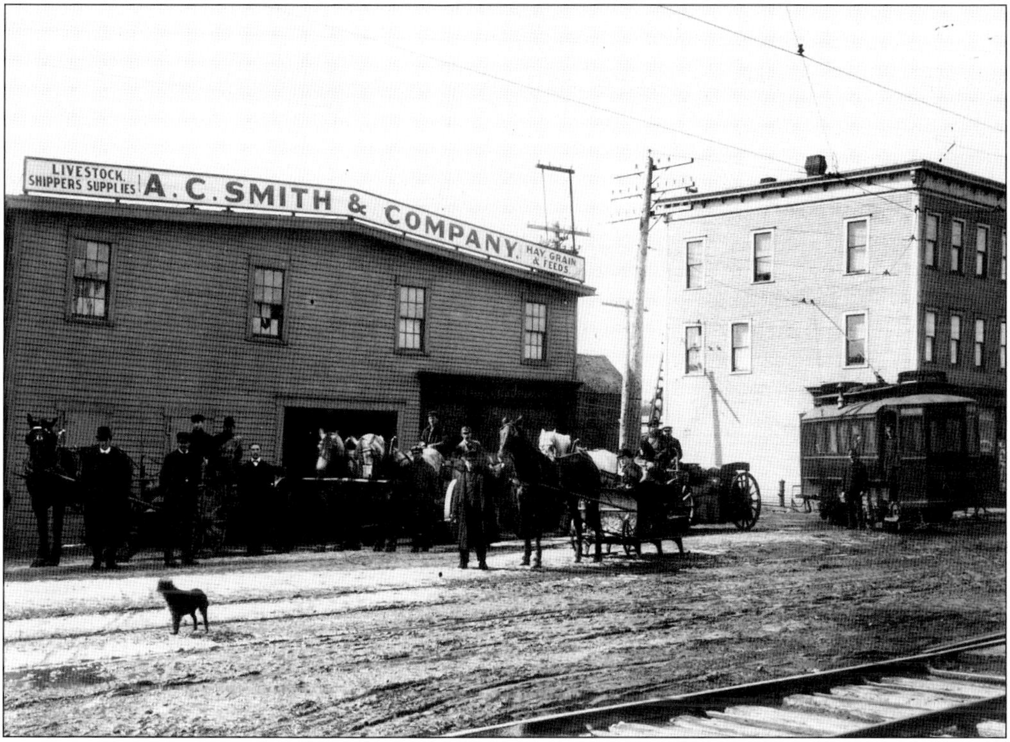

In the era of horse-pulled transportation, it was necessary to have hay and grain establishments to provide feed for the livestock. A.C. Smith provided this service to local residents and to incoming and outgoing shipments of cattle from his Union Street establishment prior to 1932. (Provincial Archives.)

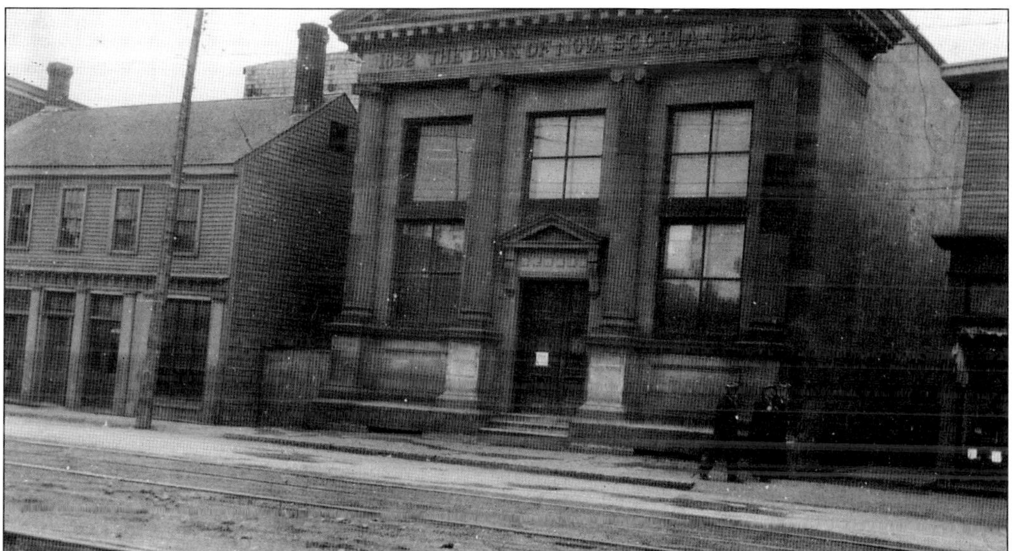

At the turn of the century New Brunswick banks were formidable buildings, designed to convey solidity and reliability, but this factor did not save this structure when Union Street disappeared. Nor was Cameron's Barbershop (to its right) spared, though both businesses moved to other Saint John West locations. (Allan Family Collection.)

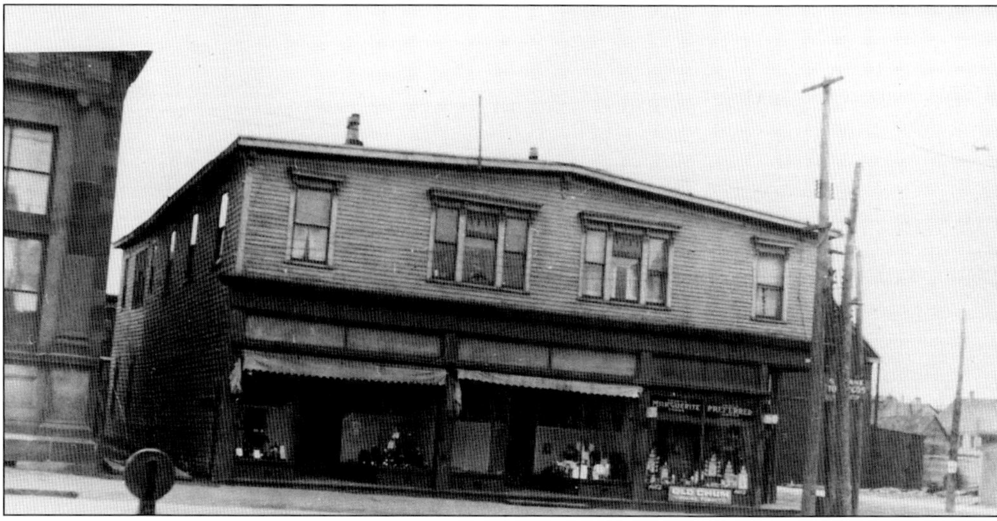

The Ideal Store on Union Street in lower Saint John West. Hymie Garson was a progressive merchant who chose this area for his store as he believed it would grow to be the liveliest business section of the city. Little did he know that the street he had chosen for the booming business he foresaw would disappear soon after this picture was taken in 1930. (Provincial Archives.)

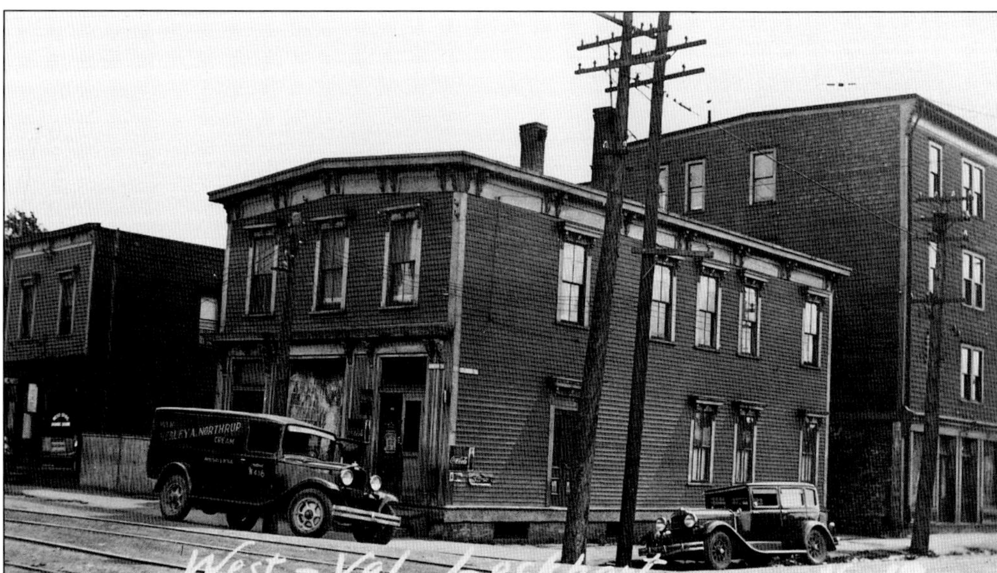

The corner of St. John and Union Streets was the location for Percy Barnes' store, the West Side Lunch, and Furnette's Store. In 1931 Hedley Northrup had switched over from the horse-drawn wagon to the truck to deliver his milk products (see p. 94). (Provincial Archives.)

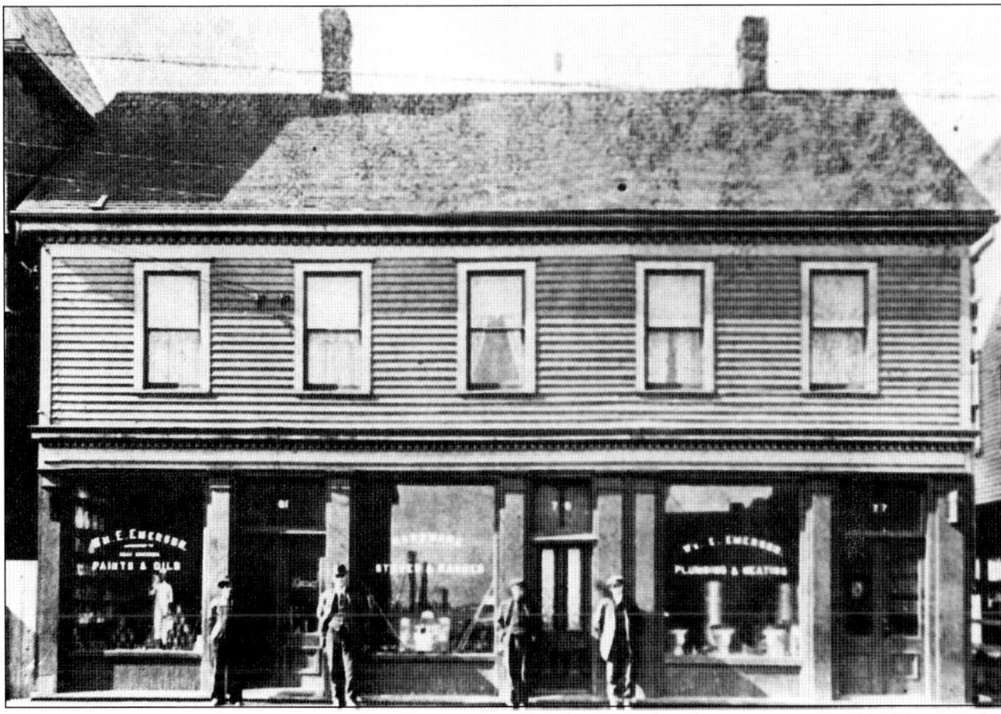

W.E. Emerson Hardware on Union Street was the leading hardware store in the Saint John West area for many years. The Emerson family became very prosperous and went on to open various branches of the successful hardware store. Well-known and upstanding members of the community, they contributed to the building of area churches and generously supported charitable and benevolent activities in the neighbourhood.

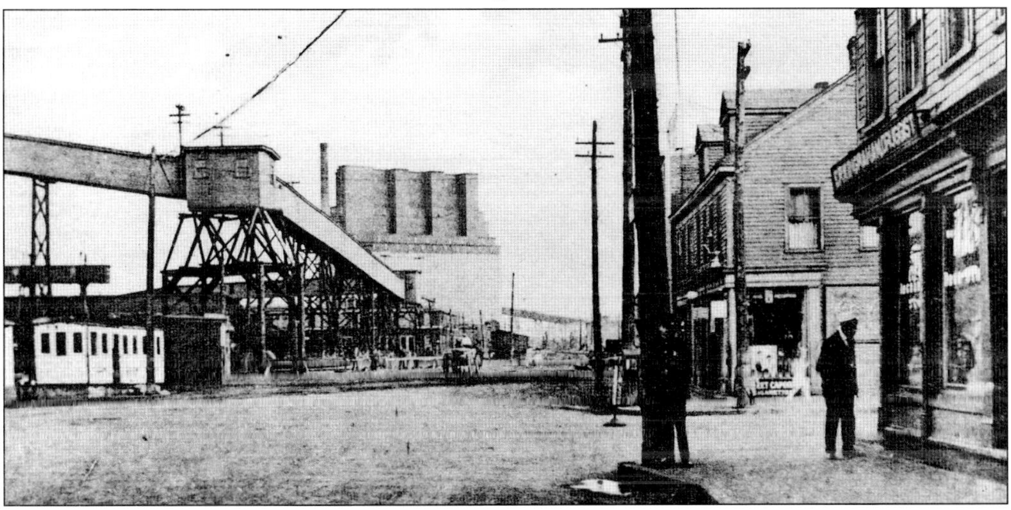

A policeman is shown "walking" the beat on Union Street at Rodney. Over to his right (on the left in the photograph) is the popular "dog cart," or hot dog emporium and quick lunch counter. These were usually obsolete street cars converted to restaurants which served the men of the law long before doughnut shops became popular. The longshoremen also enjoyed these establishments, not only for their food but also as a place to get warmed up during a sub-zero day on the docks.

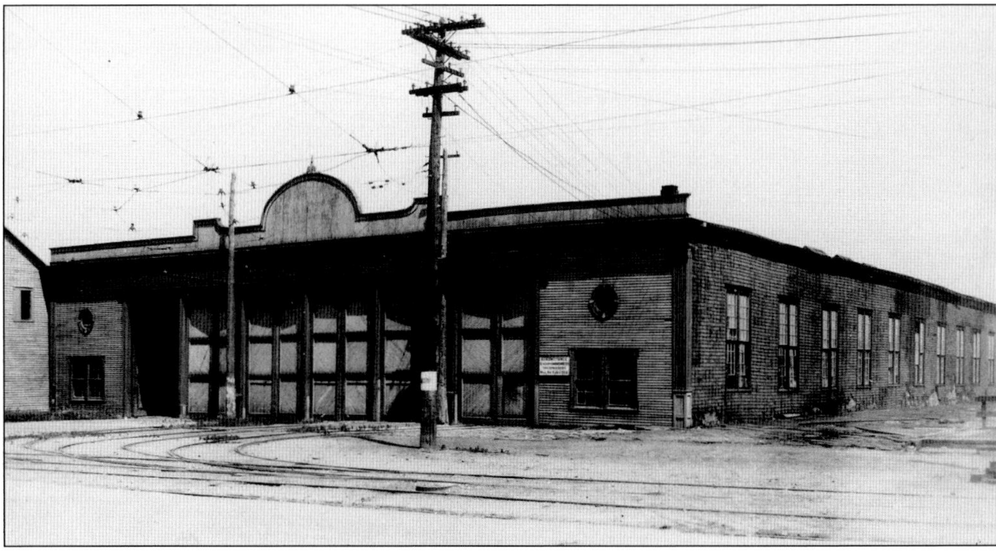

The Carleton Light and New Brunswick Power Company Car Barn on Union Street on July 28, 1928. This was the site of the first electric power generation in Saint John West. Carleton had street lights in 1884 before Saint John proper enjoyed electric lights on their streets and it was from this barn that the power was first generated by engineer D.C. Clark. (National Harbours Board.)

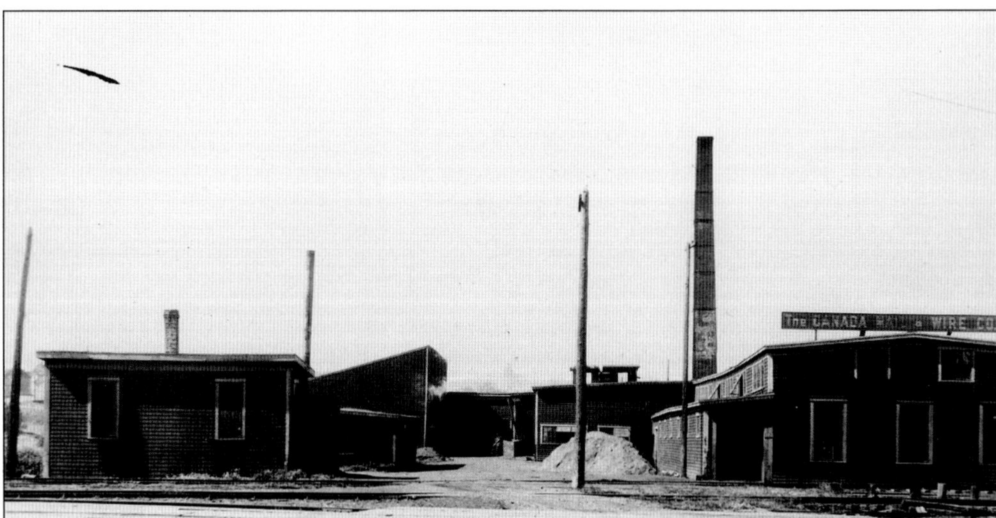

The Canada Wire and Nail Company Ltd. on July 30, 1928. The company was known across Canada for its high quality horseshoe nails, but it disappeared when Union Street was torn out for harbour development. (National Harbours Board.)

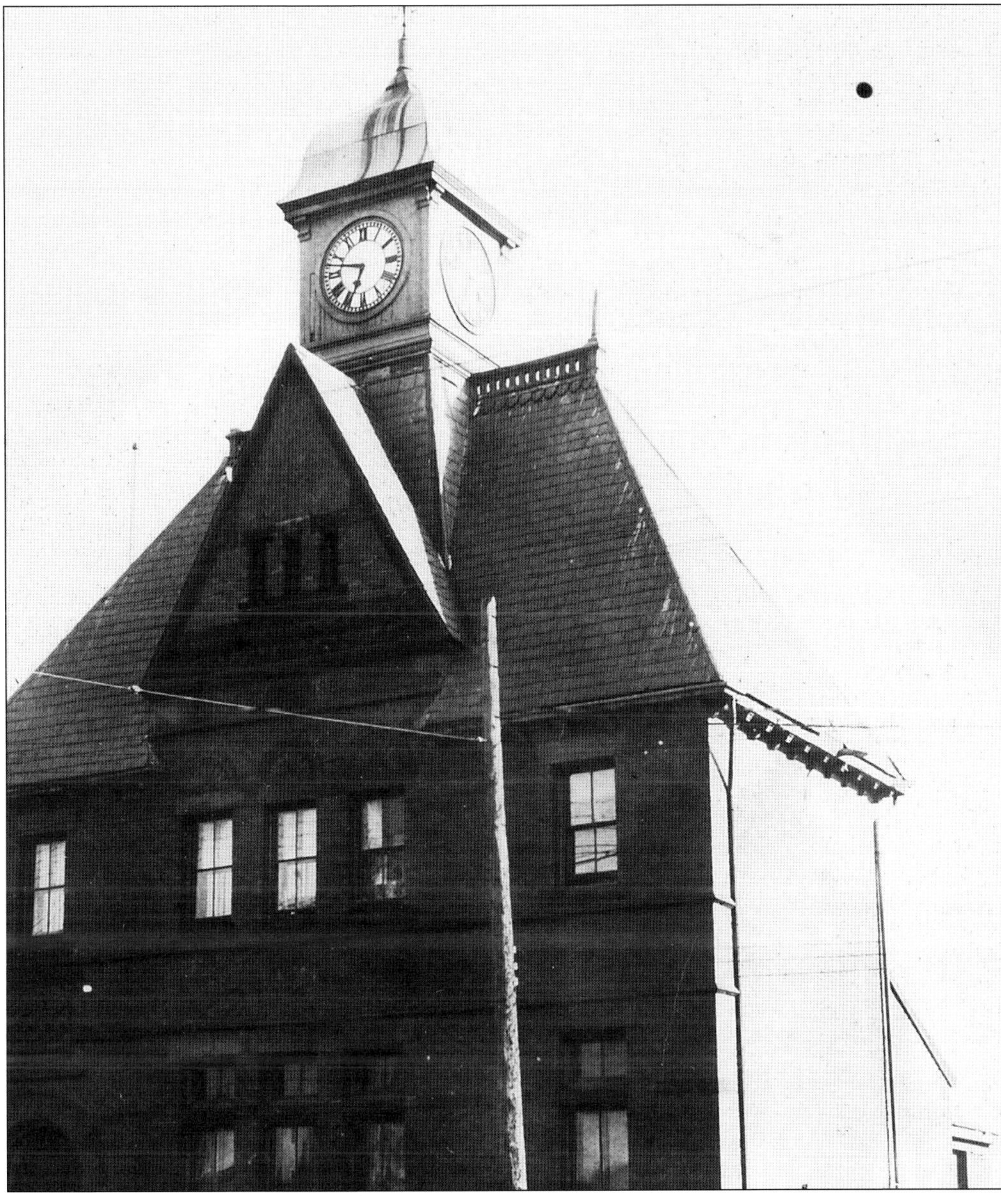

The post office on Union Street West was torn down and later rebuilt a few blocks west on King Street. The four-faced clock originally set in the tower of the post office was moved to the octagonal tower of St. George's Anglican Church three blocks west where its mechanical components still measure the hours to this day. It is the only mechanical clock still in operation in the city, all others having been electrified. The post office clock replaced an earlier clock that had been installed in the 1890s. Local folk tales indicate that the original clock was installed when the minister of the church caught four of his parishioners playing poker. He promised to keep their errant ways secret from their wives if they would install a four-faced clock in the newly constructed tower of the church. Three of the four kept their word, and for many years the church had only a three-faced clock. However, when the post office was torn down in 1932, the clock they gave replaced the old church clock, and St. George's has had a four-faced clock since. You can see the clock as it is today on p. 116. (Allan Family Collection.)

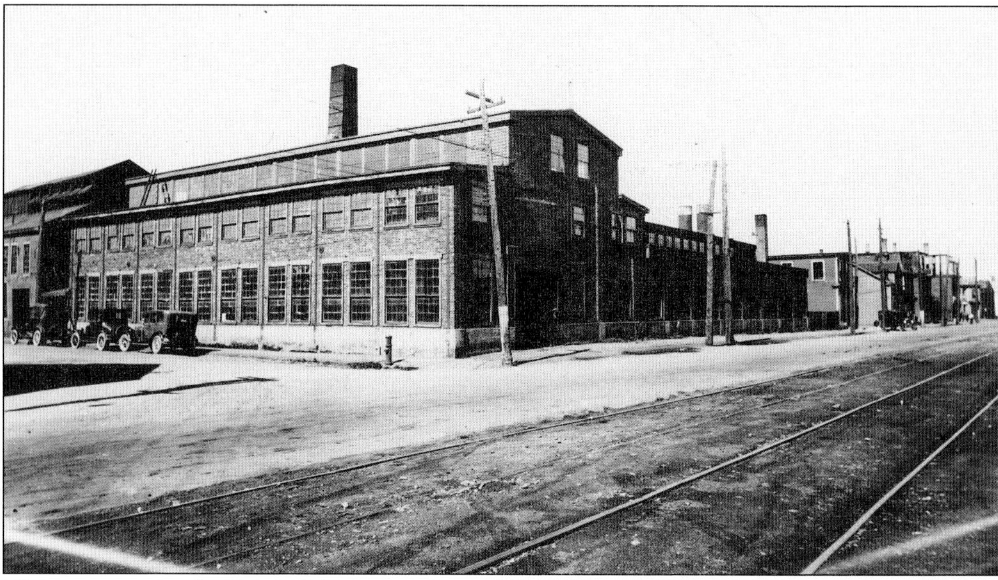

The Union Foundry, named for its Union Street location, was one of the major Saint John concerns that did metalwork for the local shipping and railway industries. When the port expansion forced it to move, it did not relocate in the Saint John West area and many jobs were lost—another example of the considerable economic and social disruption caused by the port development. (National Harbours Board.)

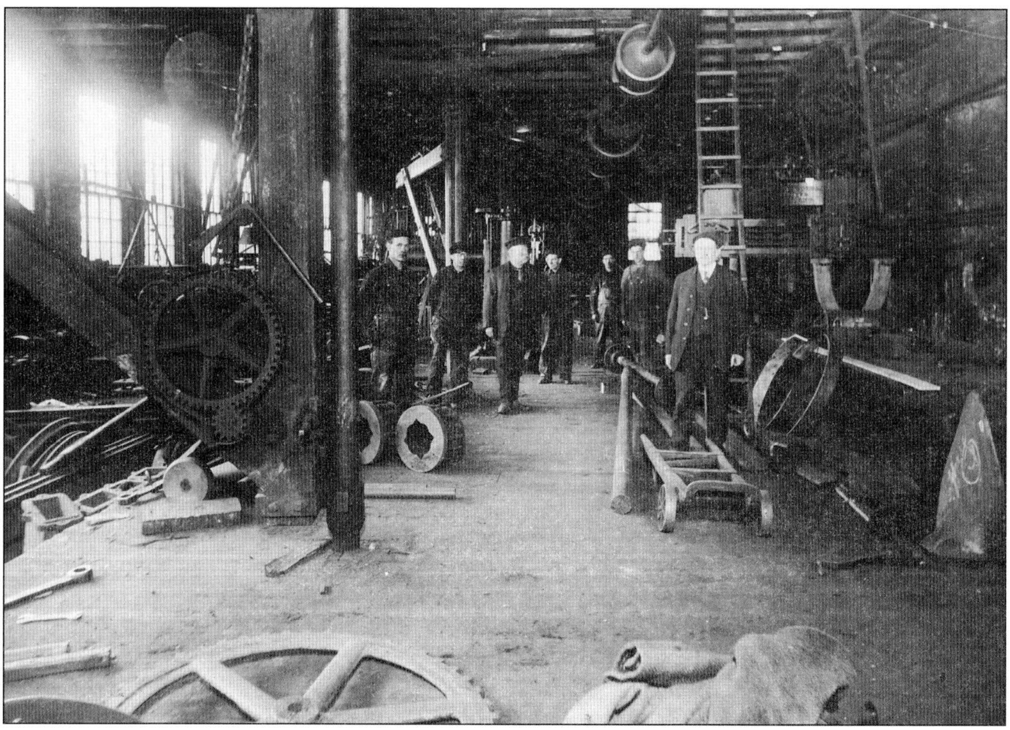

The busy port at Saint John West and the many ships that passed through it meant many hours of work for a foundry and its skilled workers. That the Union Foundry specialized in ship's machinery is obvious from this interior view. (George Cameron Collection.)

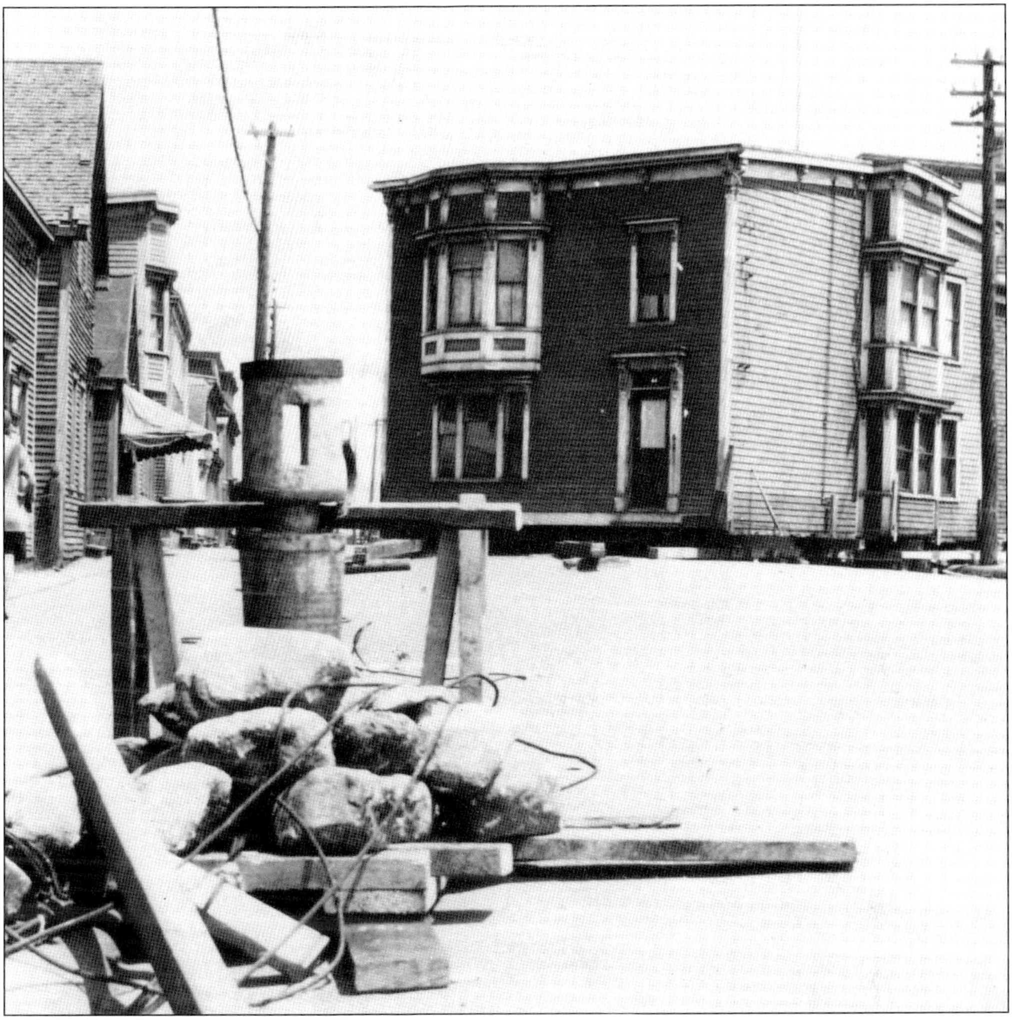

When it came time for Union, Middle, and lower King Streets to be torn down, some of the houses were moved on skids to other areas of Saint John West. In most cases they survived the move and still stand to this day. (Roy H. Makenney Collection.)

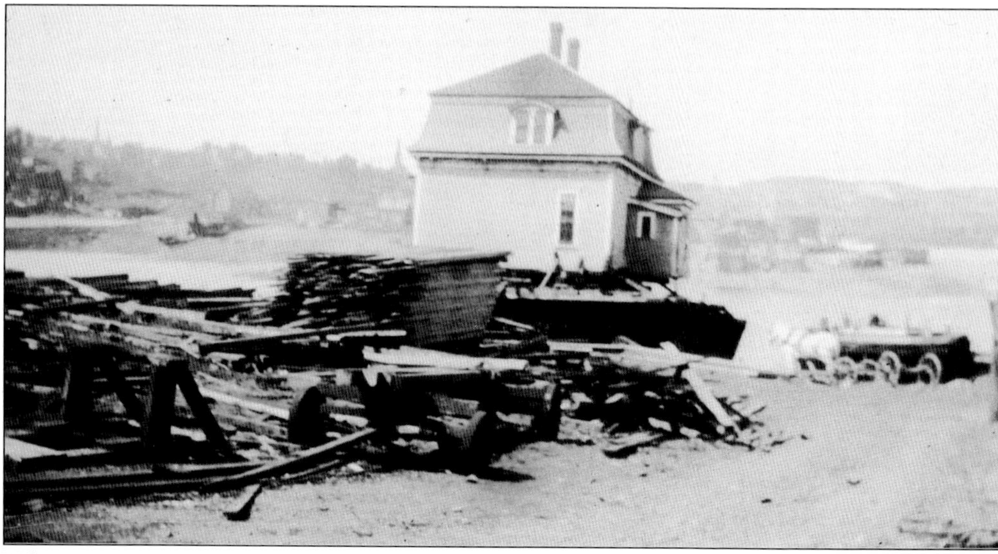

When it was convenient to do so, a house would be moved to the edge of the harbour, rolled out at high tide to a scow, towed up river, and then rolled back onto the land and pulled along the streets to a new location. (Allan Family Collection.)

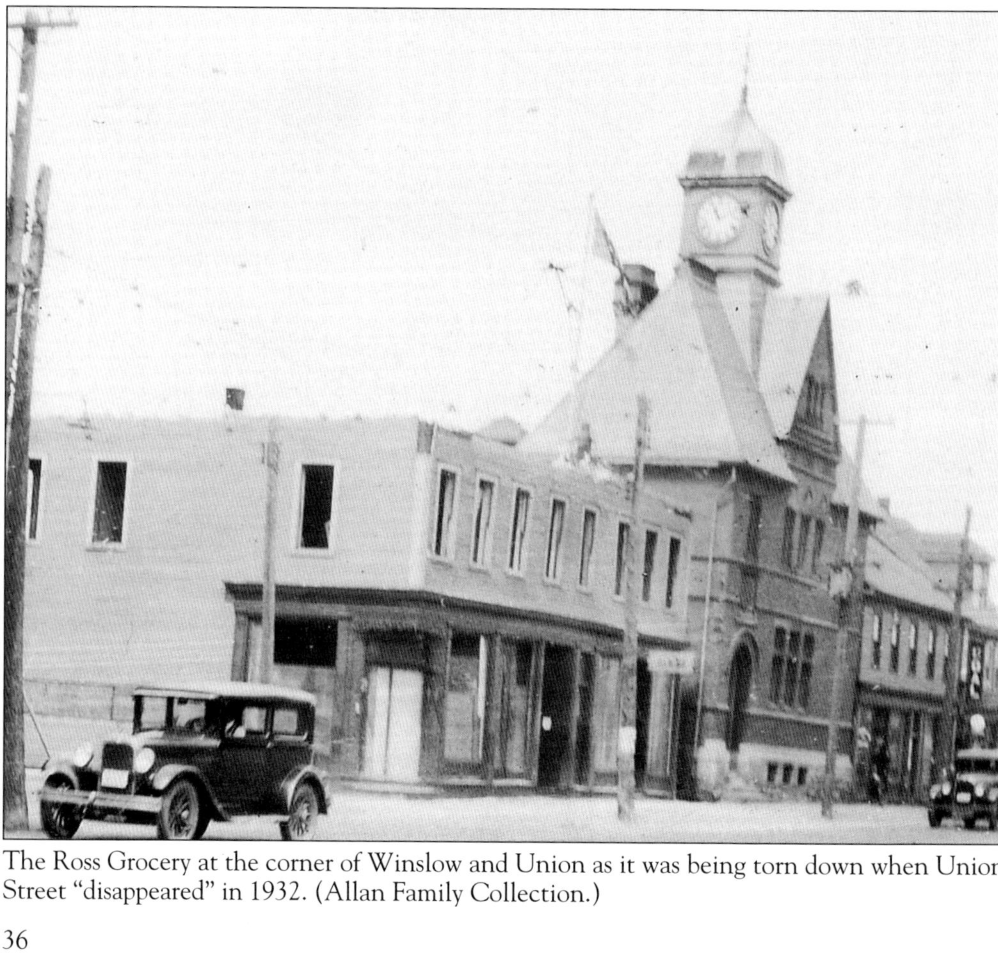

The Ross Grocery at the corner of Winslow and Union as it was being torn down when Union Street "disappeared" in 1932. (Allan Family Collection.)

Four

King Street West Disappears

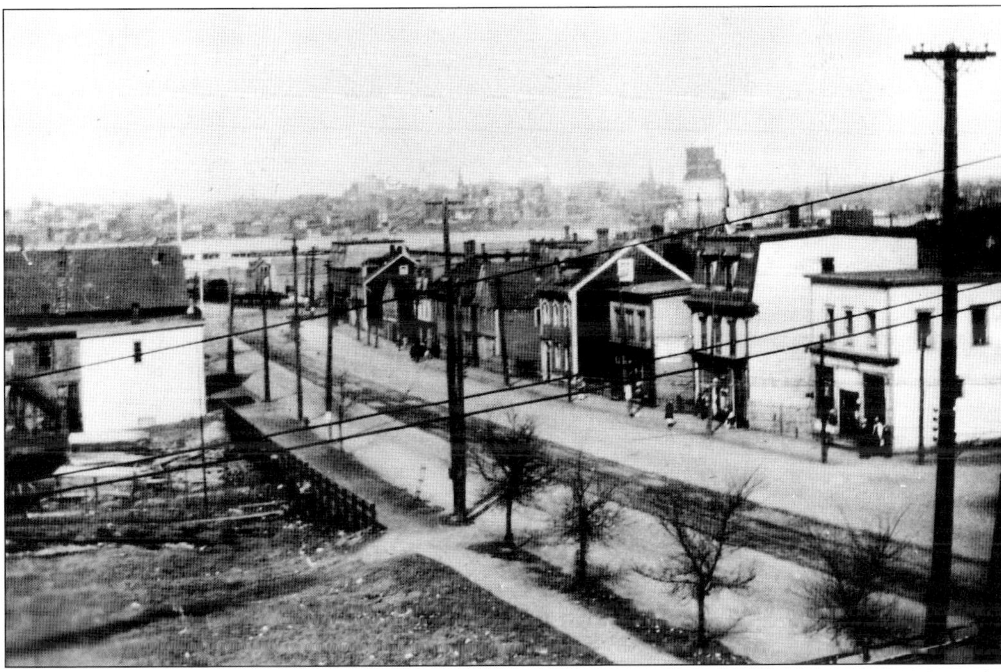

King Street in Carleton began at the harbour near Pier 1 and ran up a grade parallel to the Saint John River at right angles to Union Street. It terminated abruptly at the bluff on what was known as Courtenay Hill, a name supposedly taken from the fact that couples courted on this hillside overlooking Saint John West. The lower end of King Street disappeared along with Union Street as part of the port development. Prior to that it was home to a mixture of houses and mercantile concerns on the right side and houses and businesses such as lumberyards and fish plants on the left side, the latter depending on the tides that allowed vessels to float into the wharves beside the plants. The huge grain elevator on the horizon is not part of the West Side but is actually located across the harbour in the south end of Saint John proper.

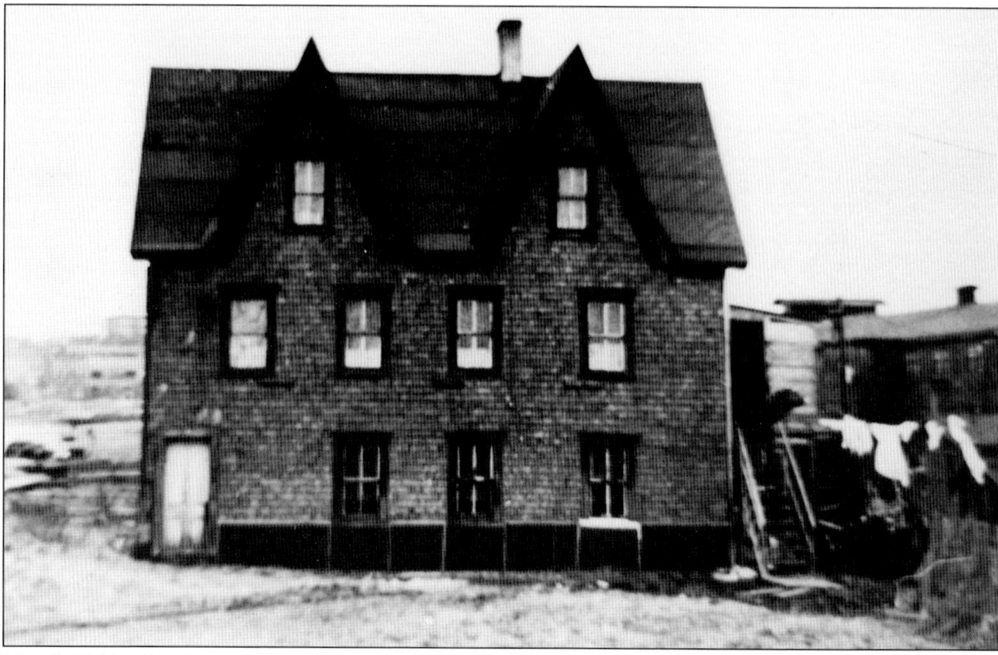

Until 1854, the Saint John Common Council appointed the mayor from among the elected councillors. In 1854, James Olive, who was born and lived in this stretched version of a "carpenter gothic"-style home (a style popular in Saint John), became the first mayor elected by the citizens. This home stood on lower King Street. (Gerald Keith Collection.)

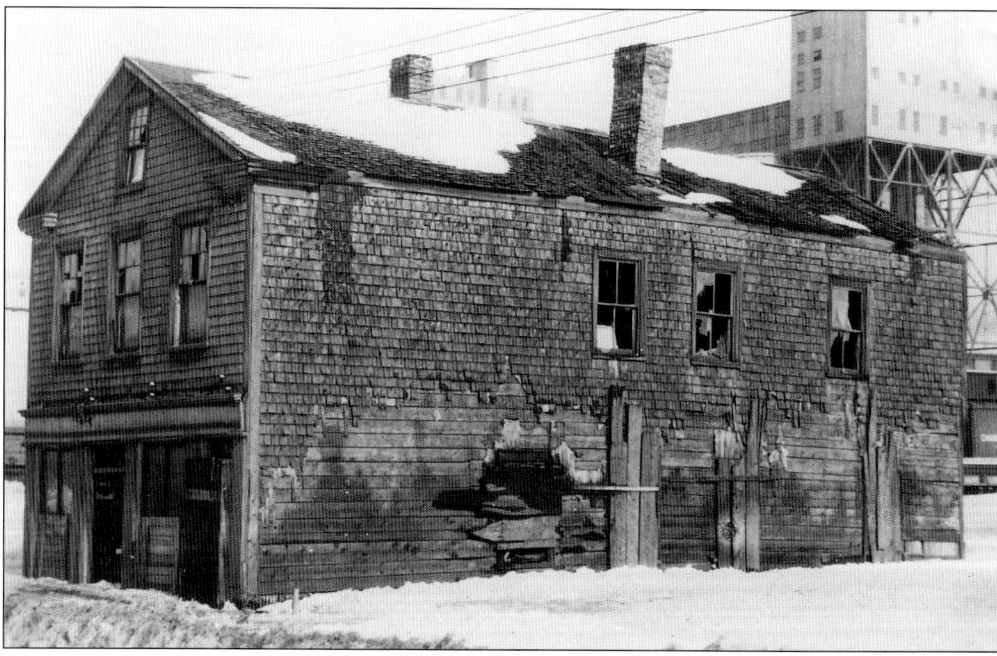

Lambert's was one of many merchants in the King Street neighborhood catering to residents who worked at the port. Most merchants would let port workers run up bills during the summer which they would pay off when work became plentiful with the arrival of ships around the first of December after the Saint Lawrence froze up. (National Harbours Board.)

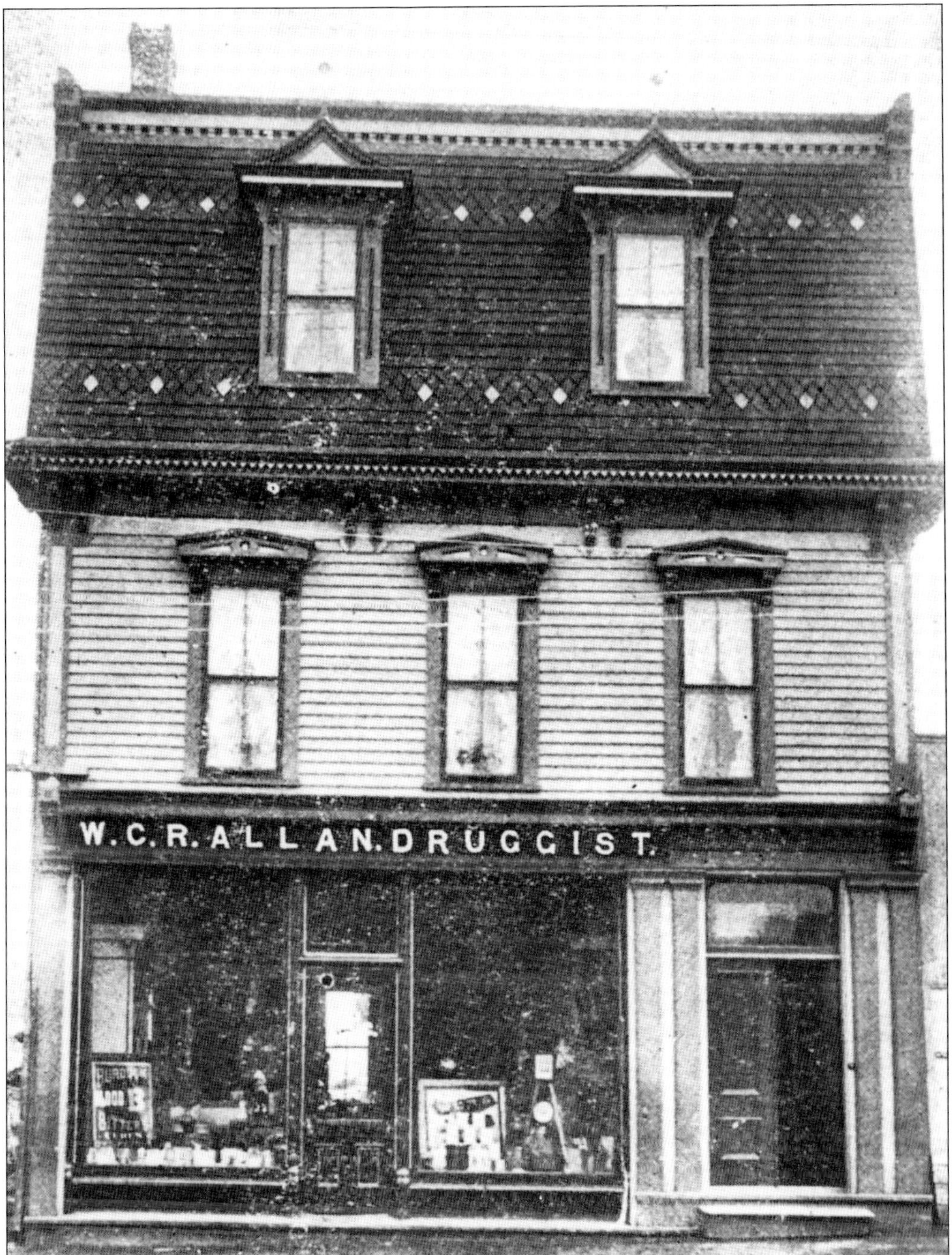

W.C.R. Allan advertised that he was a druggist and seedsman. His patent medicines were sold across Canada from this store on King Street.

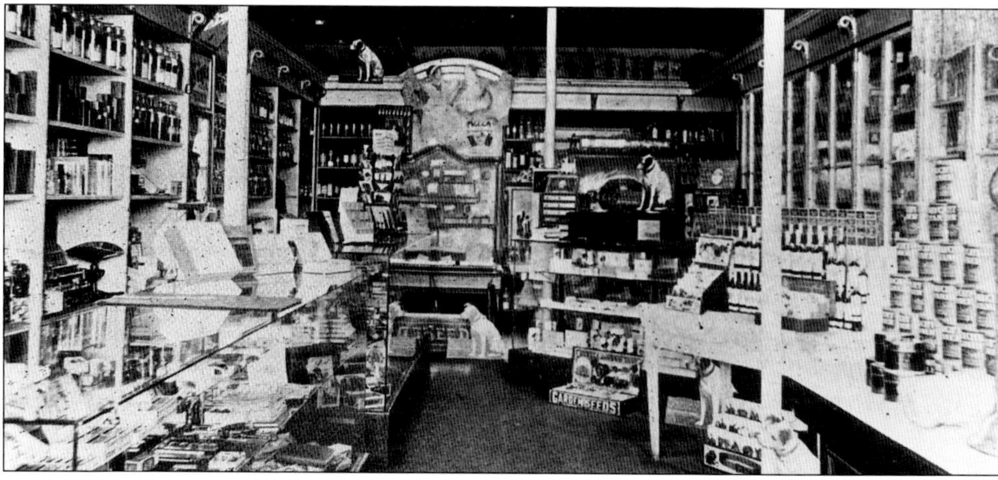

The interior of the W.C.R. Allan Drugstore photographed around 1904. On the packed shelves can be seen the huge variety of seeds Allan advertised as well as many of the popular perfumes and toilet articles of the day.

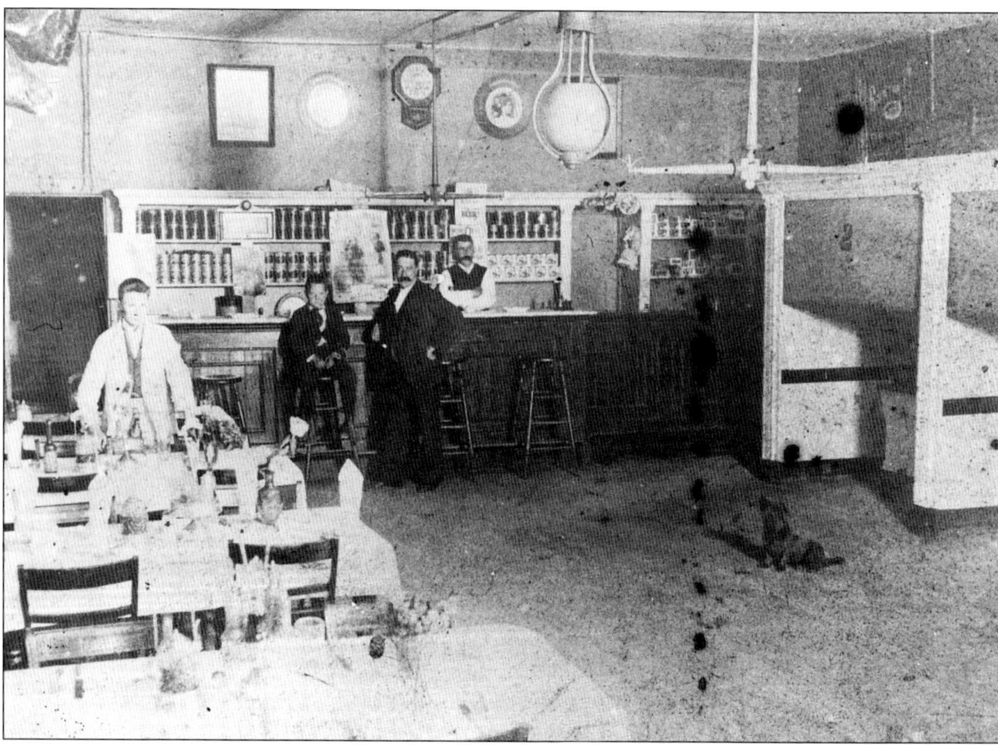

Barry Dykeman is awaiting customers to fill his well-arranged tables at the Chowder House on King Street in this early 1900s photograph. The tall, walled booths on the right-hand side of the restaurant ensured privacy for seafood lovers. Gas lamps still lit this store although power was available in Saint John West by this time. (Dorothy Fair Collection.)

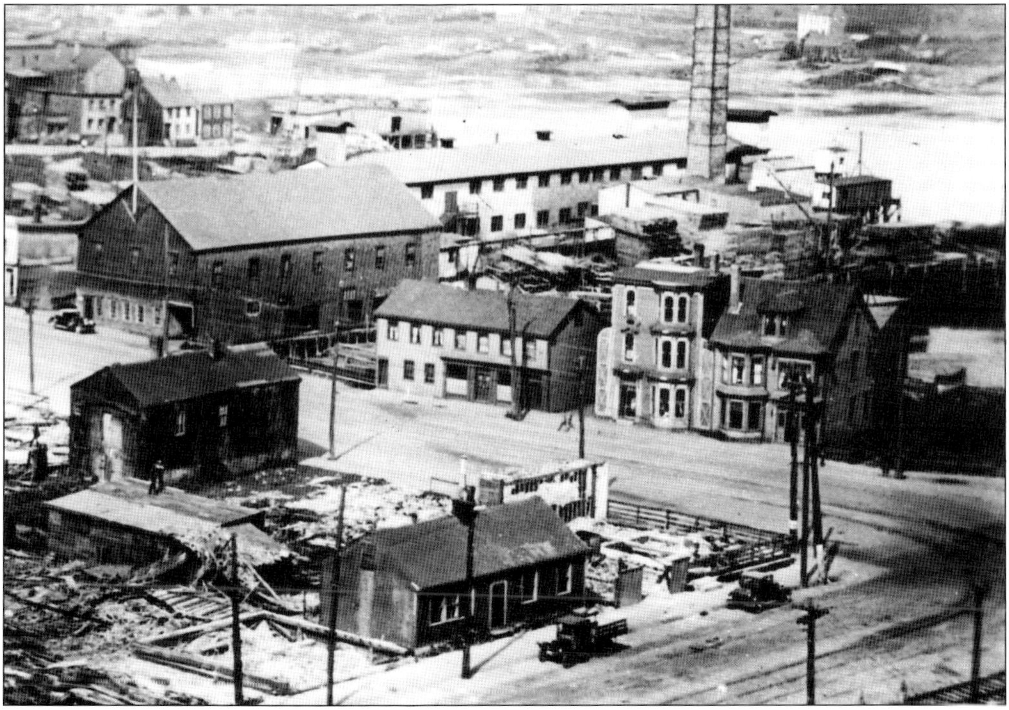

This aerial view of lower King Street shows, from left to right: Mulchay's store, the J.M. Driscoll Lumber Mill, Lewis Conner's fish factory (nearest the tall smoke stack), Lane's boarding house, and Robert Adams Jewelery.

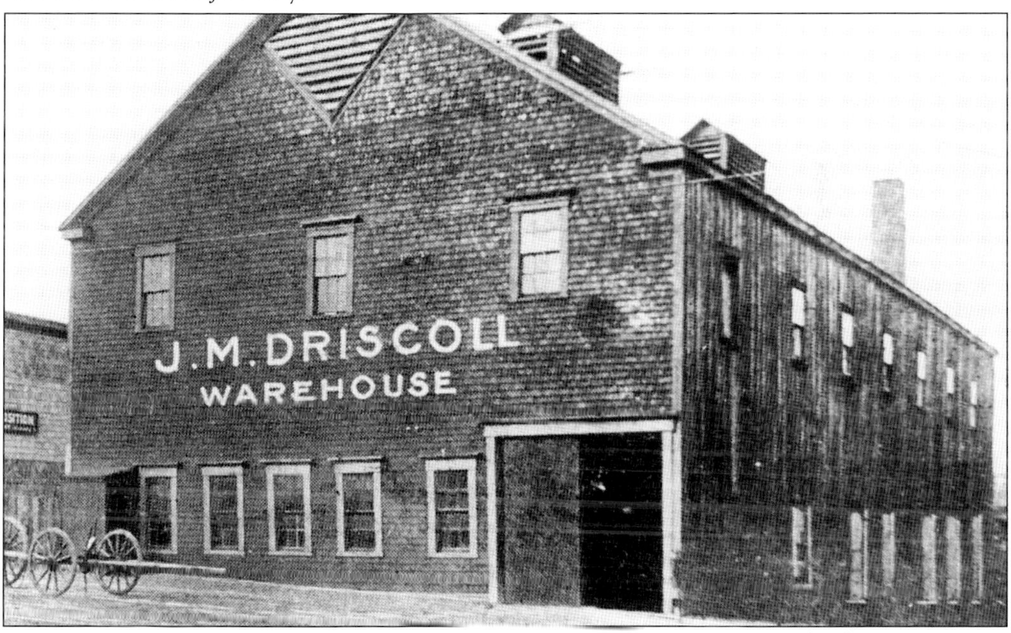

The J.M. Driscoll Lumber Mill took advantage of the high and low tides in the Saint John area. They would float barges loaded with lumber right up to their mill on lower King Street, and then let them settle on the mud flats so they could be unloaded onto wagons such as the one shown at the left of this picture.

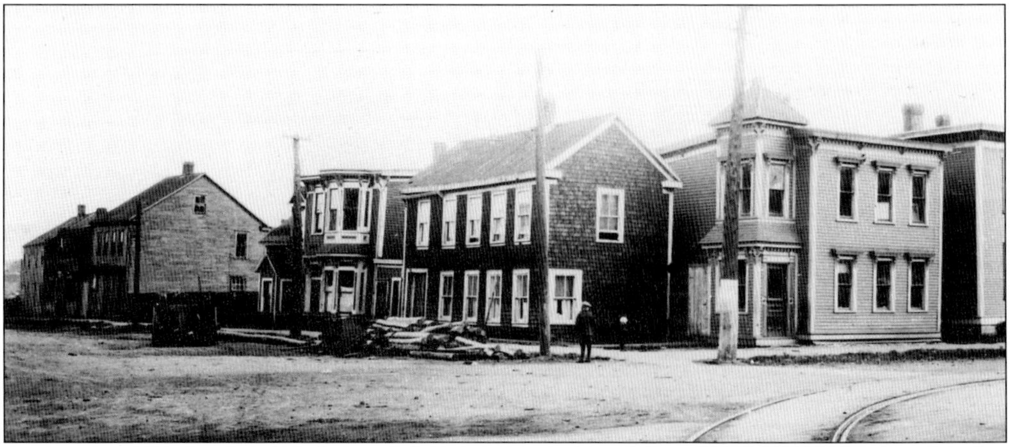

Homes built in this area were usually constructed by the owners during the summer months when work at the port was scarce. Many were able to scavenge lumber here and there from port operations. Some had experience as shipbuilders and managed to turn out well-appointed homes in styles typical of Saint John at the time. (National Harbours Board.)

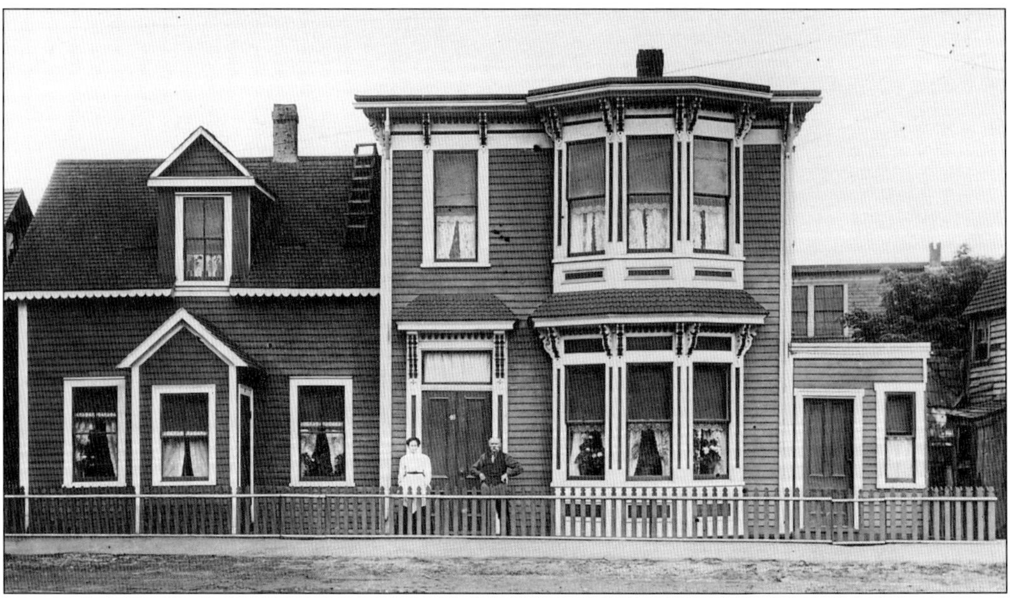

Hiram Nice and his wife in front of their home at 48 King Street. In the previous picture Hiram's house is the third one from the left. Note the geraniums in the window—always a popular flower with Saint Johners, the geranium is now the city's official flower. (Ann Nice Collection.)

Five

King Street Is Rebuilt

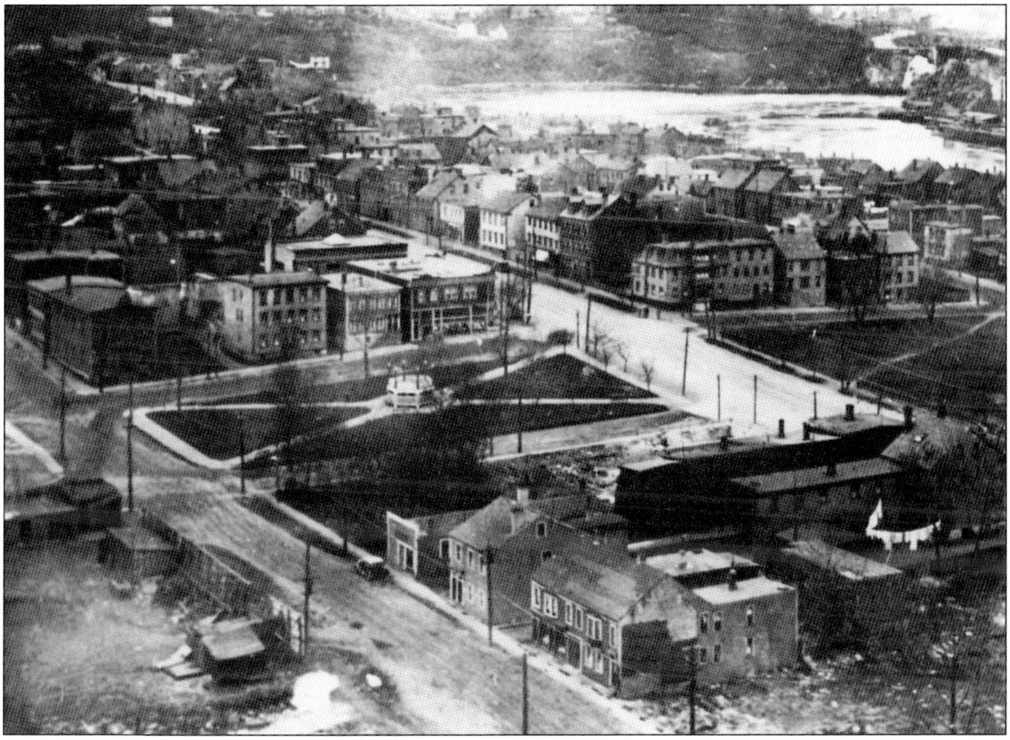

Prior to the demolition of Union Street and lower King Street, upper King Street was primarily residential in nature. At the east end of the street nearest the harbour was a small park called Tilley Square with a bandstand where the Carleton Cornet Band gave summer concerts. On the west or upper part of the street was Fire Station Number 6 and St. George's Anglican Church. The latter had been built in 1821 and was and is the oldest church in Saint John in continuous use. On the heights above King Street was another park officially known as King Square West, but locally known as Courtenay Hill. Courtenay Hill was a rocky tangle of birches and alder bushes that a turn-of-the-century futurist predicted would one day be paved with a marble street 200 feet wide and have the government house, the diocesan cathedral, and a huge public observatory grandly located on its brow. It remained undeveloped, however, and has provided a great place for kids to play and for couples to court. It has also long been used as a great vantage point for viewing the Reversing Falls which are just visible in the upper right hand corner of this photograph. It is at these famous falls that the Saint John River ends its 450-mile run from the northern portion of the state of Maine to the Bay of Fundy and that the tides and the river fight daily for supremacy, creating rapids that run both ways. (McMulkin Collection.)

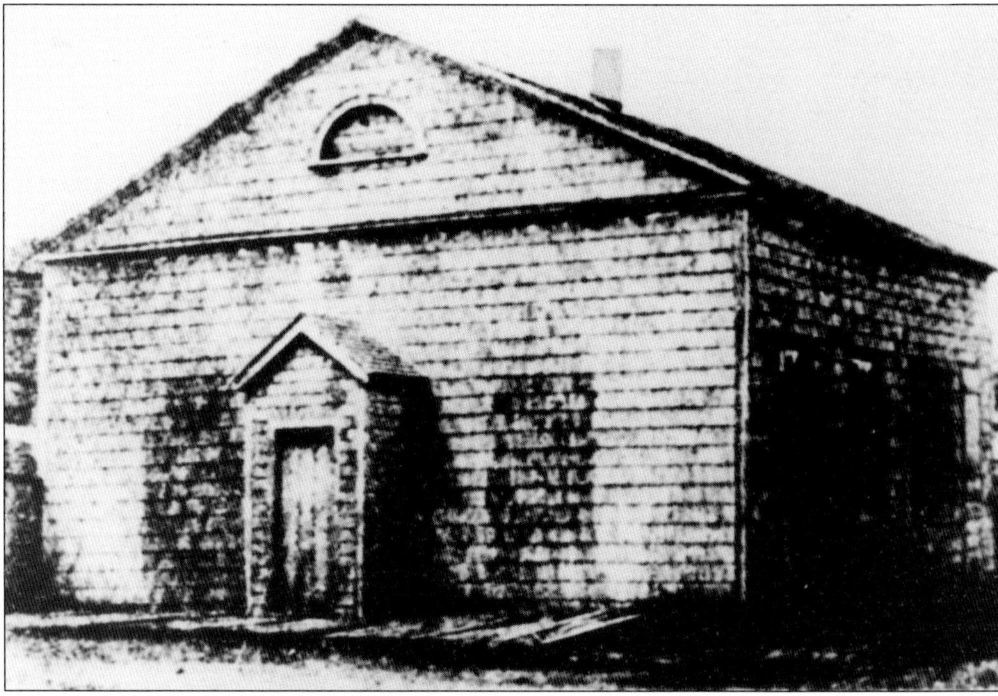

This is the only known photograph of the first church that was built in Saint John West when it was still known as Carleton—the Free Baptist Meeting Hall on King Street. The building also served as the initial home of many other faiths in the area before they established their own churches.

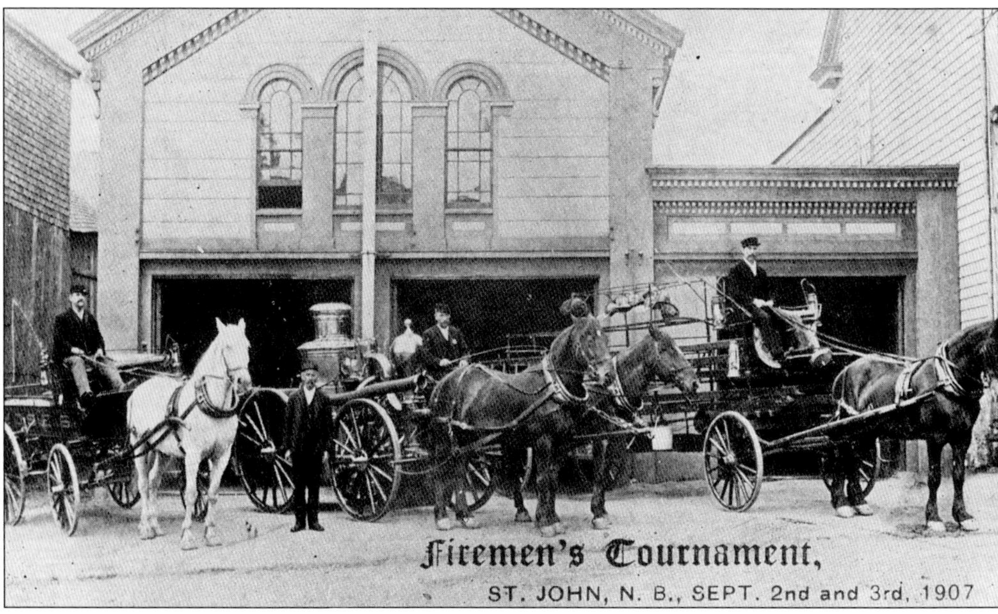

At the Firemen's Tournament held on September 2 and 3, 1907, the men of the King Street West Fire Station are ready to join in the festivities. From the left, Mr. Brittain is the driver of the horse cart; Mr. Lemon and Mr. Christopher are in charge of the fire engine; and Mr. Carvel is the driver of the hook and ladder.

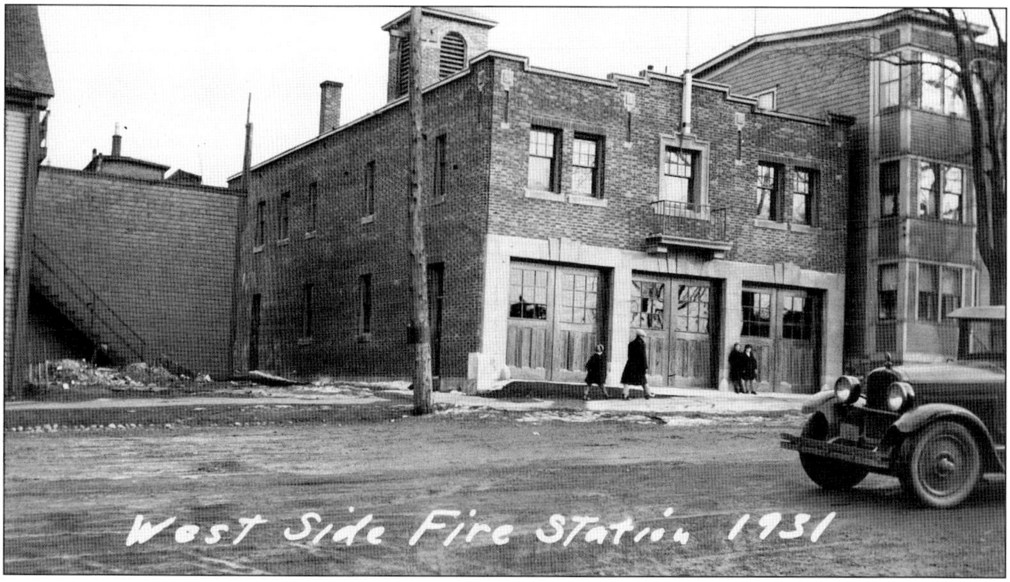

Not nearly as interesting architecturally as its predecessor, the 1931 West Side Fire Station was part of the rebuilding of King Street. Citizen protest has meant that it has survived closure despite a decline in the area's population and business life since the 1960s. (Provincial Archives.)

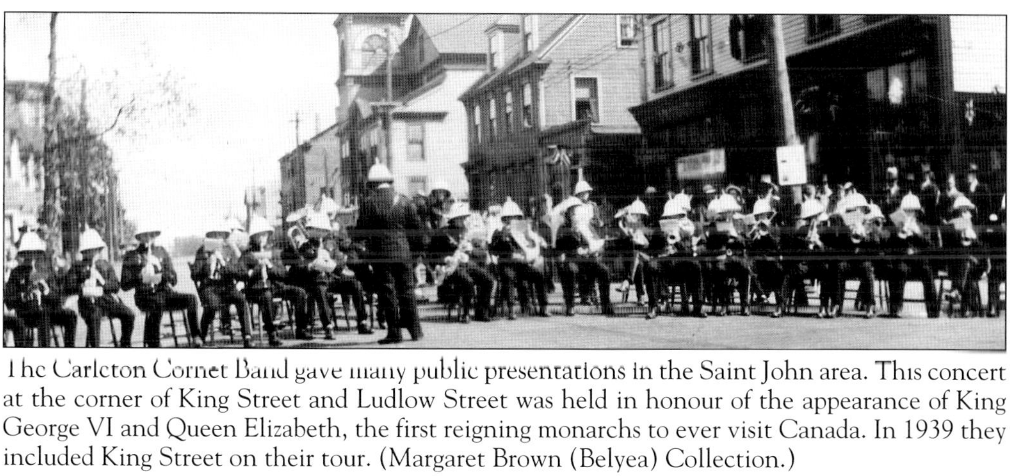

The Carleton Cornet Band gave many public presentations in the Saint John area. This concert at the corner of King Street and Ludlow Street was held in honour of the appearance of King George VI and Queen Elizabeth, the first reigning monarchs to ever visit Canada. In 1939 they included King Street on their tour. (Margaret Brown (Belyea) Collection.)

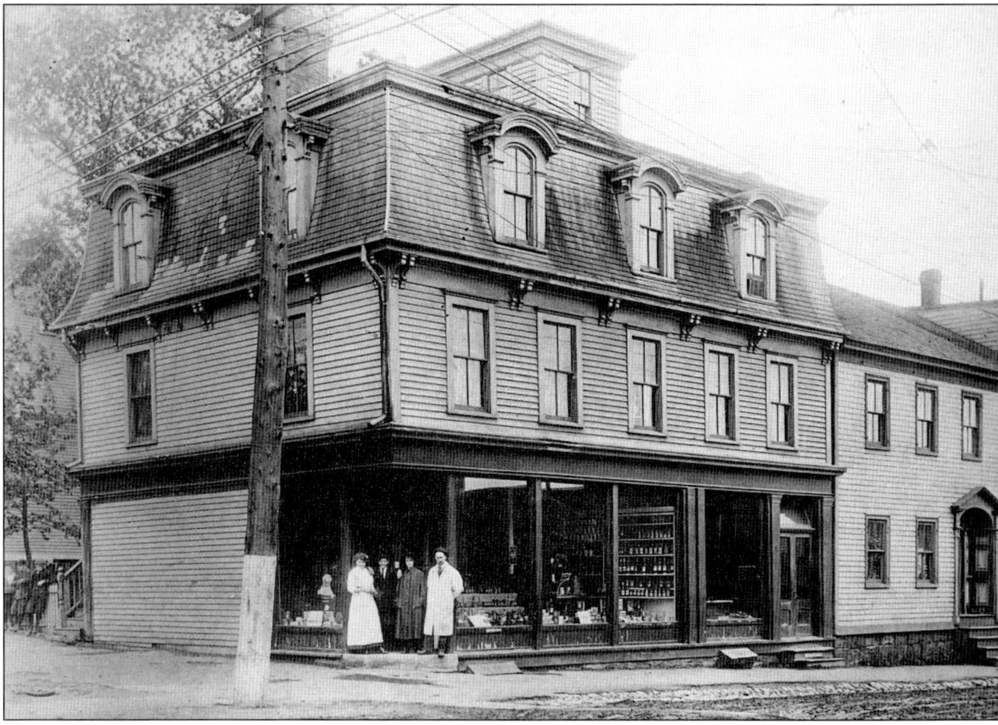

Charlie and Jim Hamm's grocery store at the corner of King and Ludlow Streets about 1917. To the right is Wetmore's Bakery. This building (still standing) is said to have had the greatest turnover of business concerns in Carleton. (Spurge Allaby Collection.)

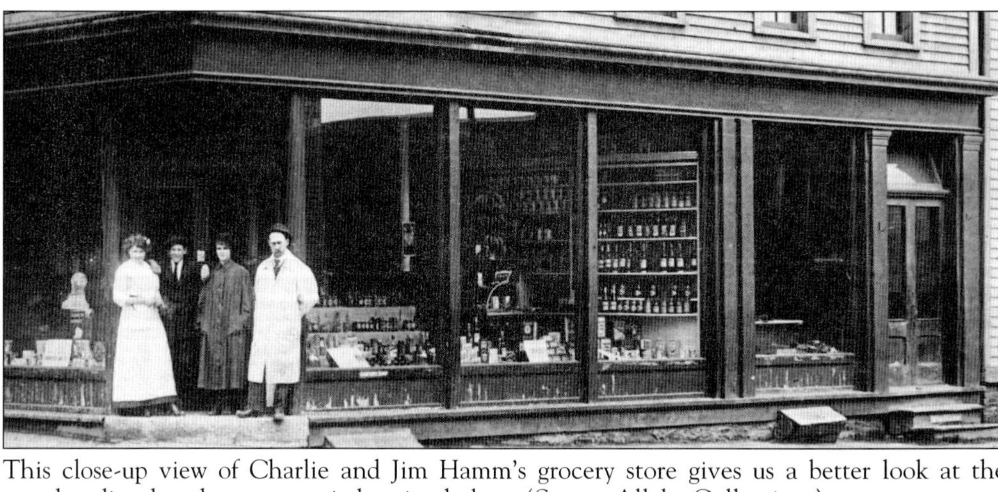

This close-up view of Charlie and Jim Hamm's grocery store gives us a better look at the merchandise that the store carried on its shelves. (Spurge Allaby Collection.)

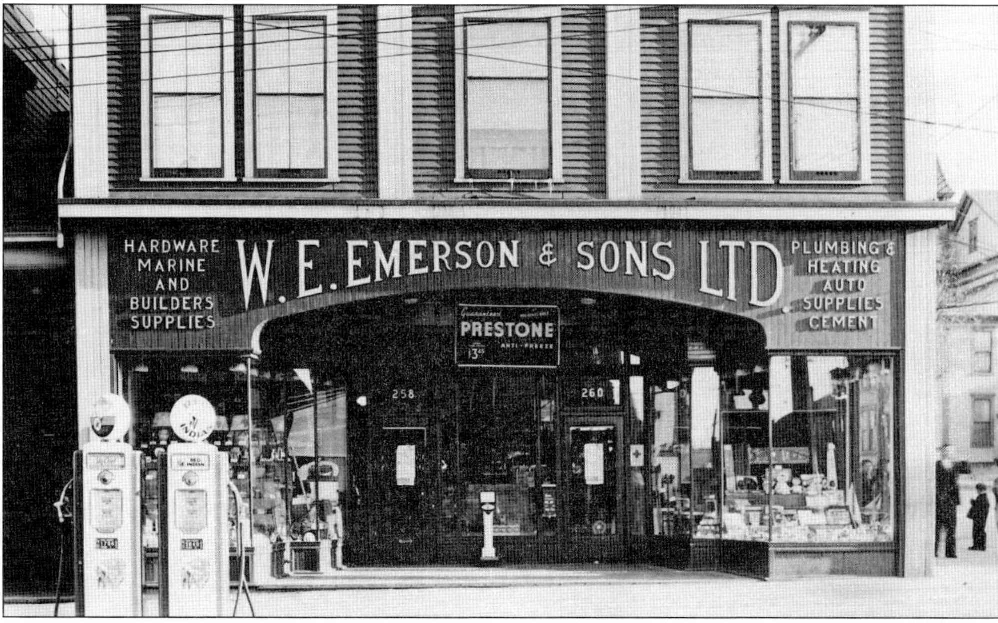

The W.E. Emerson and Sons Ltd. store at the corner of King and Ludlow Streets was the leading hardware store in the Saint John West area. As was common with such stores at the time, the lower level would be used as the sales floor, and the upper level would be made into apartments, thereby producing the maximum revenue possible for the business. (Provincial Archives.)

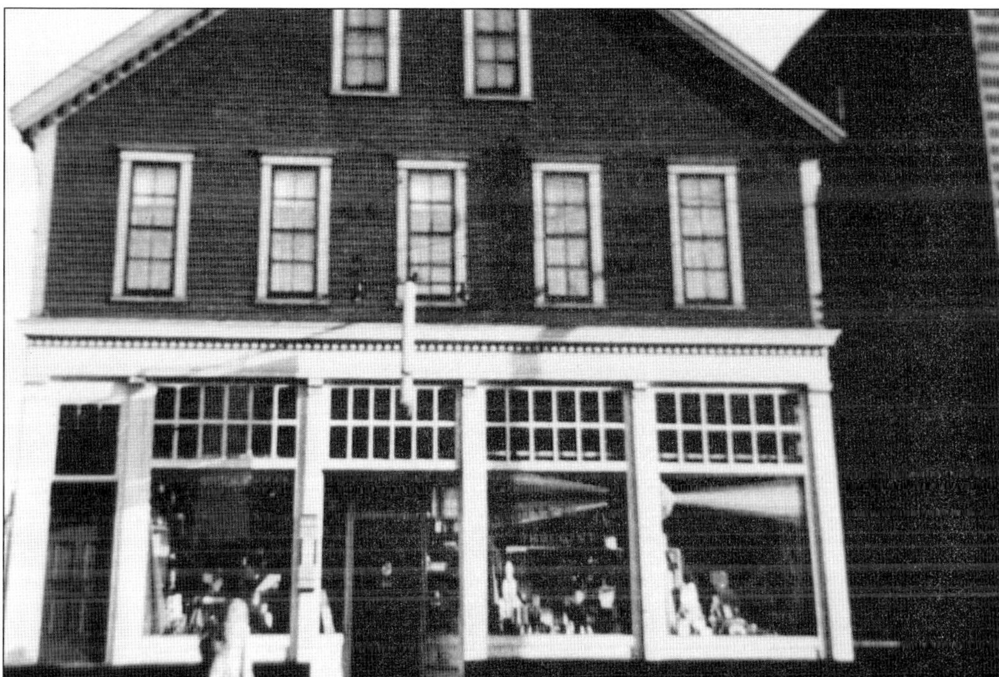

T. Giles Allan, brother of W.C.R. Allen, whose drugstore is shown on p. 39, operated this drugstore on the upper portion of King Street after the 1932 destruction of Union Street. (Gerald Keith Collection.)

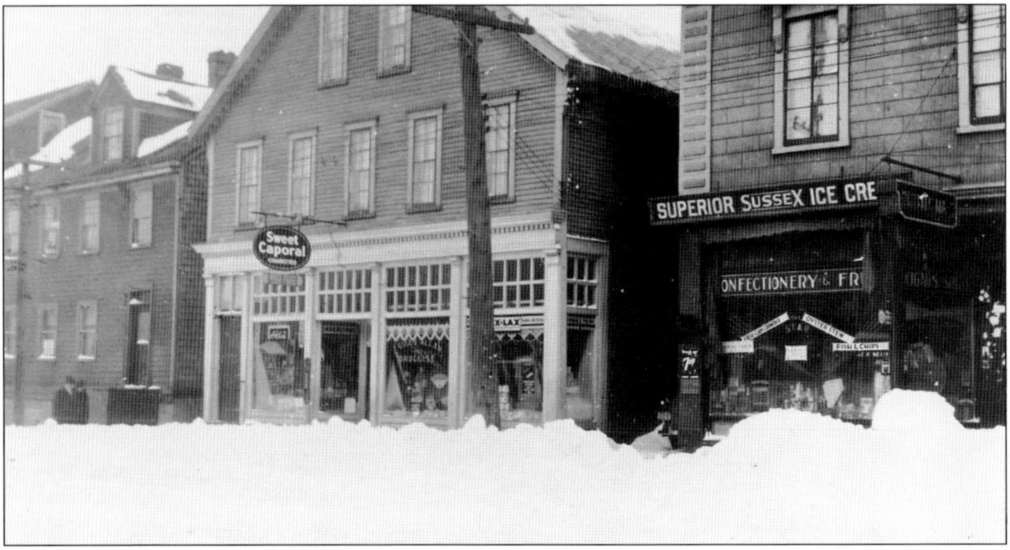

Next to Allan's Drugstore was the Star Ice Cream Parlour and Lunch Counter, the most popular eating spot on King Street. The "Superior Sussex Ice Cream" shown on the sign later won an award for the best ice cream in Canada during a national competition. (Allan Family Collection.)

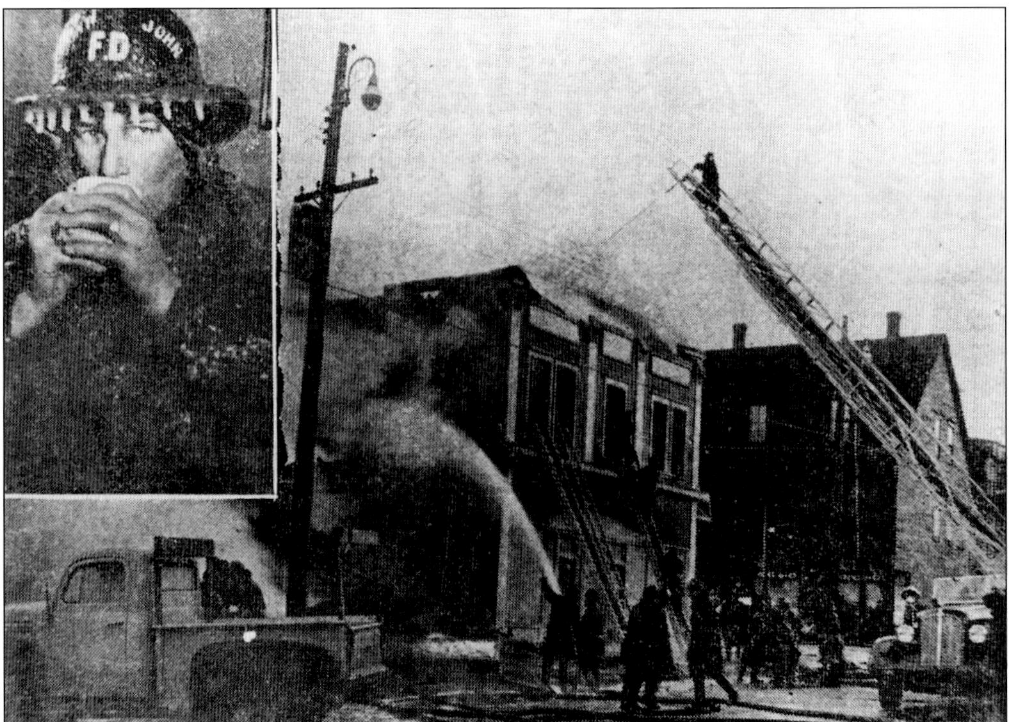

Early in November of 1957, a fire destroyed W.E. Emerson, the Star Restaurant, and the adjacent post office on the upper King Street level. These businesses survived less then thirty years after being moved from their Union Street locations as a result of the port expansion. (*Evening Times Globe*.)

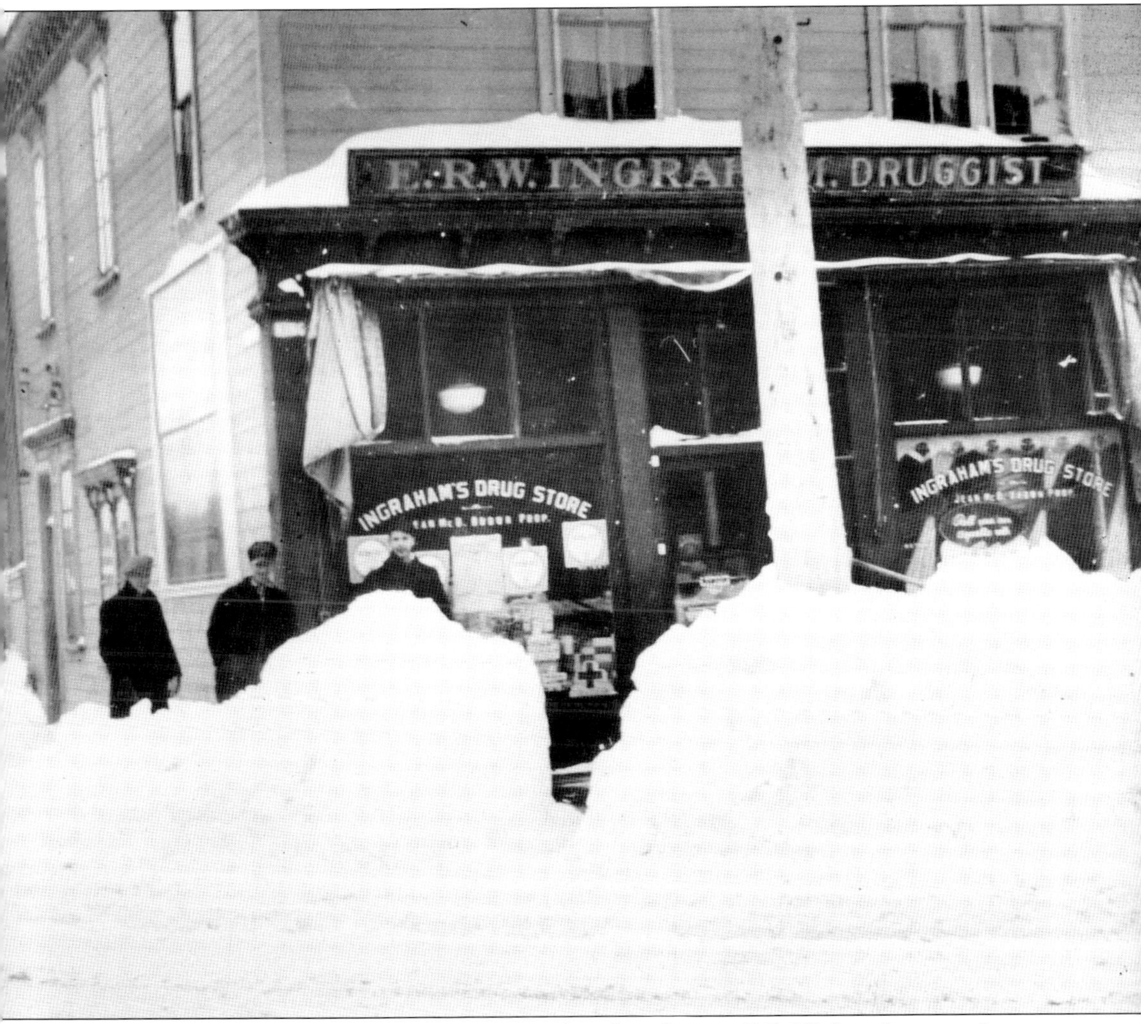

Ingraham's Drug Store on the corner of King and Ludlow Streets. E.R.W. Ingraham was known as "Duphie" by his friends and customers and there are many stories about his operations on Union Street, and later on King Street. During the winters when the business was at the Union Street location it is said that "Duphie" used to throw buckets of water onto the stoop of his store so it would freeze and discourage street car passengers from waiting in the entrance and blocking customers. At King Street a story is told of "Duphie" selling a man a beautiful cigar. Just as the customer proceeded to light his cigar, "Duphie" tapped him on the shoulder and pointed to a "No Smoking" sign in the store. The man protested vigorously. "You sold me the cigar, why can't I smoke it in the store?" he asked angrily. "Duphie" pointed to his wide range of merchandise and said, "I also sell Exlax." The point was taken and the man left the premises. (Allan Family Collection.)

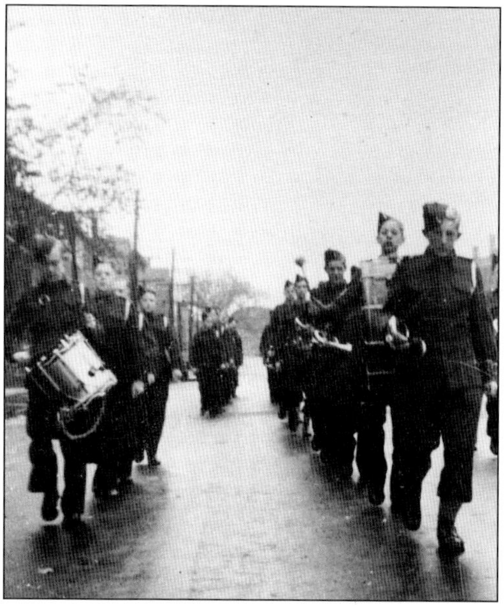

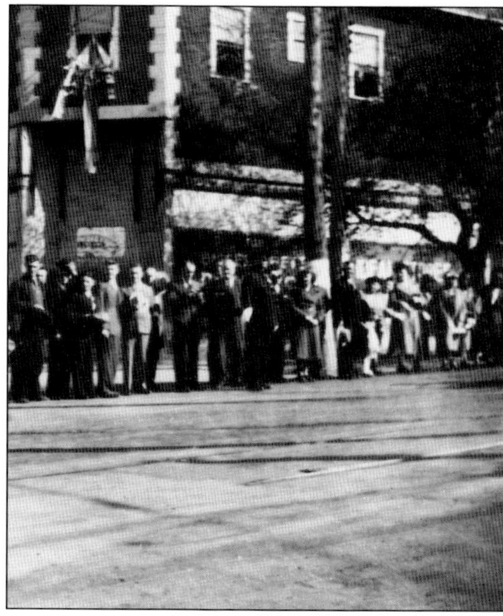

Left: Public events such as this parade including the New Albert School Band often took place on King Street West. (Malcolm Harned Collection.)
Right: The royal visit to Saint John on June 13, 1935, included a parade down King Street West and thousands gathered to watch the King and Queen go by. (Margaret (Belyea) Brown Collection.)

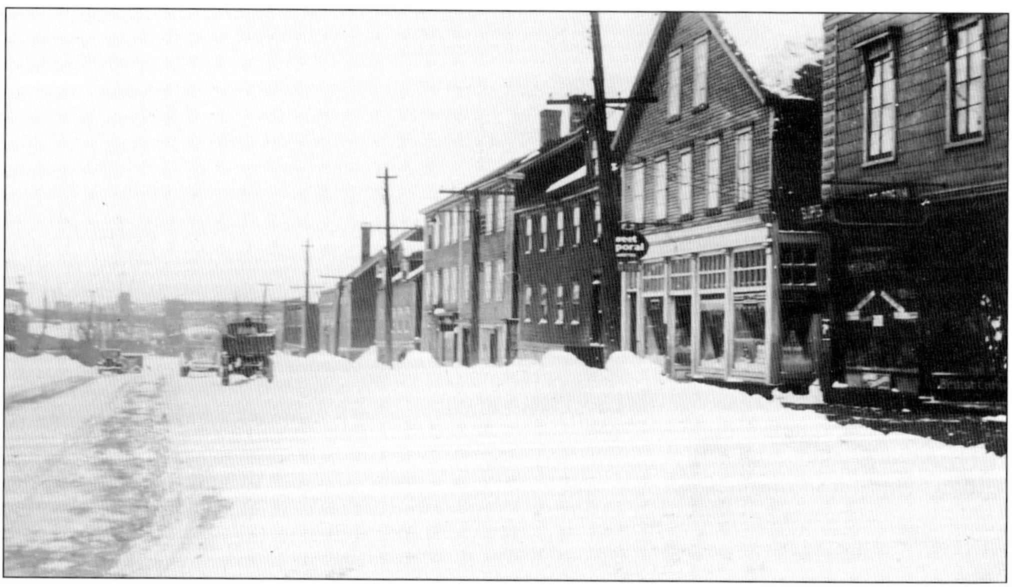

Winter visits King Street West but business carries on as usual. From the bottom of the street are the Ideal Store, the Bank of Nova Scotia, Iliffe Shoe Repair, Leslie's Barbershop, McCarthy's Ladies Wear, Charlie Meisner's Barbershop, Allan's Drugstore, and the Star Restaurant. (Allan Family Collection.)

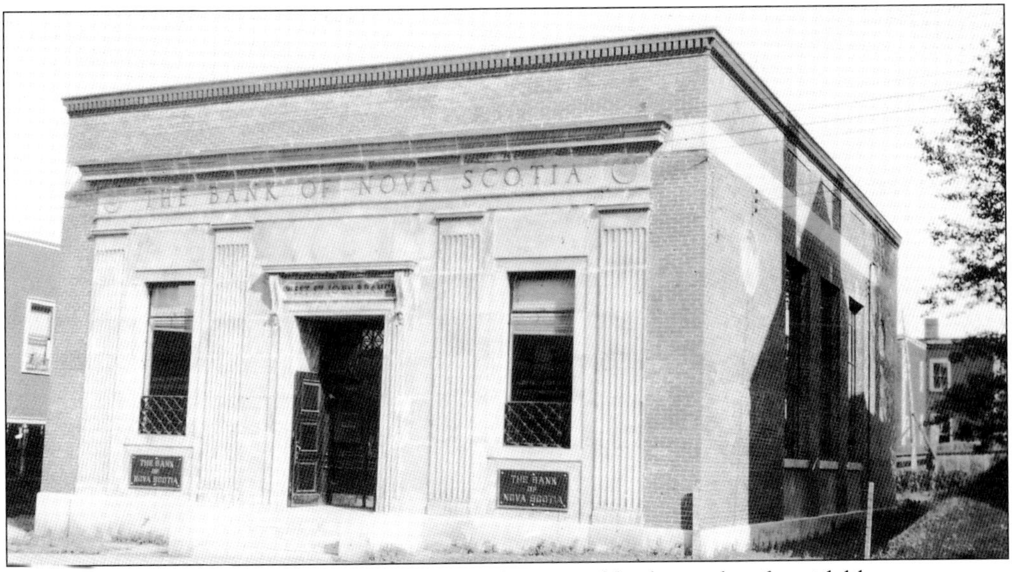

The Bank of Nova Scotia moved from Union Street and built another formidable structure on King Street in 1932. (Allan Family Collection.)

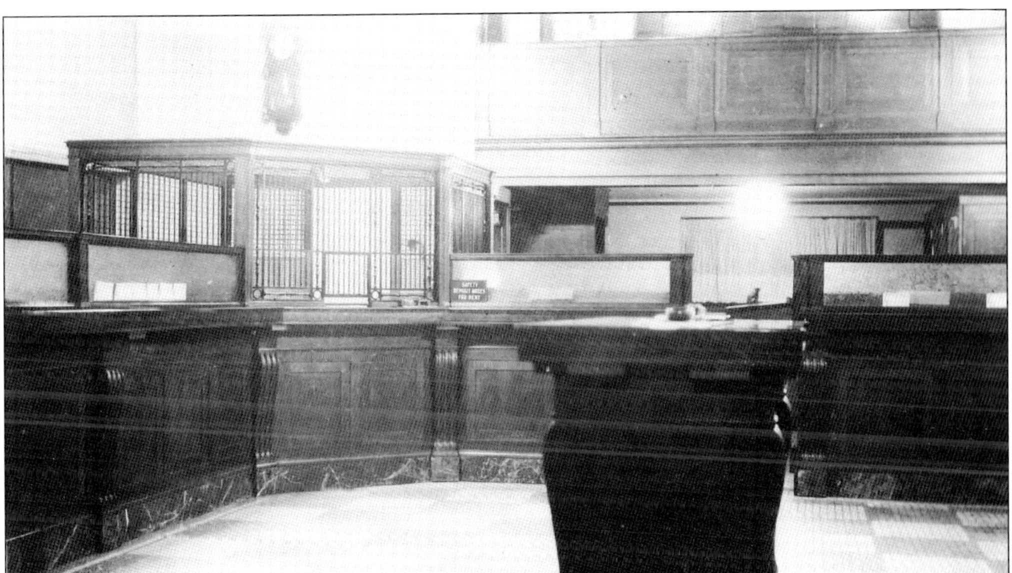

This is the interior of the very staid Bank of Nova Scotia with the well-protected teller's cage. Millions of dollars passed through this bank every year as a result of the port and railway operations which were the lifeblood of Saint John West. (Allan Family Collection.)

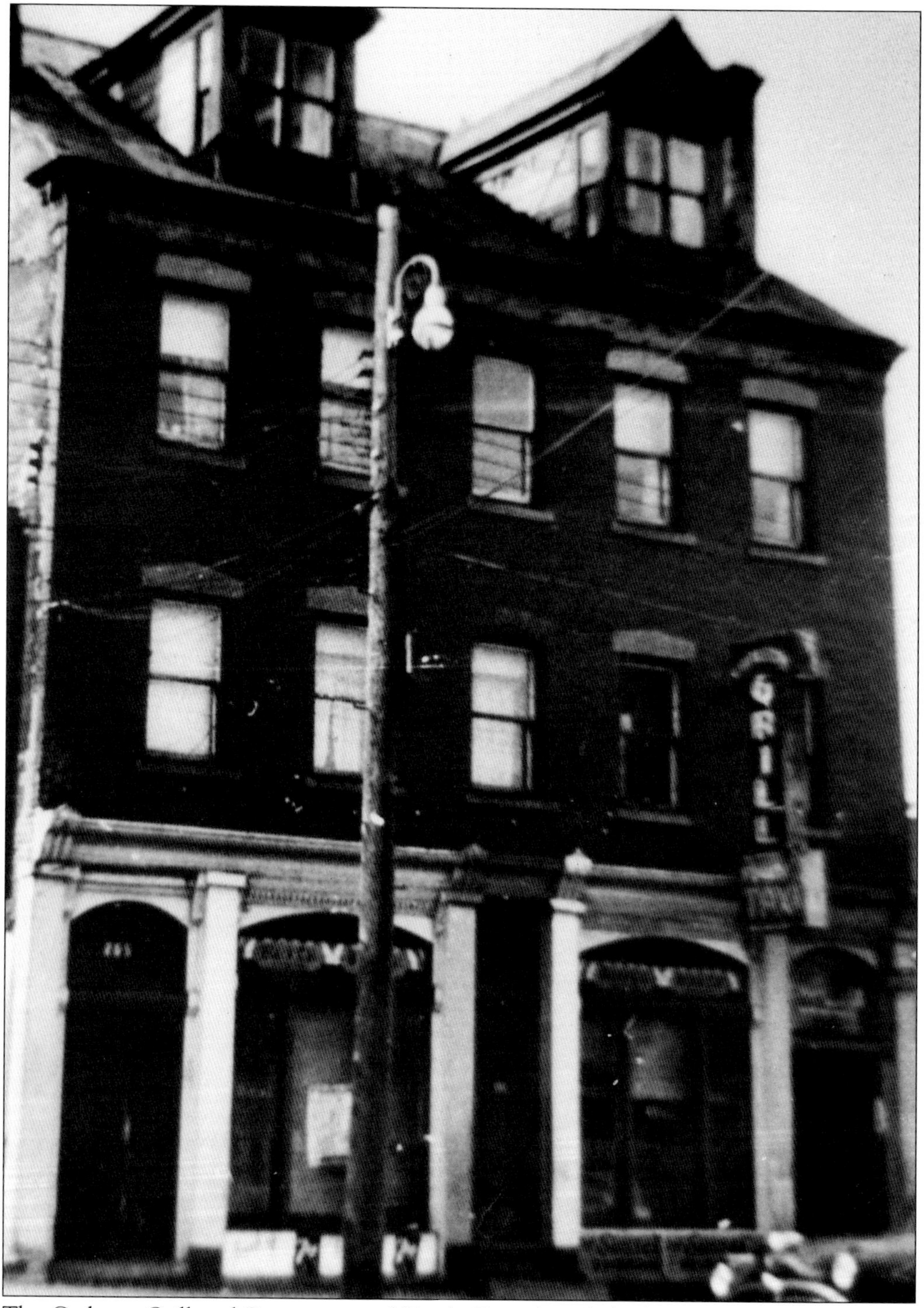

The Carleton Grill and Restaurant and Fundy Taxi shared the lower level of this building on King Street while the upper level had rooms to let by the day, week, or month. These rooms weren't always used for sleeping as sailors coming into the port well knew. (Gerald Keith Collection and Provincial Archives.)

Six

The Great Port Fire of June 22, 1931

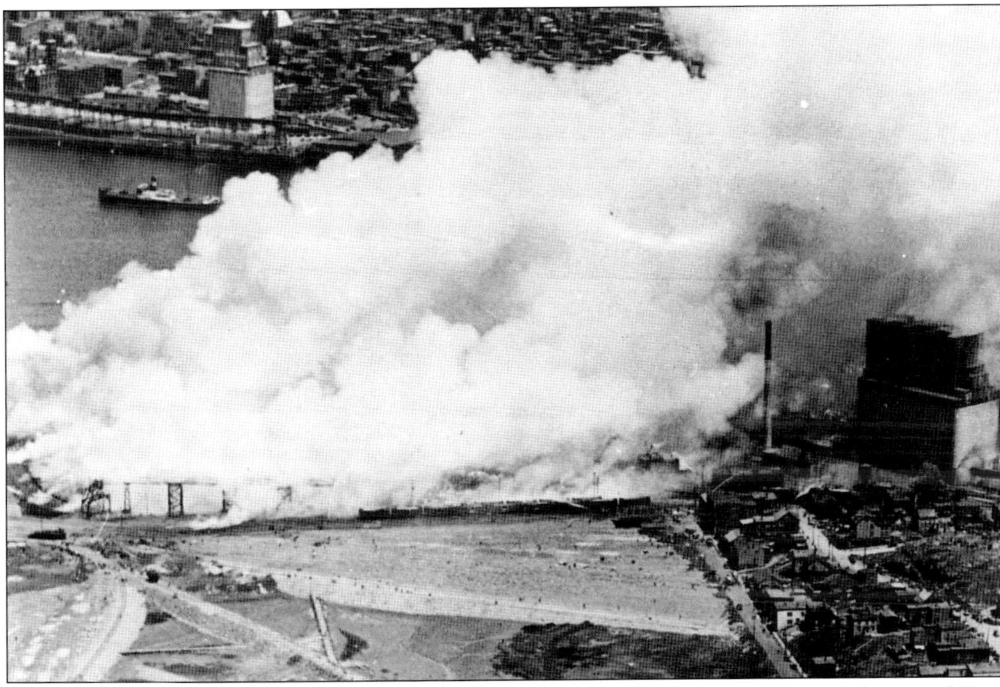

A disastrous fire swept through the port on the afternoon of June 22, 1931, and destroyed Piers 8 through 14 and the grain elevators that served them. In some ways this conflagration proved more of a boon than people realized when they saw the smoke rising over the harbour on that June day, for it was just at the beginning of the Depression years and the rebuilding and repairing provided some much-needed work for West Siders Area tradesman set to work repairing the ruined piers, sheds, and railway property, while those on welfare could earn an extra $2 per day by helping to tear down the cribwork of the old piers and the metalwork of the elevators that had to be replaced, as well as pulling out the old steel spikes and gathering the metal to be sold for scrap. In addition, many West Siders feeling the pinch of the Depression visited the blackened piles of lumber and were able to saw off pieces and take them home to burn to keep their families warm. So all in all what looked like a tragedy turned out for the better of Saint John West—ships' berths were rebuilt and boom years were just around the corner with the coming of World War II. What these pictures remind us, however, is that at the time most people were concerned with just surviving the Depression. (National Harbours Board.)

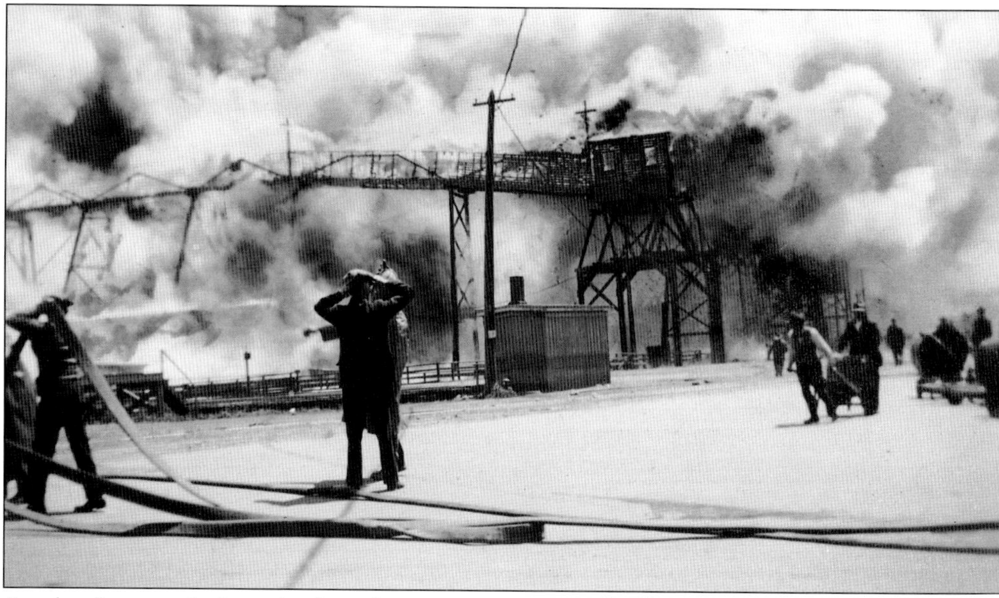

As the fire raged through the afternoon, tenement dwellers on Protection Street whose homes were threatened by the flames tried to gather their possessions and get them out of harm's way. Most of them weren't able to save very much from their homes. (Dorothy Campbell Collection.)

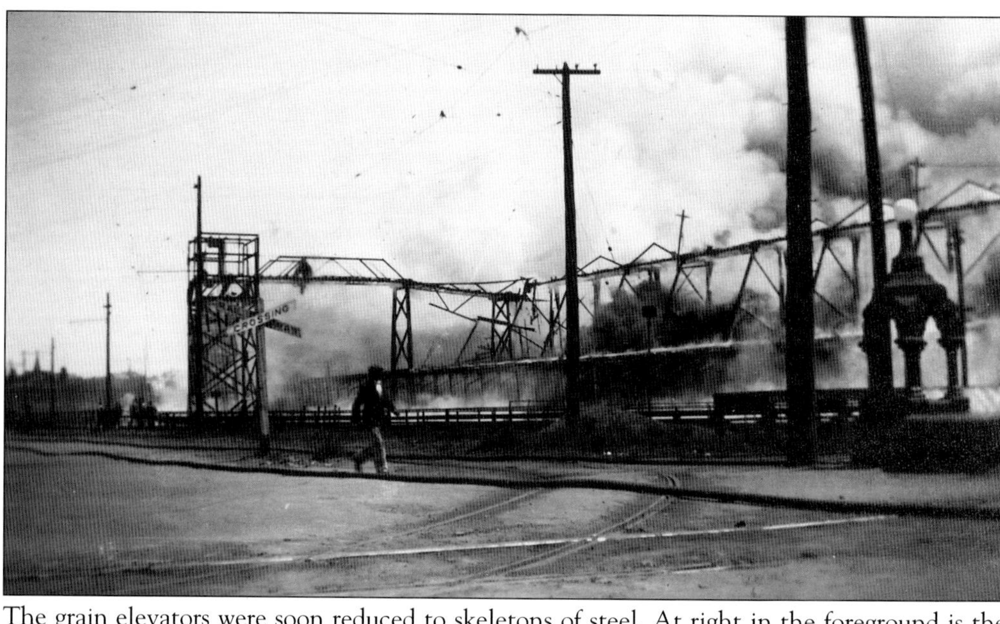

The grain elevators were soon reduced to skeletons of steel. At right in the foreground is the Band of Mercy Fountain placed by members of St. Jude's Church as a humane effort to give the horses (and men) that worked around the port a clean drink of water. This fountain still stands in Saint John West although not at this location. (Dorothy Campbell Collection.)

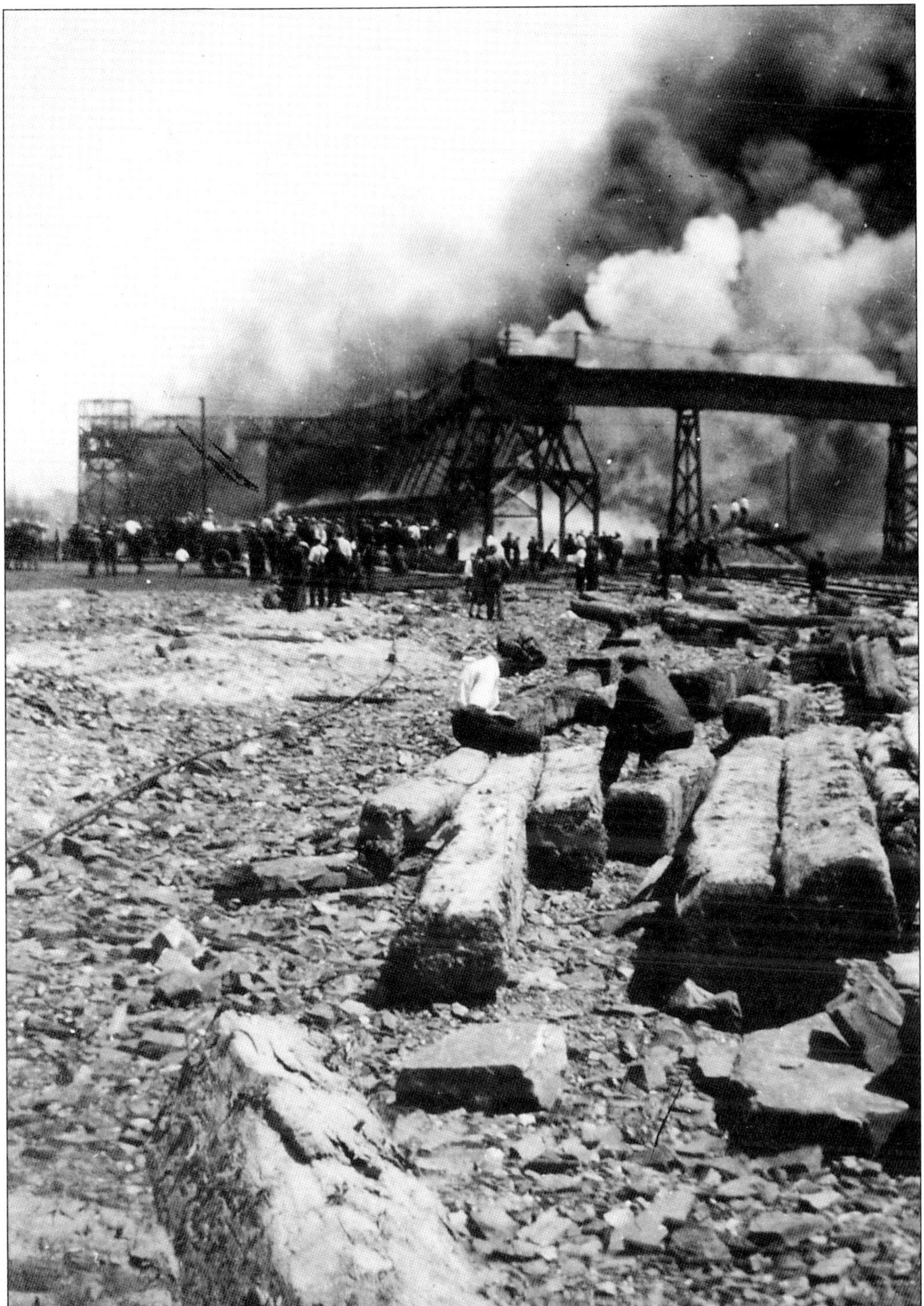

The boys sitting on the logs washed up from previous wharf construction work seem oblivious to the fact that $10 million worth of destruction is going on as the grain elevators burn behind them.

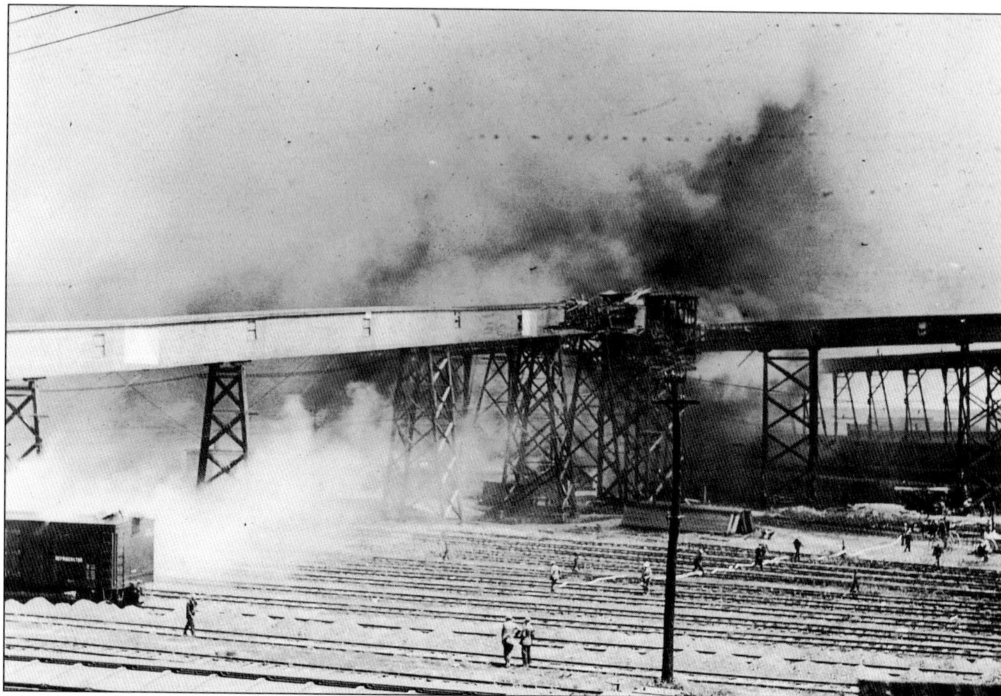

Even fire-fighting equipment could not escape the intensity of the flames—a new fire truck that was parked on the wharf fell through the weakened planking and disappeared into the depths of the harbour during the Great Port Fire of 1931. (Eleanor James Collection.)

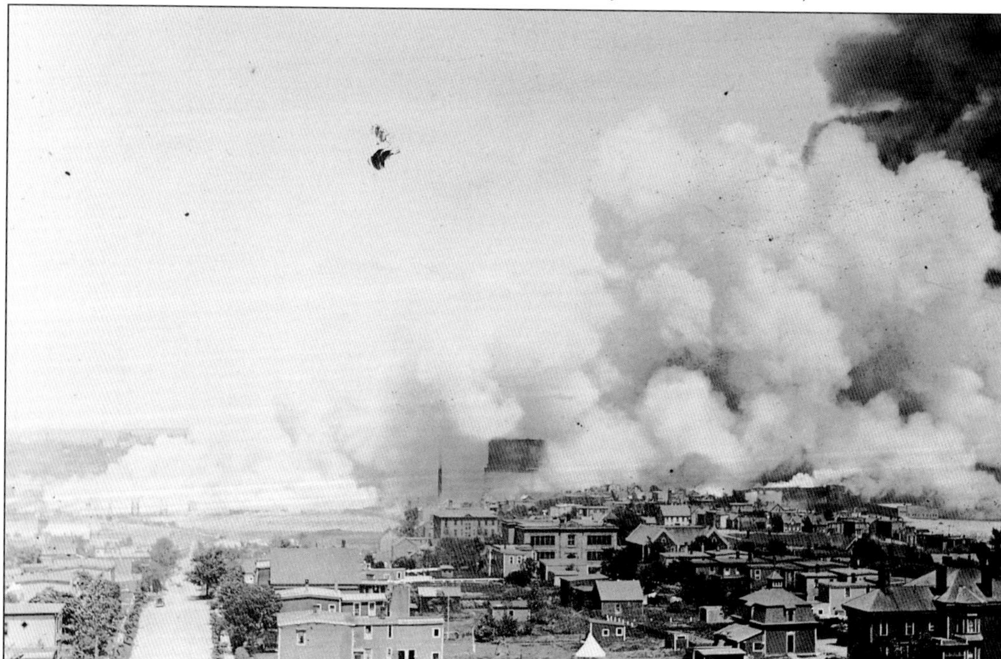

This view taken from the heights at Martello Tower shows the fire as it burns its way from the centre of the harbour towards Pier 14 at the extreme south end of the harbour, destroying everything in its path. (Eleanor James Collection.)

Seven

Postcard Views of Saint John

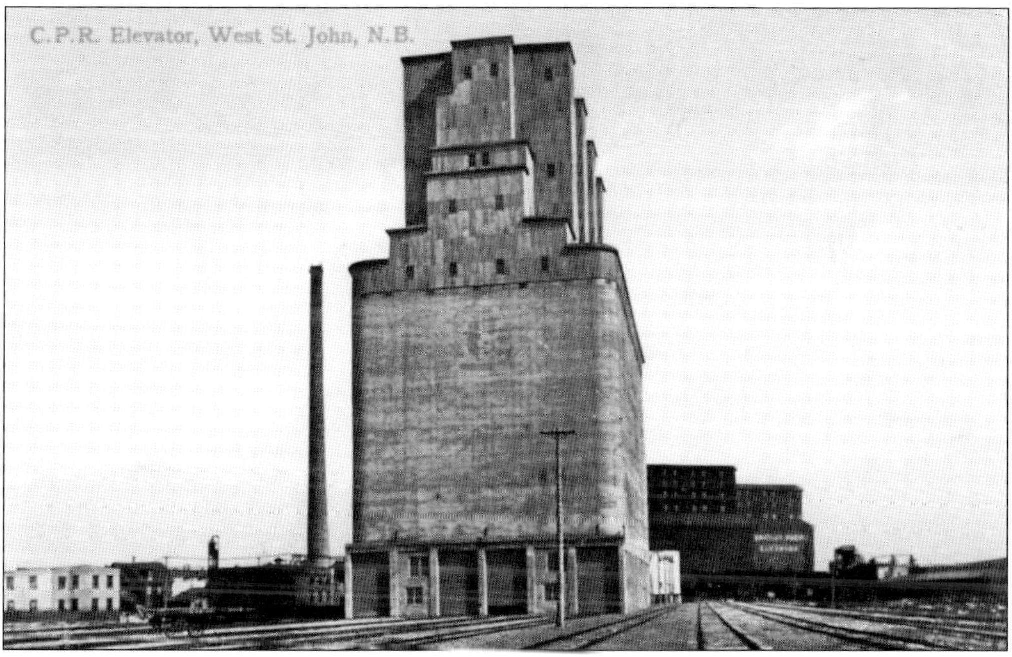

At the turn of the century, local photographer Isaac Erb took many pictures in the Saint John area. The images were often hand coloured and were used extensively as picture postcards in the heyday of the postcard as a quick method of communication. The glass negatives now belong to Jamie Wilson of Wilson's Studio, who has given permission for the use of Erb's images in this compilation. This postcard shows the Canadian Pacific Railway grain elevator in Saint John West. (Erb Collection.)

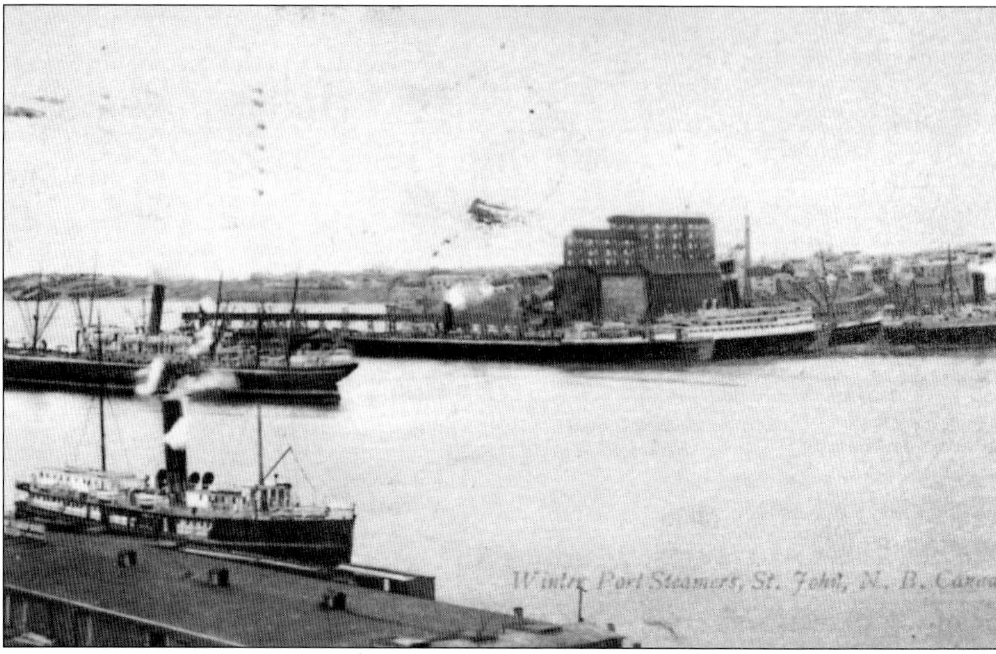

In 1906 it only cost 1¢ to send this winter view of the Saint John harbour looking from the city centre toward Carleton at Sand Point. (Erb Collection.)

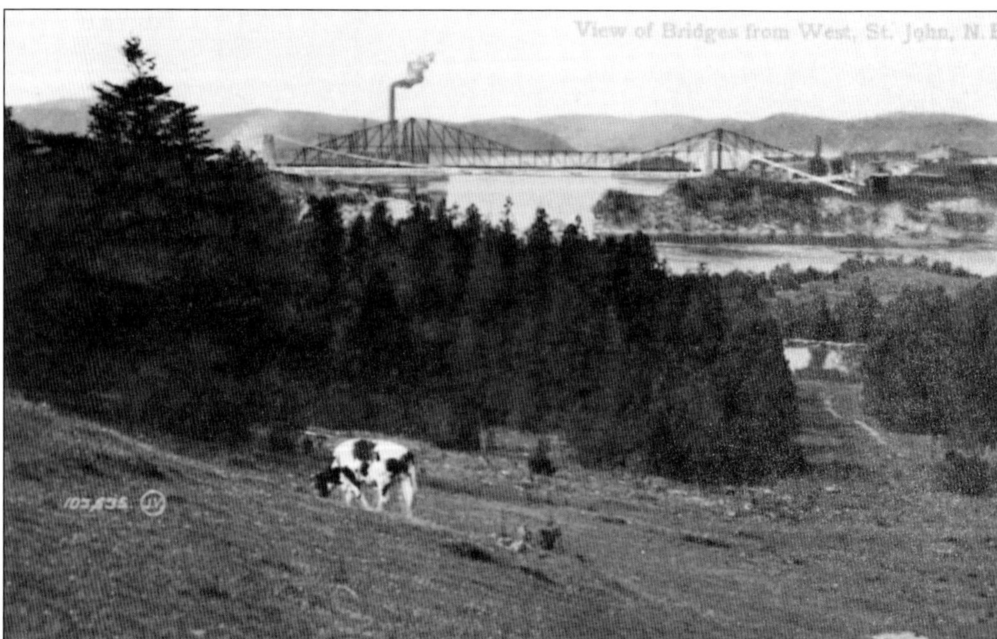

Taken from the heights of Carleton, this is a view of the suspension bridge which spanned the Reversing Falls between 1853 and 1916. (Erb Collection.)

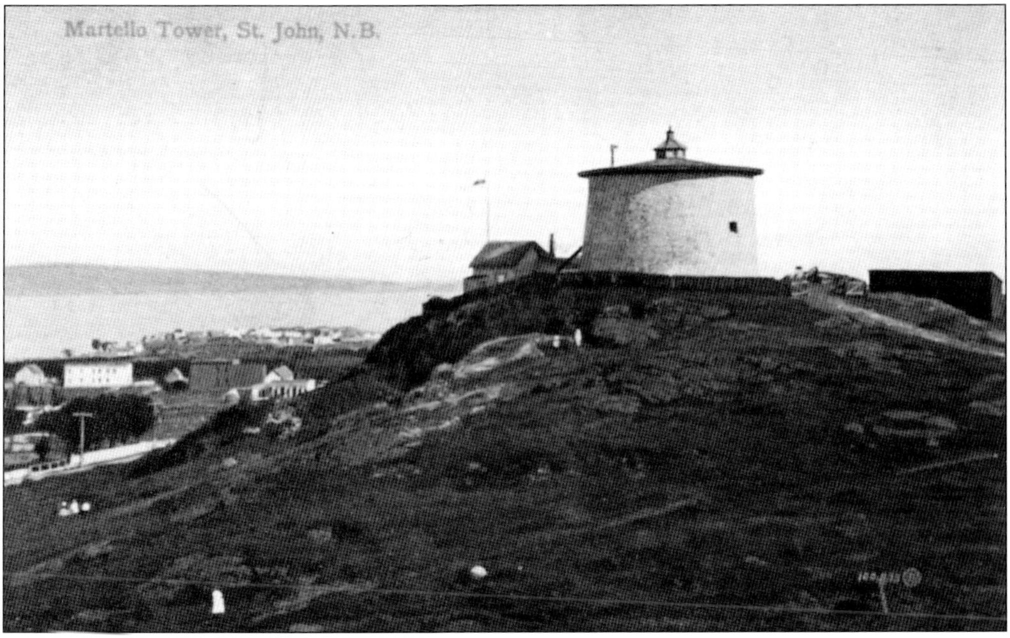

Martello Tower has stood on Carleton Heights overlooking Saint John West since the year 1813 when it was built as a defence against American attack, and yet not one shot has ever been fired from the site. It is one of only a dozen such defences still in existence. (Erb Collection.)

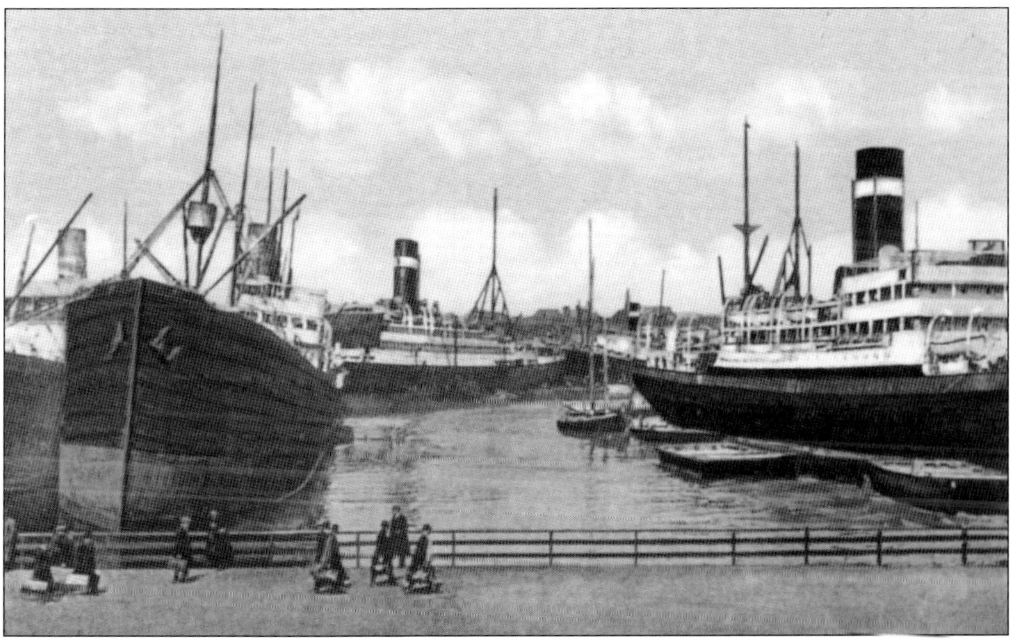

In the winter months during the port's "golden age" activity was such that when the St. Lawrence froze over sometimes as many as two or three steamers would be tied side by side in the Saint John West area awaiting unloading. (Erb Collection.)

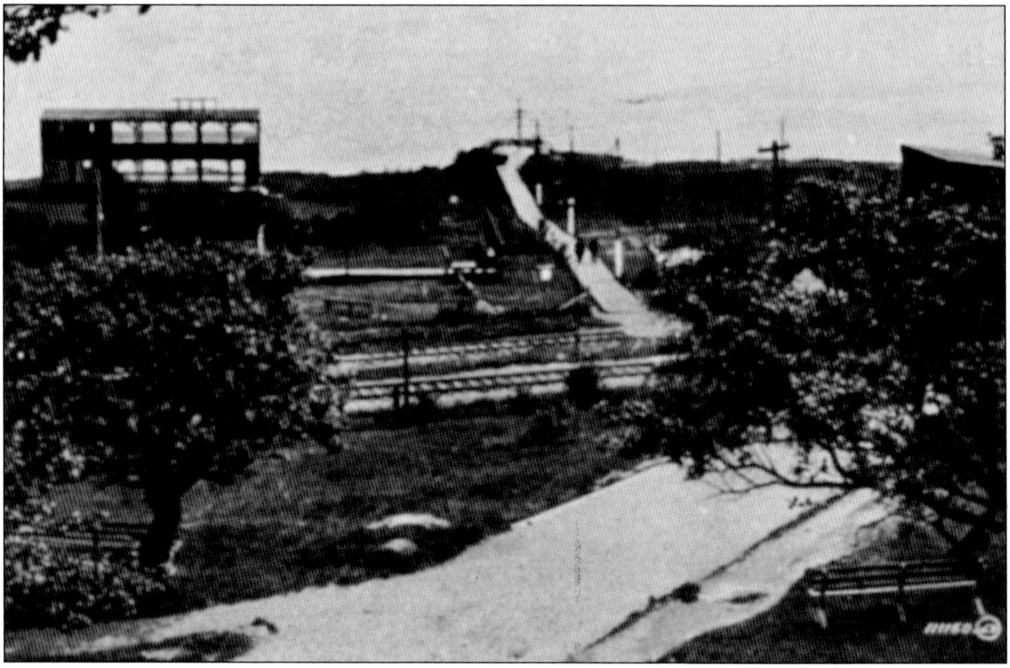

When the residents of Carleton wished to escape to the country they had only to walk 20 minutes west, and along the Fundy coast to the 14 acres of beauty at Seaside Park. Those too young or old or too eager to get there to walk could take an open-air streetcar to the park, which was a private development of the Street Railway Company. (Erb Collection.)

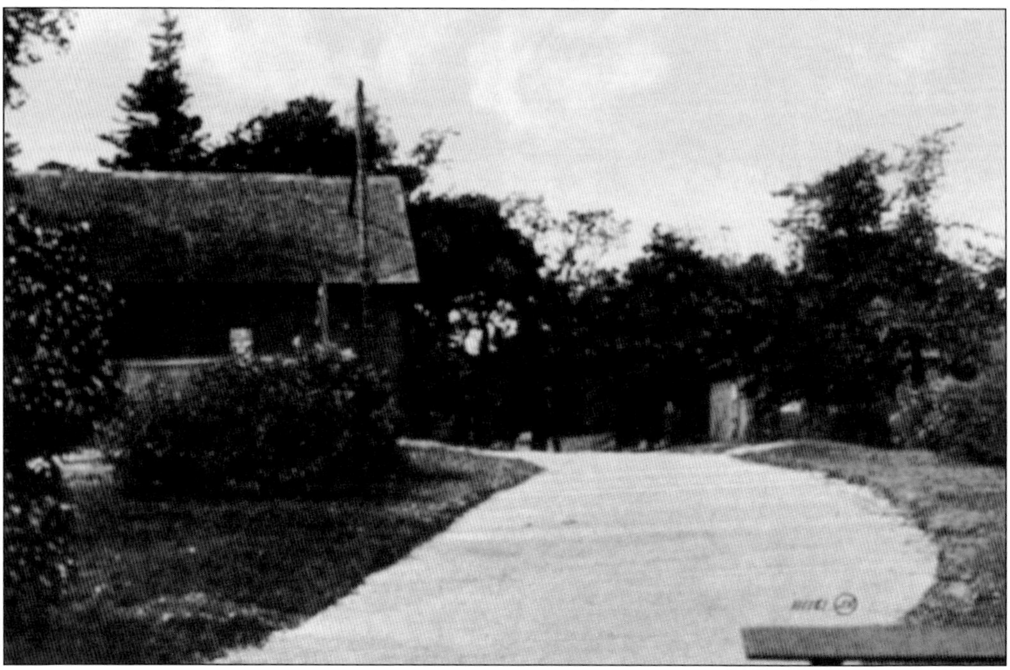

Amongst its many facilities, Seaside Park included a dance hall, a canteen, and for a time a merry-go-round. It overlooked the Bay of Fundy about a mile from where Carleton or Saint John West ended at the city line, and the parish of Lancaster began. (Erb Collection.)

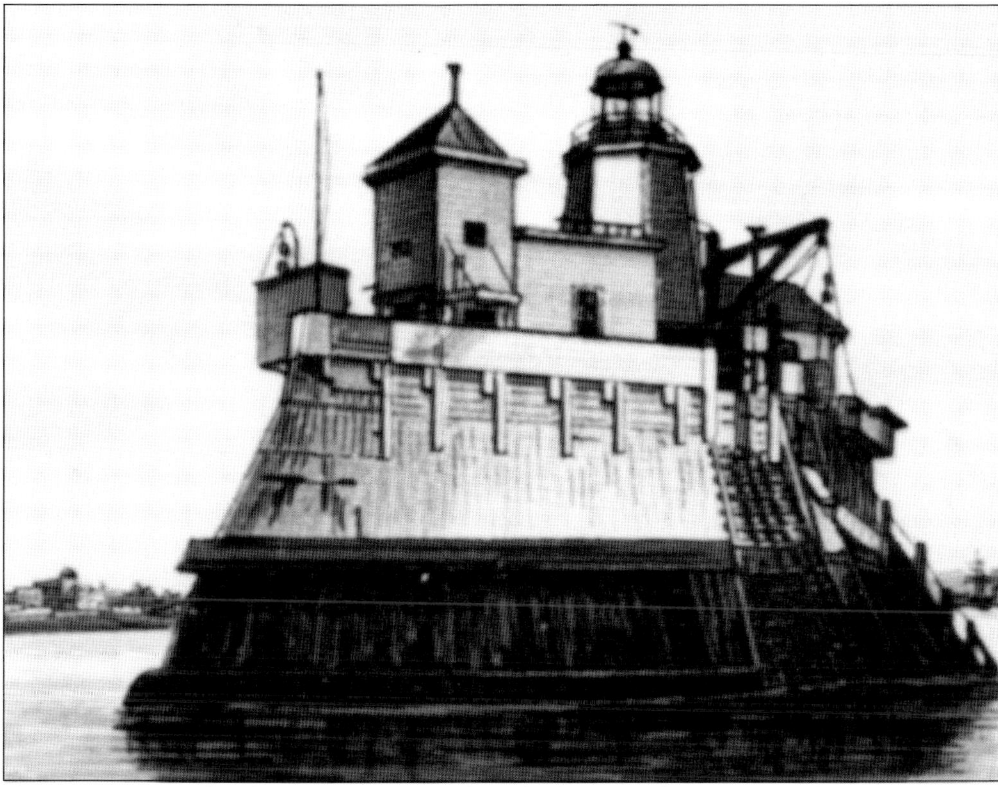

Ships coming into berth in Saint John Harbour had to pass the Beacon Light. It was built on a rocky outcropping in the harbour as a warning to ships whose captains did not know of the danger of the shoals when covered by the 26-foot tides of the Fundy. (Erb Collection.)

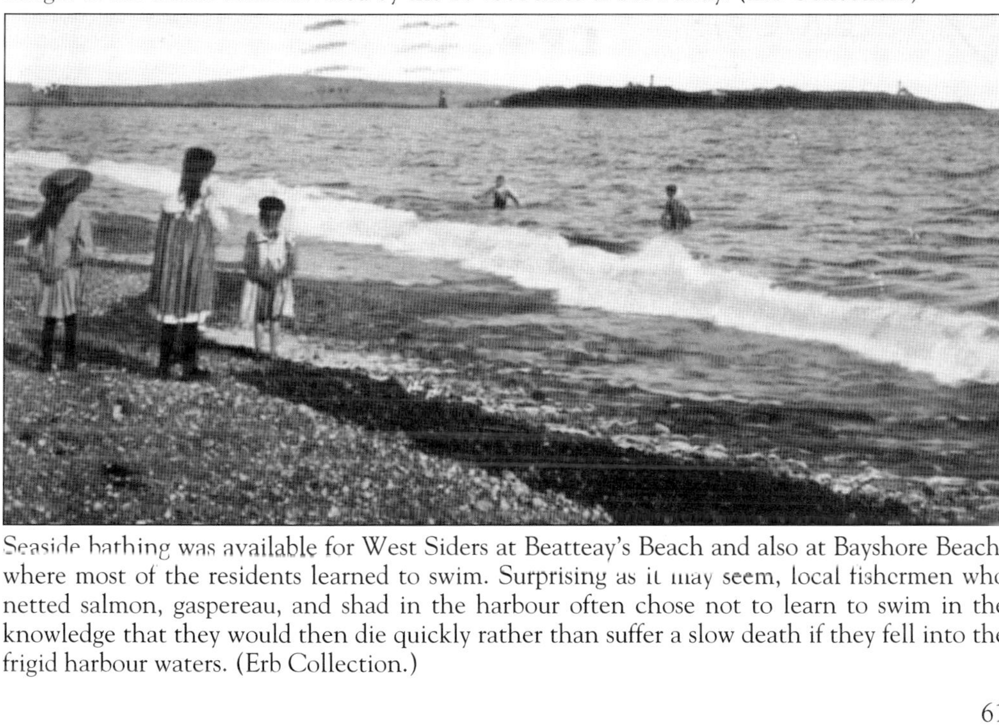

Seaside bathing was available for West Siders at Beatteay's Beach and also at Bayshore Beach, where most of the residents learned to swim. Surprising as it may seem, local fishermen who netted salmon, gaspereau, and shad in the harbour often chose not to learn to swim in the knowledge that they would then die quickly rather than suffer a slow death if they fell into the frigid harbour waters. (Erb Collection.)

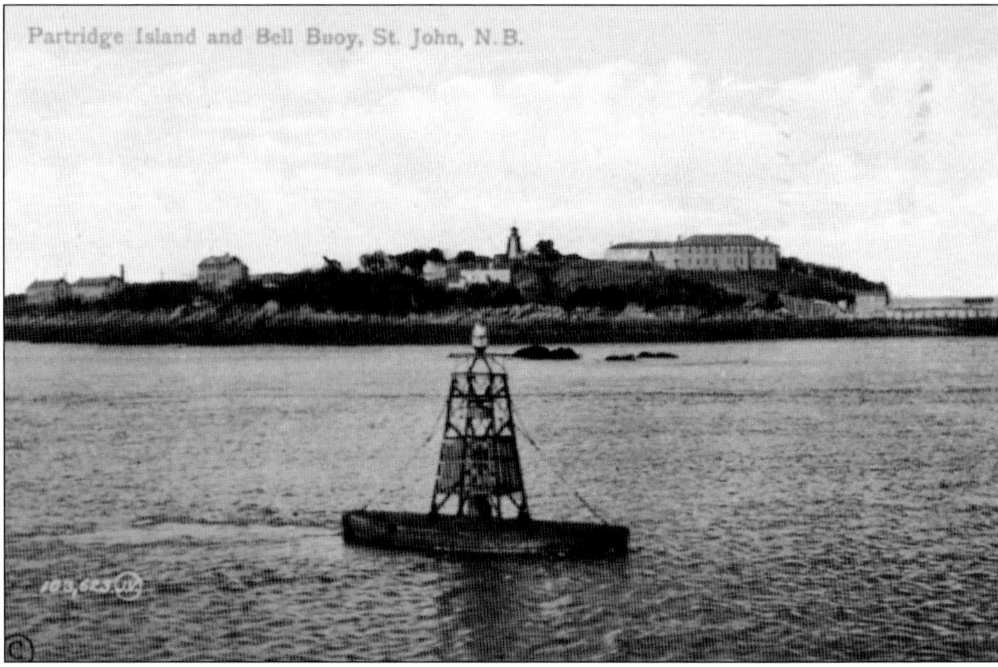

Partridge Island at the mouth of Saint John Harbour was the landing place for thousands of Irish immigrants who came to the city following the 1845–1847 famine in Ireland. Many settled in Carleton and along the Fundy coast and became the longshoremen and fishermen of the area. (Erb Collection.)

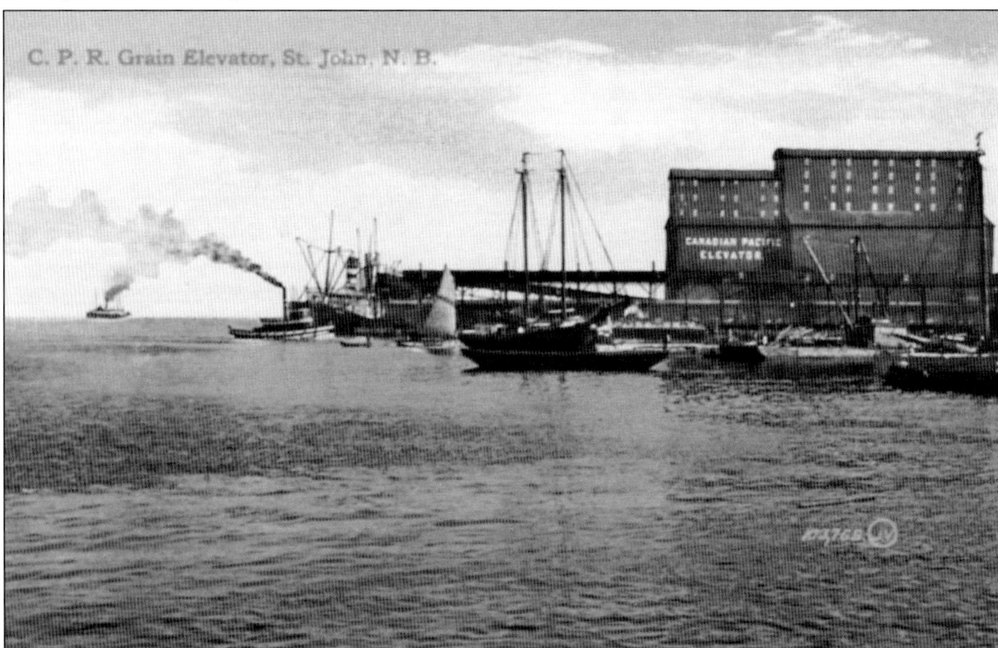

Photographs taken from ship to shore are rather rare, as are photographs of fishermen in action in and around Saint John Harbour. This is a view of the West Side of Saint John Harbour in the days when wooden ships were being gradually replaced by steel vessels. (Erb Collection.)

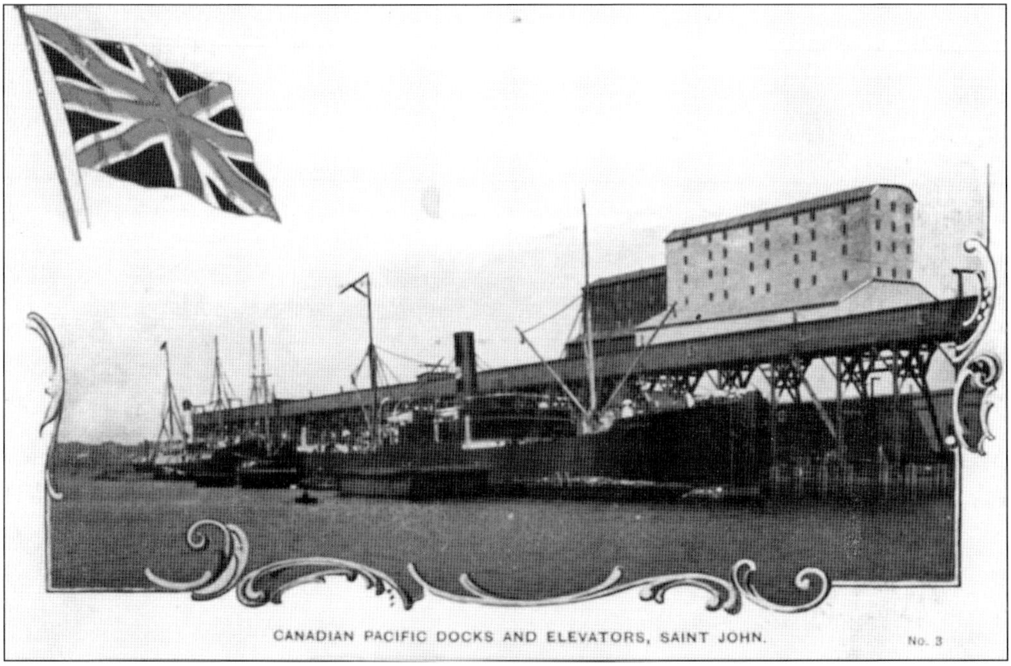

The Canadian Pacific Railway docks and elevators in Saint John West are shown in this very patriotic postcard. Note the Union Jack—the flag of the United Kingdom—in the upper left. (Erb Collection.)

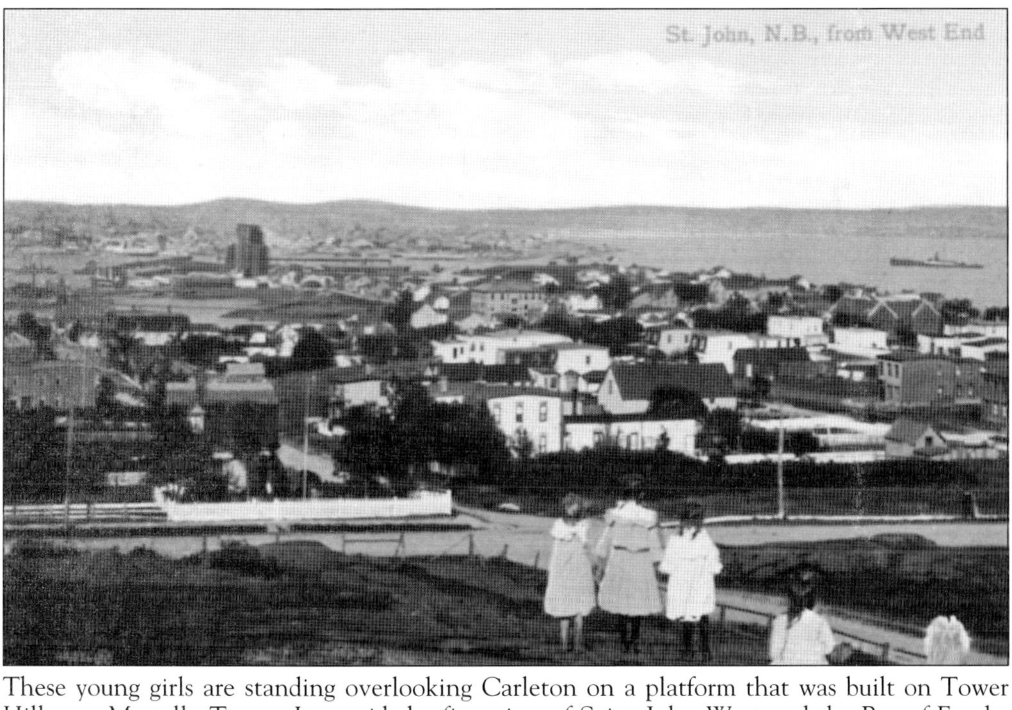

These young girls are standing overlooking Carleton on a platform that was built on Tower Hill near Martello Tower. It provided a fine view of Saint John West and the Bay of Fundy. (Erb Collection.)

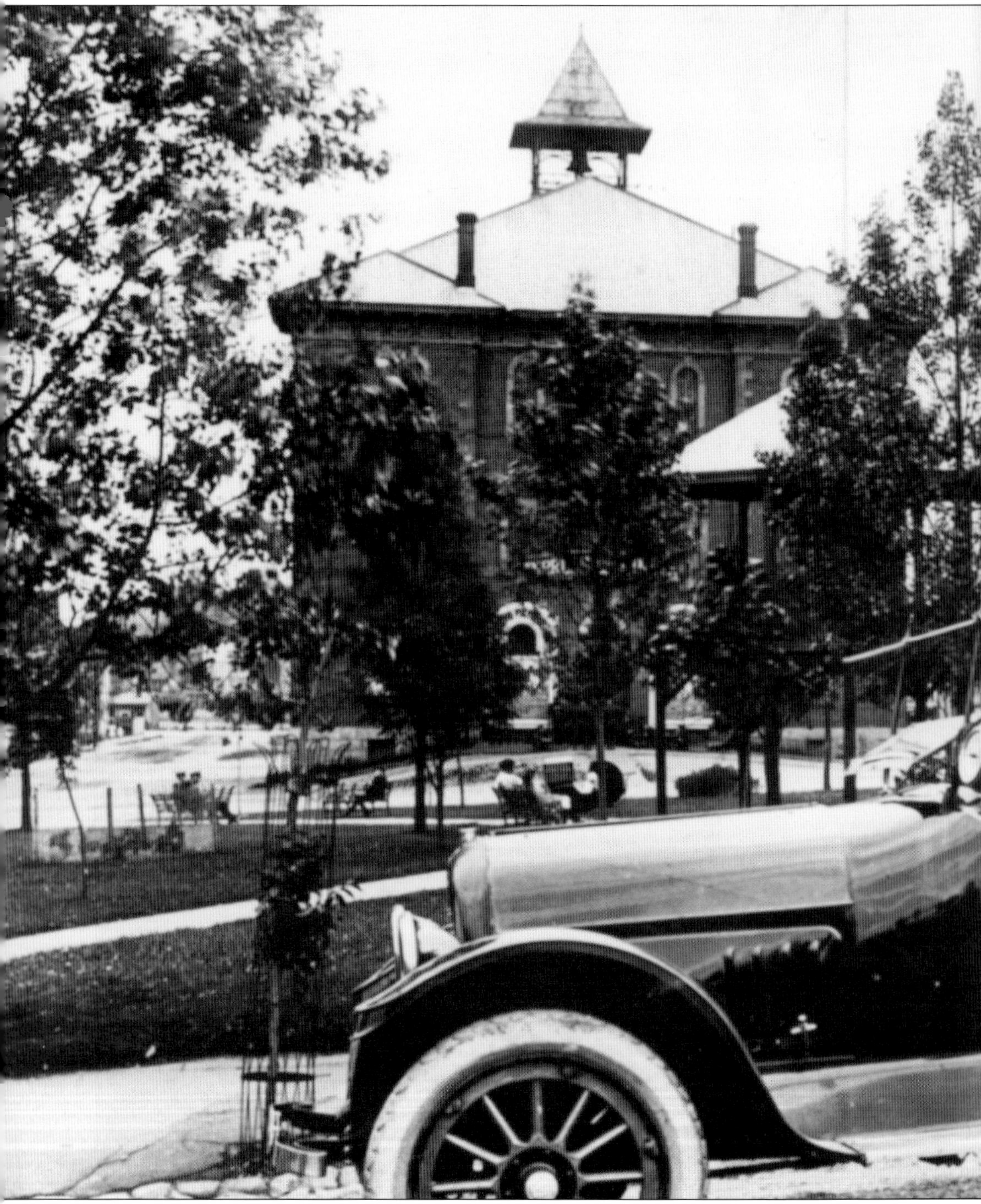

Paul Lenihan picked this photograph up at a flea market. At the time he had no idea what it represented but he recognized the Carleton Public Hall in the background and knew Fred Miller would be interested in the shot. After a lot of searching Fred discovered that the car was that of foundry owner George Waring. His wife and daughter are in the back seat and a chauffeur is at the wheel. In the background is Tilley Square and behind the square is the

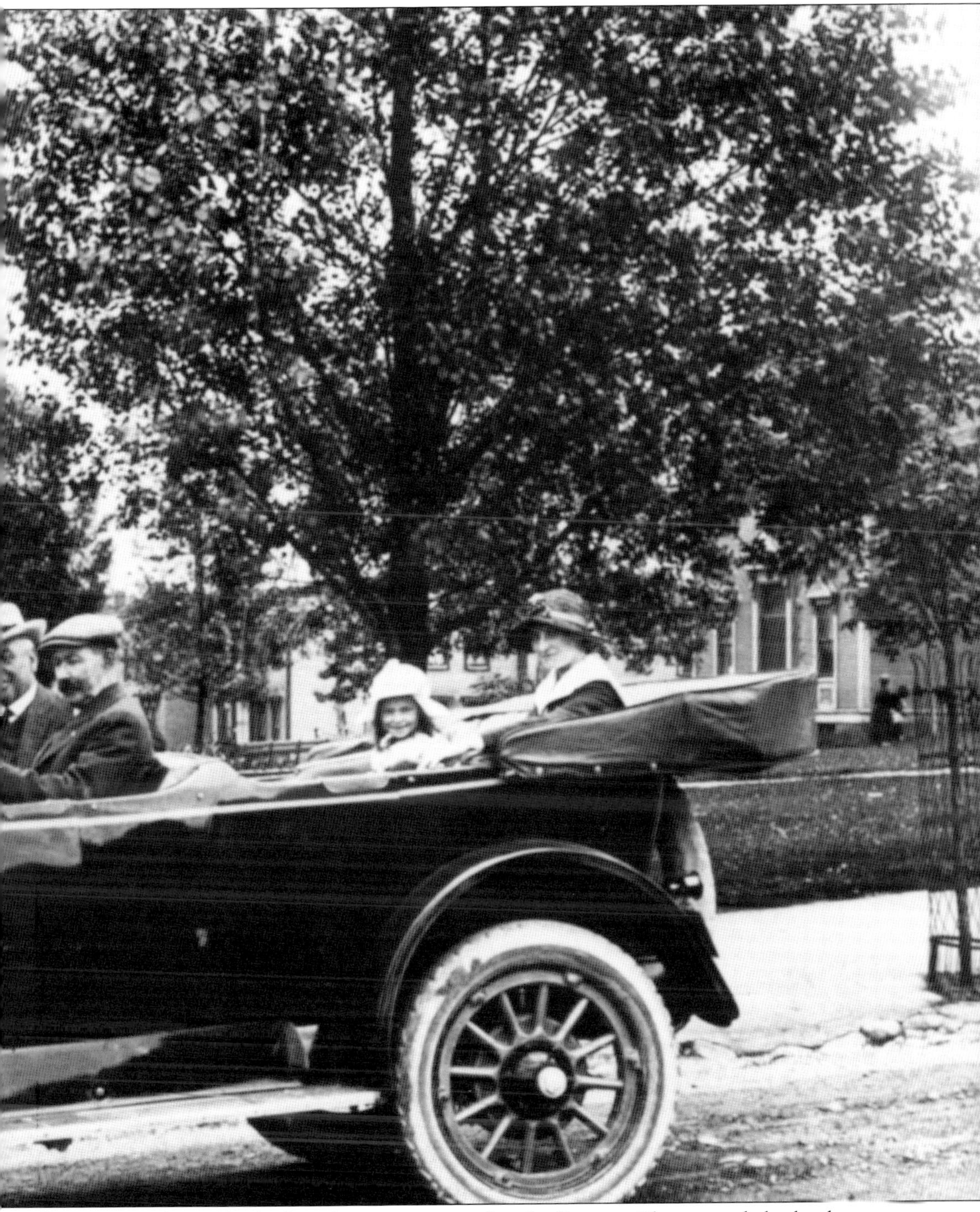

Carleton Public Hall, which at that time was used as the Empress Theatre and also by the water department, the health department, and by the police, who had a lockup in the basement. The hall had a huge auditorium that was at various times used for musical presentations, revival meetings, and lively temperance rallies that kept Saint John West "dry." The third level of the hall was destroyed by a fire in the mid-1920s. (Paul Lenihan Collection.)

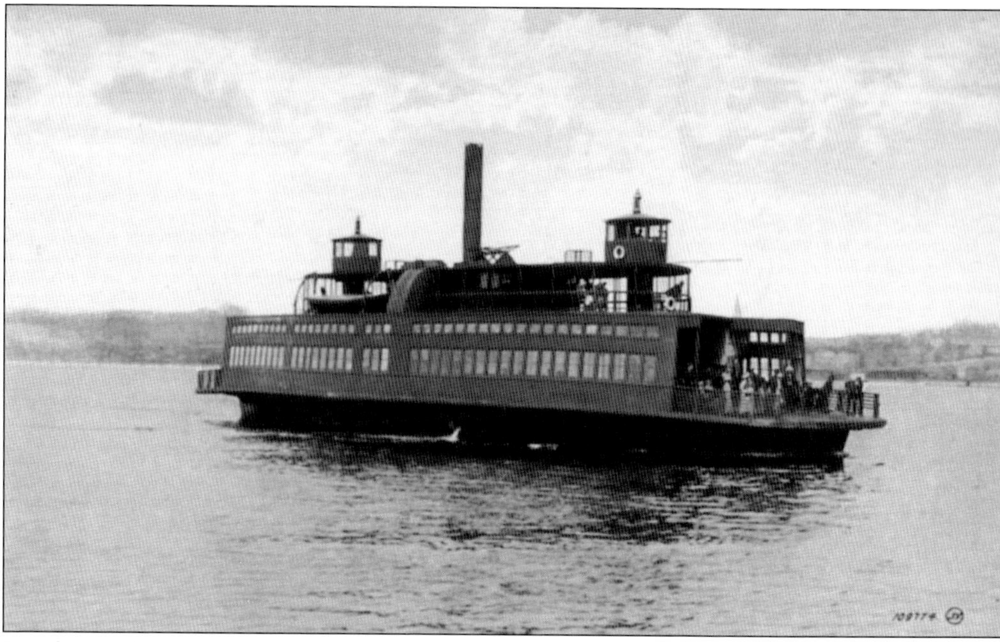

Residents of Carleton who wished to go to central Saint John could travel by ferryboat. A book of tickets cost 20¢ for ten. Old records tell us that passage for an elephant was 25¢, but as elephants were banned from crossing the Reversing Falls suspension bridge when the circus came to town the ferry was guaranteed a few four-footed passengers! (Erb Collection.)

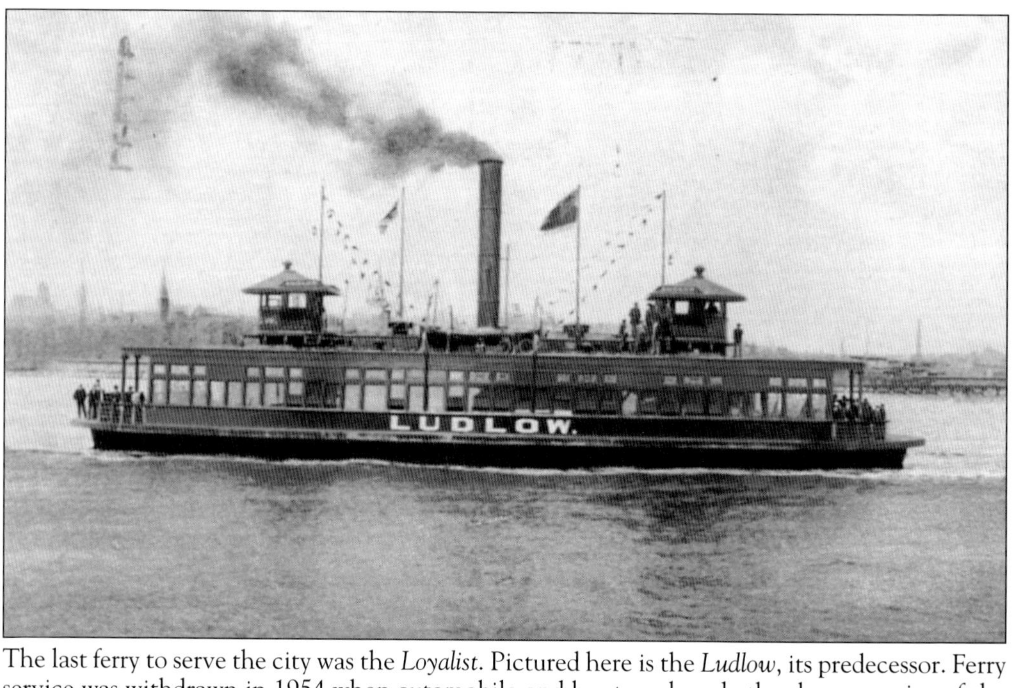

The last ferry to serve the city was the *Loyalist*. Pictured here is the *Ludlow*, its predecessor. Ferry service was withdrawn in 1954 when automobile and bus travel made the slower service of the ferry less practical. (Erb Collection.)

Eight

Businesses Large and Small

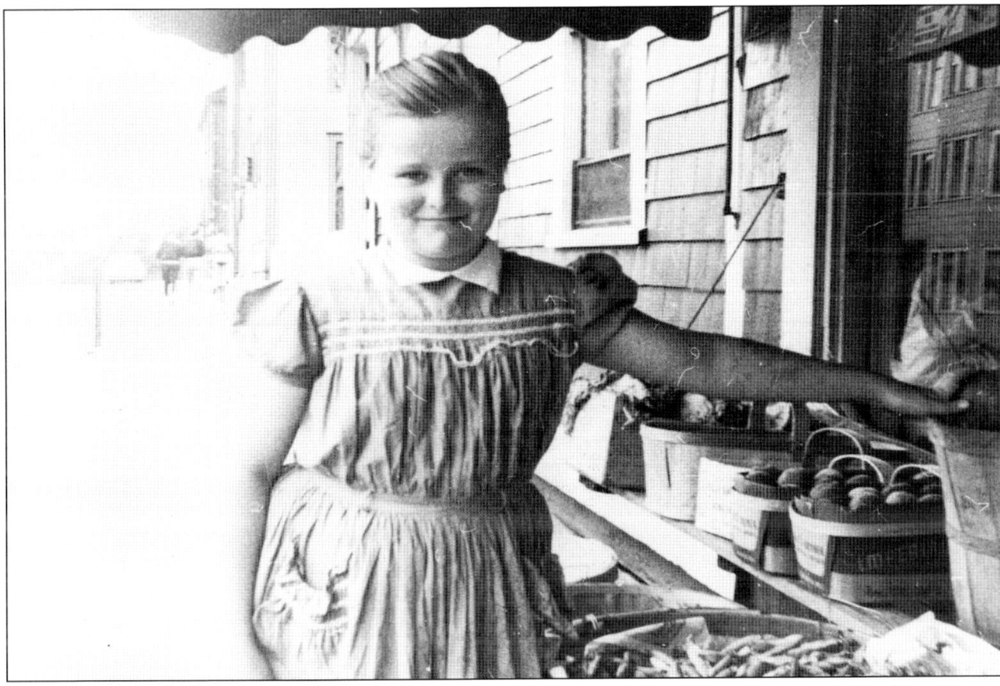

In the photograph above Janie Parks is standing in front of Art Chase's store on Ludlow Street. The store was adjacent to the Ludlow Street Baptist Church. (Doug Parks Collection.)

Though the railway and the port were the main businesses in the Saint John West area through the 1880s, there were many other businesses scattered along the streets. Some of these were small, family-owned enterprises—primarily grocers, shoemakers, clothiers, hardware stores, small restaurants, ice cream parlours, and the like. There were no large businesses in the area in terms of today's definition of a large business, but there were a number of businesses that were considered large in that they employed forty or fifty "hands," as the employees were called then. These included sawmills, lumber mills, foundries, a power-generating company, a street railway system, coal distributors, and a granite works. The first salmon hatchery to be established in the province was set up in the millpond area of Carleton when government officials realized that all the debris from the sawmills and lime-burning operations located along the river were ruining the salmons' chances of swimming upstream and finding suitable spawning grounds. This section gives a look at businesses large and small that lined the streets of Saint John West and that have all disappeared.

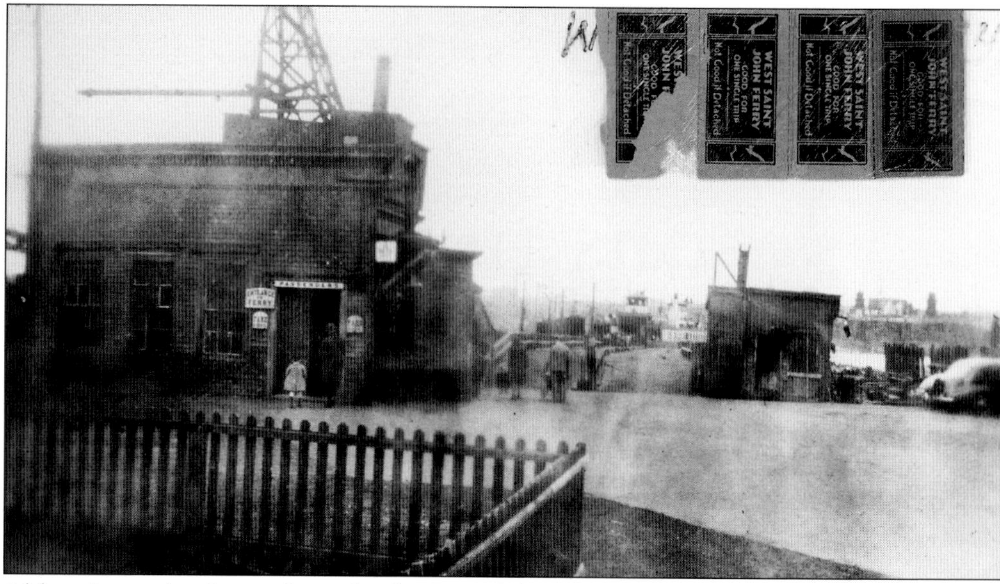

Although people who used to take the Saint John West ferry to the city remember the trips with deep nostalgia, this photograph shows that it was anything but pretty at the departure area. (Art Cormier Collection.)

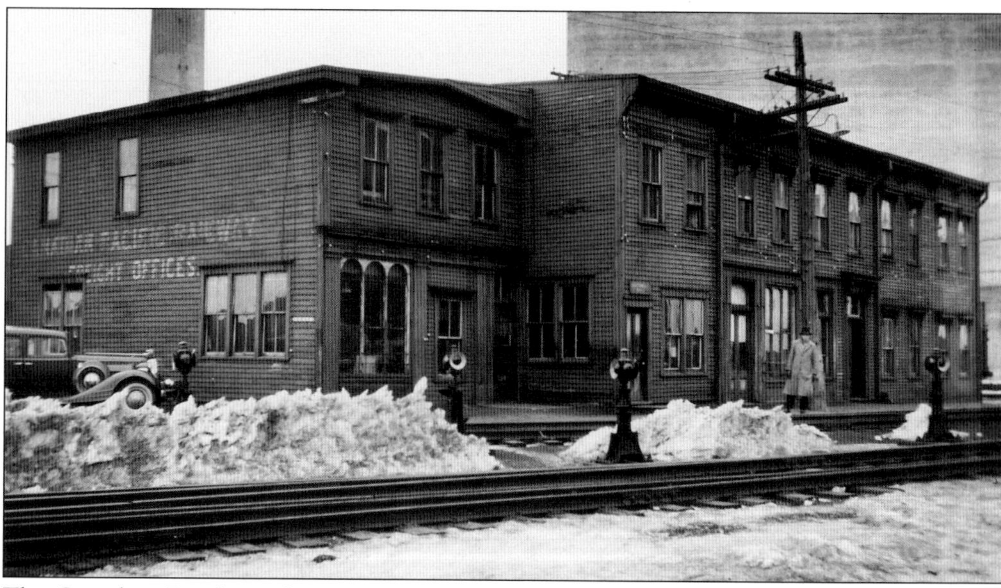

The Canadian Pacific Railway was an important employer in Saint John West. There were very few citizens in Saint John who didn't at some time work on the railway in one way or another, even if it was just shovelling snow in the winter. Canadian Pacific built several offices as business developed—this shows the last one, located at the foot of St. John Street. It was torn down in the late 1960s when the yards were moved to a suburban location in Lancaster. (Yvette (Daigle) Tobin Collection.)

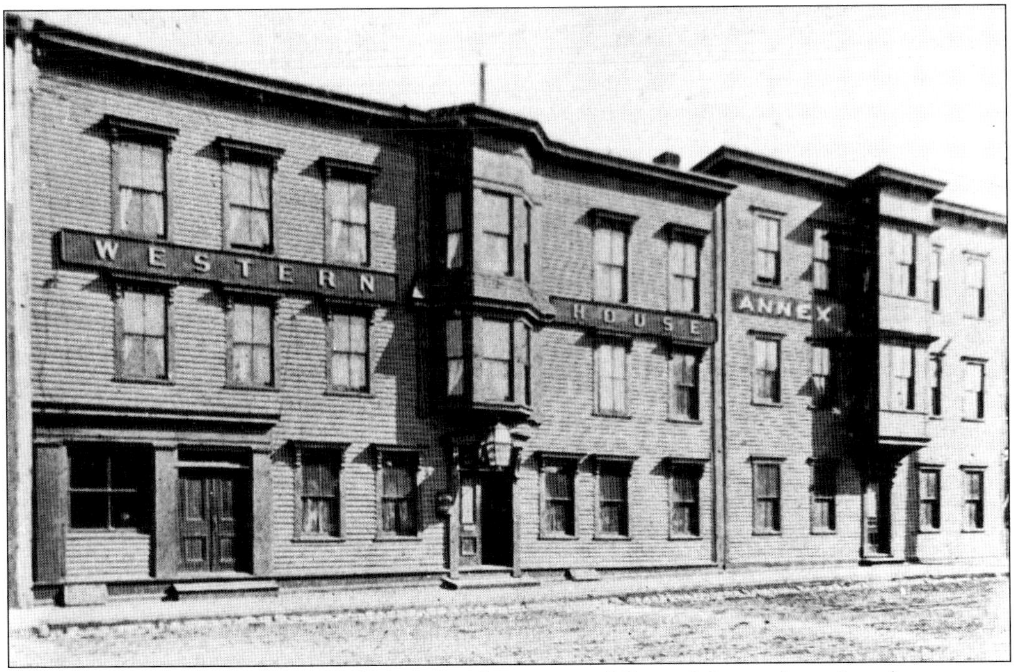

Port workers would come from the surrounding areas of Saint John and need a place to stay for the four or five months of port operations during the winter season. The Western House annex on lower Rodney Street between Union Street and Market Place was one of several choices available.

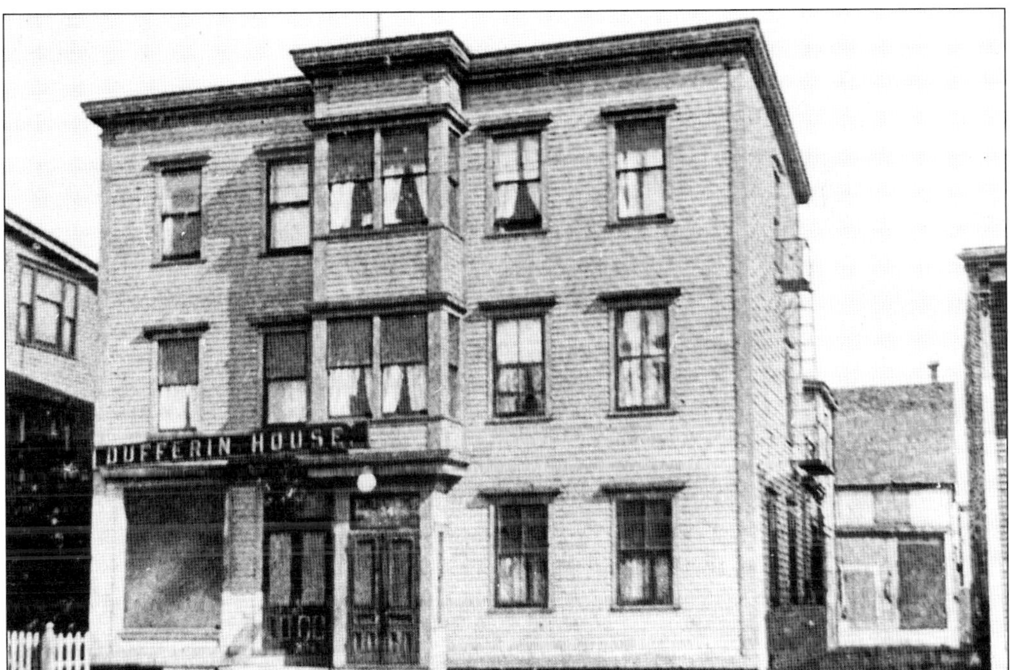

The Dufferin House on Rodney Street between Market Place and Union offered lodging to both longshoremen and visitors to the city.

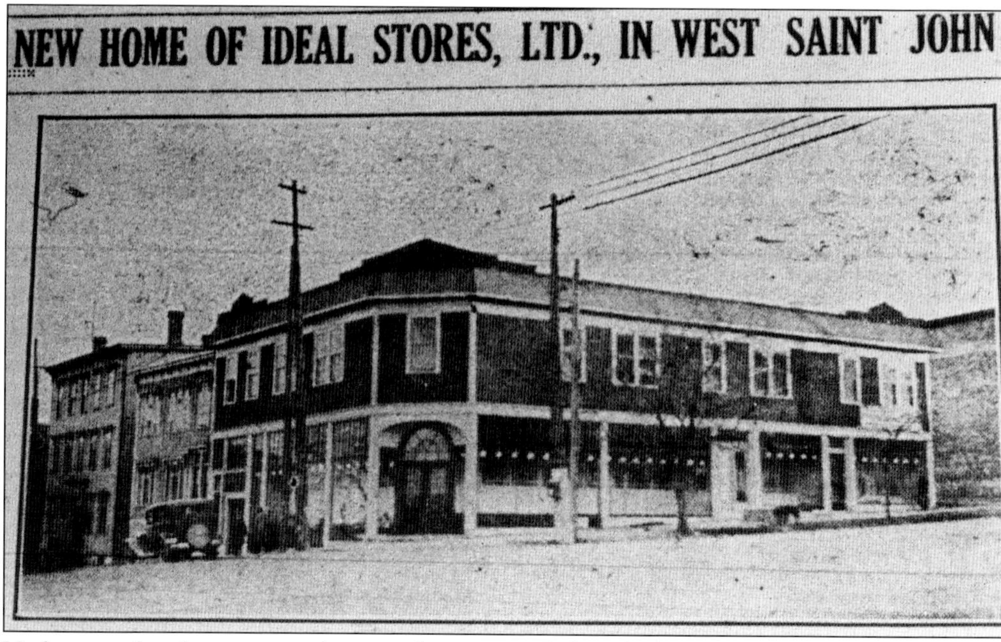
NEW HOME OF IDEAL STORES, LTD., IN WEST SAINT JOHN

Unfortunately, there is no photograph extant of the Ideal Store, which was the leading mercantile store in the Saint John West area, but this newspaper shot shows the popular store in 1930 when it moved to the corner of King and Market Place from Union Street. (*Evening Times Globe* clipping.)

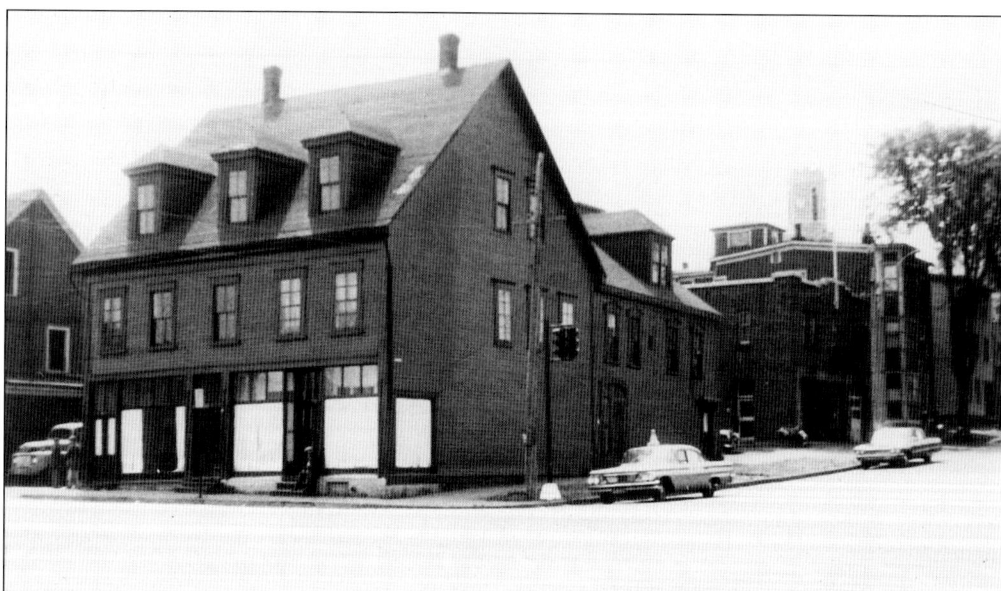

Stanley Stout's store on the corner of King and Ludlow Streets in 1964. It has since been replaced by a bank building. The 1931 fire station remains, as does the tower of St. George's Church (1821), which stands adjacent to the elm trees planted as part of the city's 100th birthday in 1883. (Allan Family Collection.)

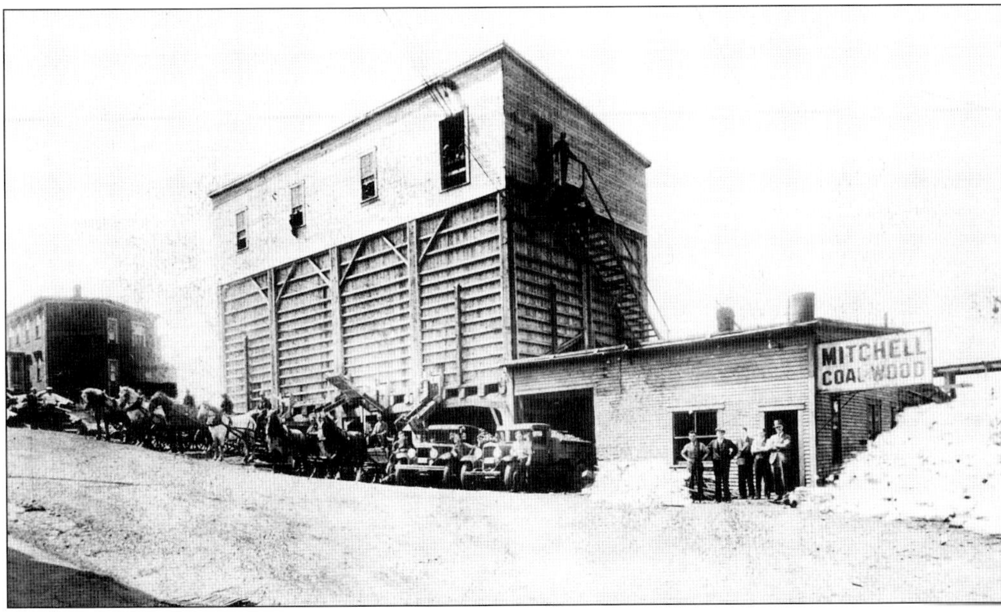

The Mitchell Coal and Wood operation on Water Street. This photograph was taken in the 1930s when horses were still as important as motorized vehicles in such businesses. (Parker D. Mitchell Collection.)

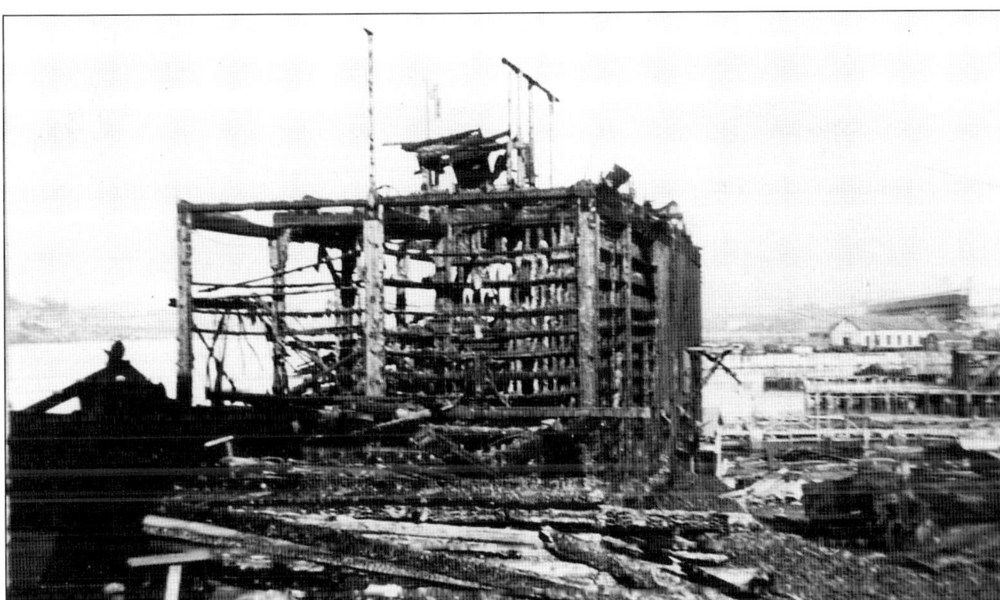

The Mitchell Coal and Wood operation managed to survive the port expansion but a fire in the 1940s completely destroyed the structure and the firm moved across the harbour to a location on Merritt Street. (Malcolm Harned Collection.)

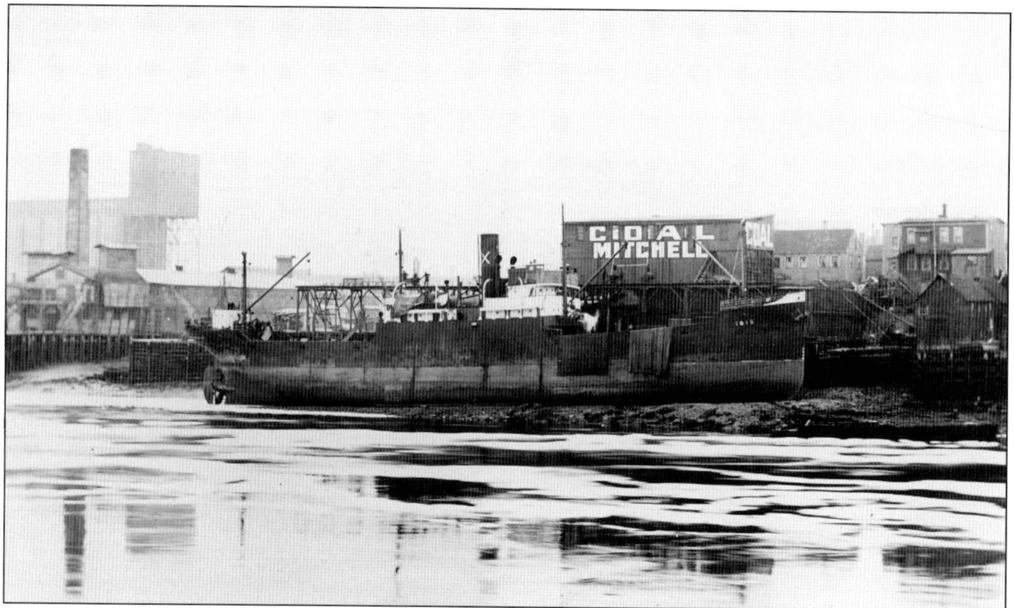

This shipload of coal is settled on the mud flats to be offloaded at Mitchell Coal and Wood. Finding a location adjacent to the tidal harbour was an important business consideration in this area. (New Brunswick Museum.)

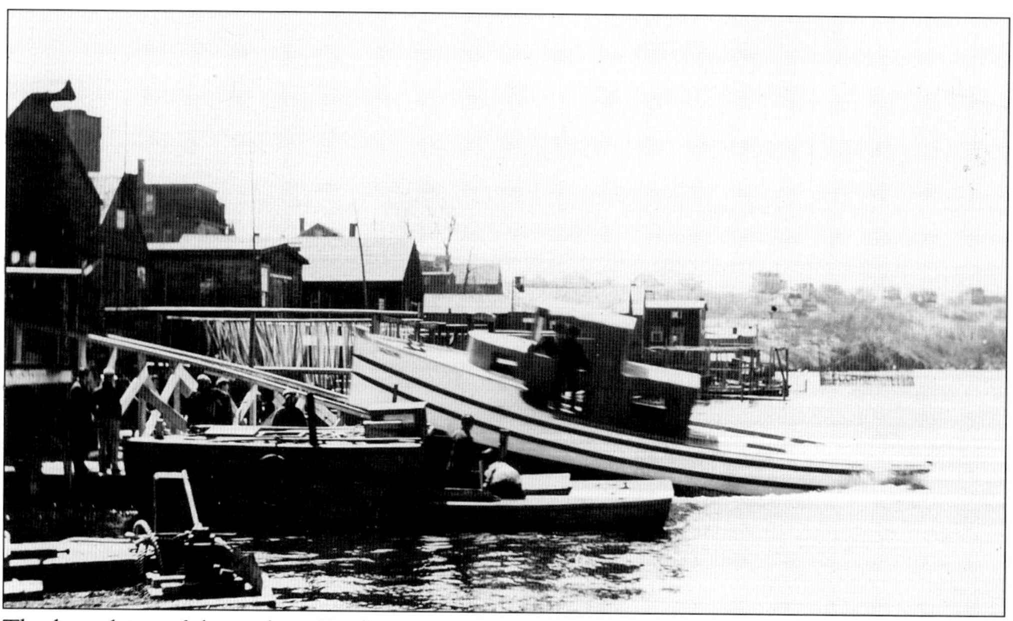

The launching of the tugboat *Perdue* in 1936. *Perdue* was built for the Parker D. Mitchell Coal Company by Leonard Harned. It is the last known boat to have been built in the Saint John West area, an area once famed for its ships that sailed the seven seas. (Mel Harned Collection.)

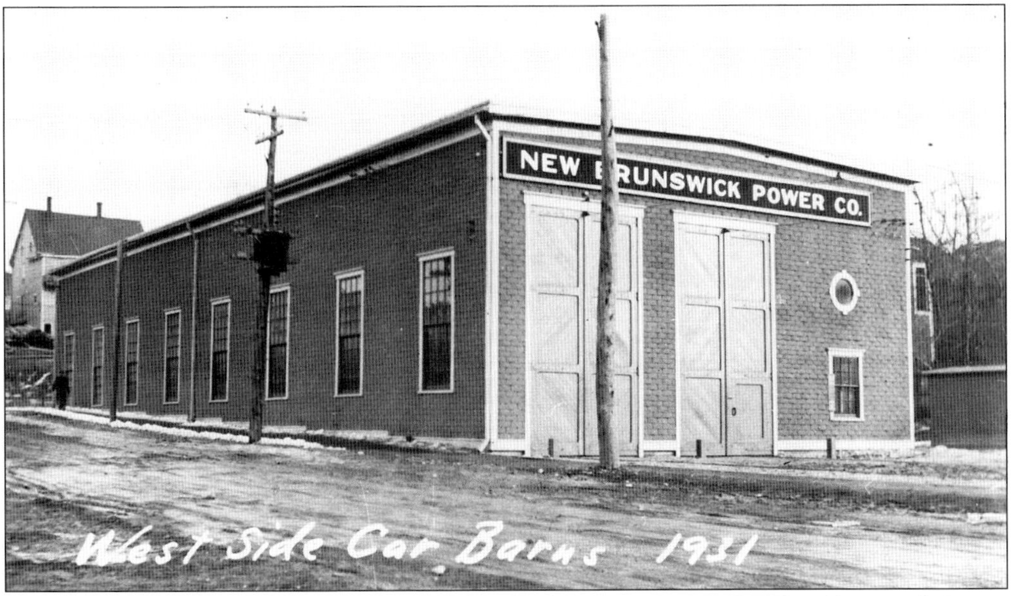

In 1931 a new set of car barns had to be built for the streetcars run by New Brunswick Power Company as their previous barn on Union Street had been torn down to make way for port expansion. There were additions made to this barn later on, when space was needed to house the buses which began operations in the mid-1940s. (Provincial Archives.)

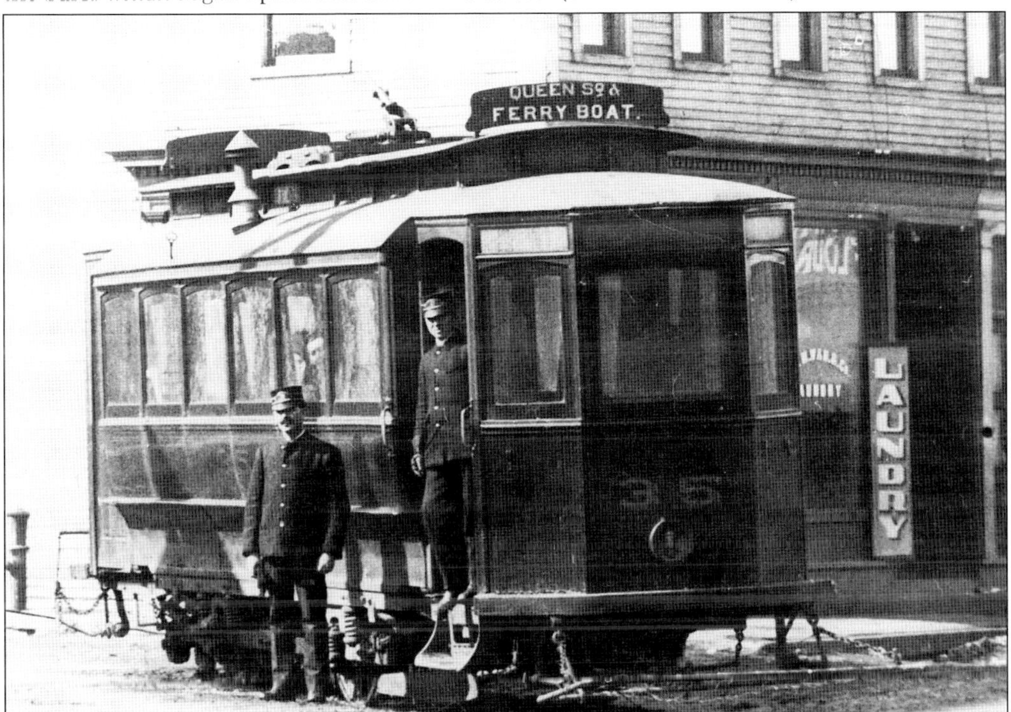

Streetcar number 35—for "Queen Square and Ferry Boat." It was built by the Ottowa Car Company—though such cars were also built in Saint John for use in the city. Cars similar to this one (with the glass removed) also served the route to Seaside Park shown on p. 60.

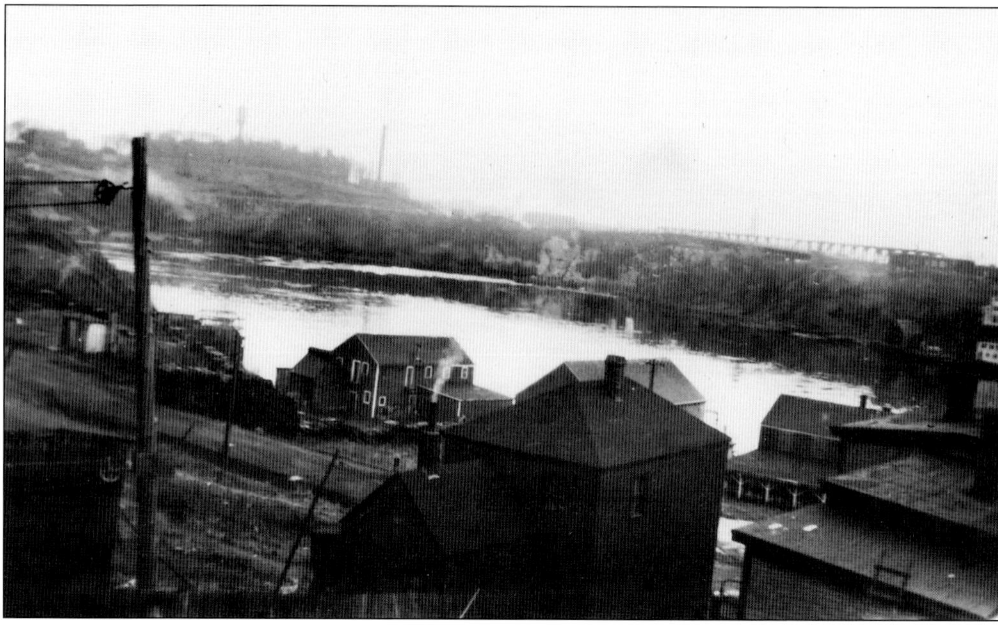

This photograph shows us the view looking west towards the Reversing Falls and the Provincial Asylum. Included in the picture are, from left to right along the shore, Flemming and Dennison Woodyard, Robertson's Fish Plant and Smokehouse, and the factory where the barrels for shipping fish to the West Indies were made. (Joan (Iliffe) Galbraith Collection.)

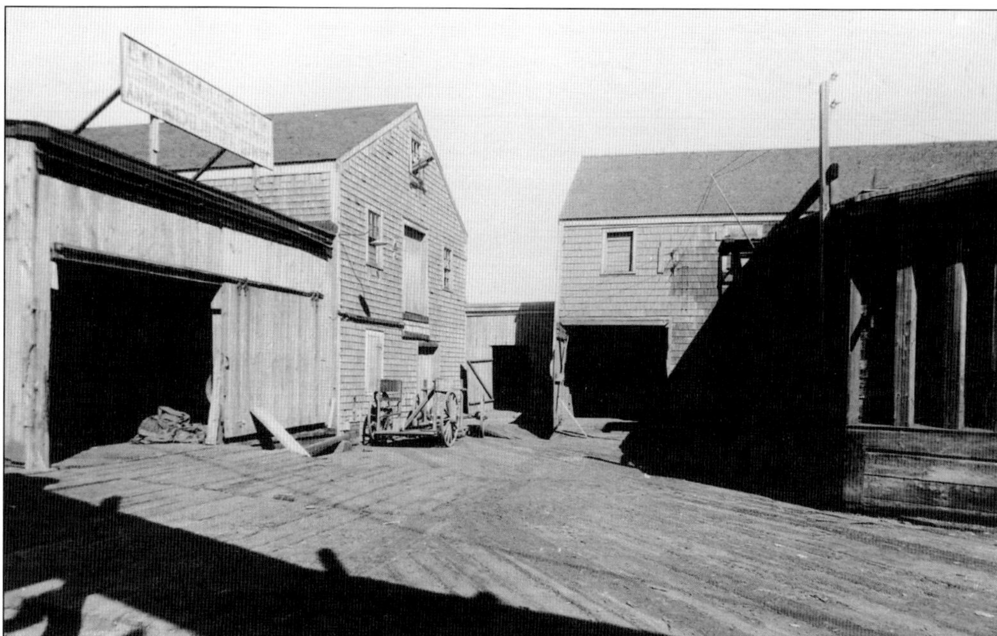

The rear portion of the Colwell Coal Yard in October 1928. Note the low-slung wagon, known as a "sloven." Such wagons are said to have been invented in Saint John to take advantage of the tidal variations that let scows rest on the mud flats. Once the scows were set on the mud flats, the "slovens" would go out to take their cargo. The "slovens" were designed with no sideboard to make it easier to transfer cargo from scow to "sloven." (National Harbours Board.)

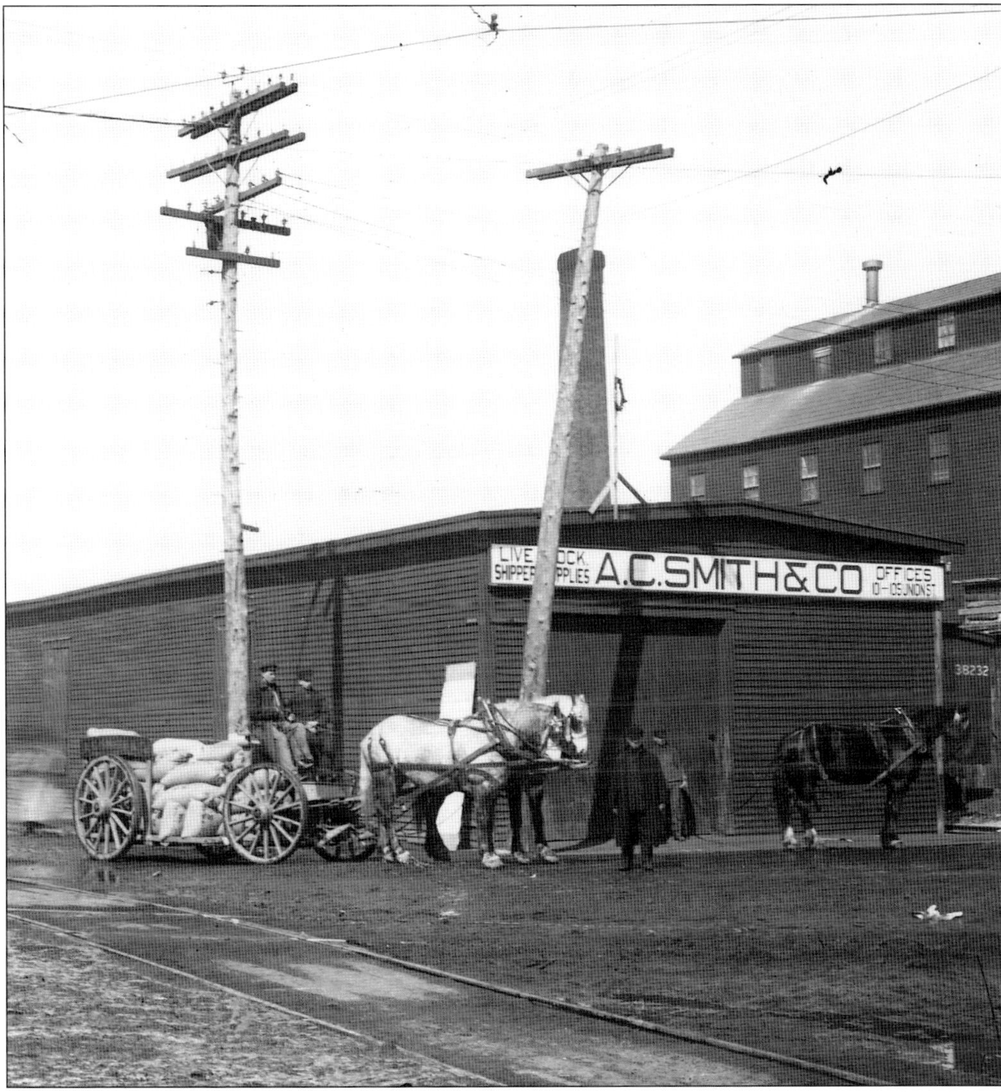

A.C. Smith and Company Ltd. supplied hay and straw to the Saint John West area when horses still outnumbered automobiles on the road. Note again the "sloven" with a stack of feed on its bed. (Frank O'Brien Collection.)

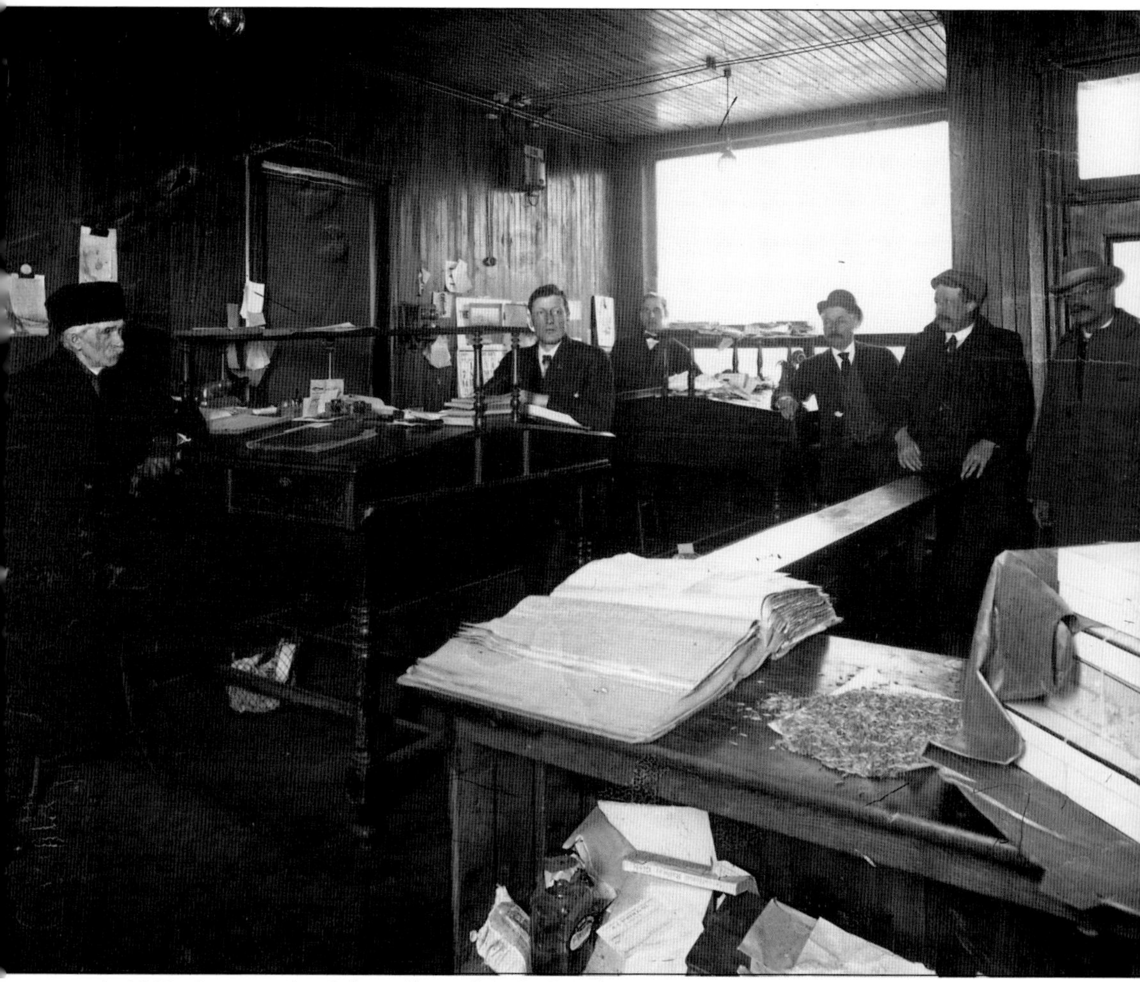

A 1909 photograph of the office of A.C. Smith on Union Street in Carleton, as Saint John West was known in this era. (Frank O'Brien Collection.)

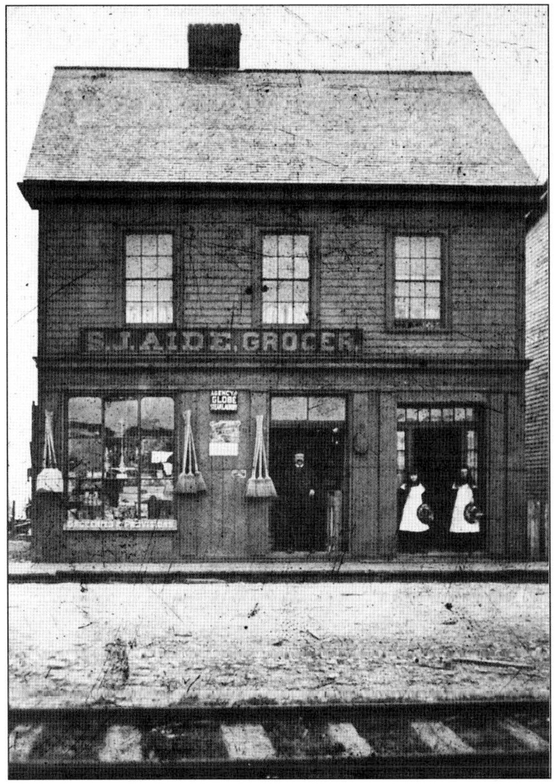

S.J. Aide Grocer was located on Protection Street on the harbour side of the main line tracks that served Carleton. This is probably the oldest of the building photographs in this section. This print was taken from a glass negative. (Margaret Morrisey Collection.)

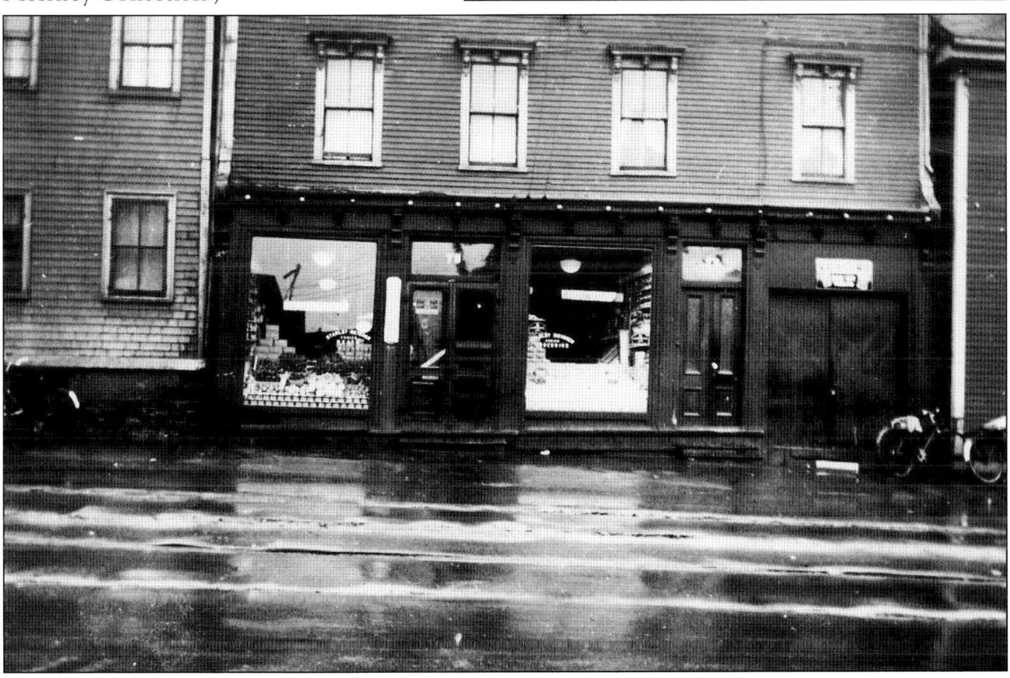

Meisner's Grocery Store was a family operation on Ludlow Street between King and Prince Streets. It served residents of the north side of the Saint John West peninsula and was a very successful business. (Shirley (Meisner) Jobe Collection.)

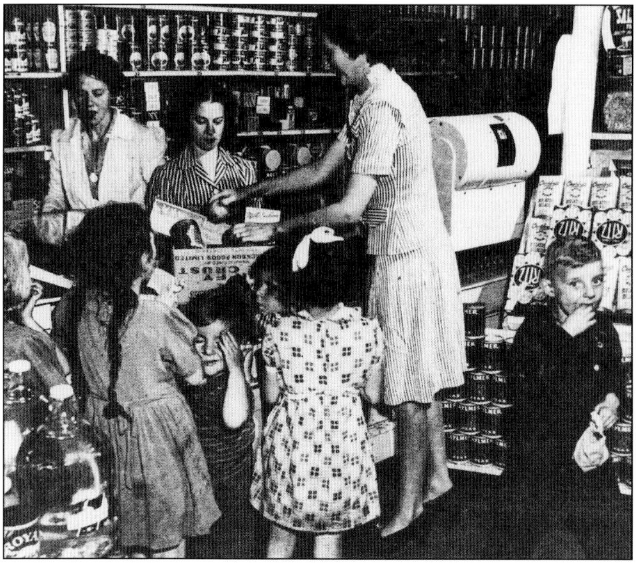

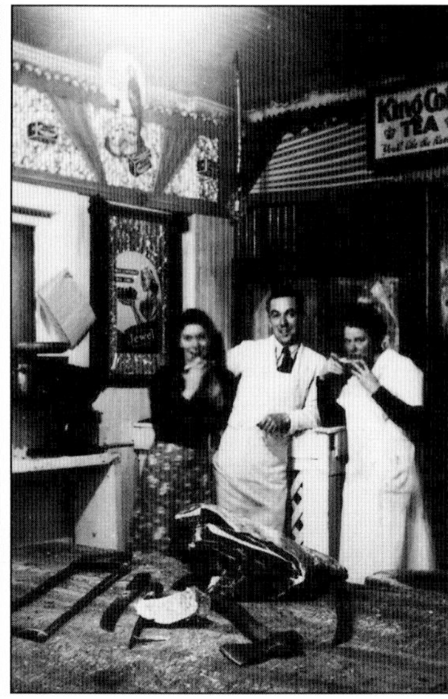

Left: Nina Belyea is shown at Meisner's Grocery Store in 1946. Note the wide range of goods available. (Nina Belyea Collection.)
Right: Shown left to right in this photograph are Marjorie Nice (clerk), Dan O'Riley (meat cutter), and Veleda Meisner, wife of owner Stanley Meisner. (Shirley (Meisner) Jobe Collection.)

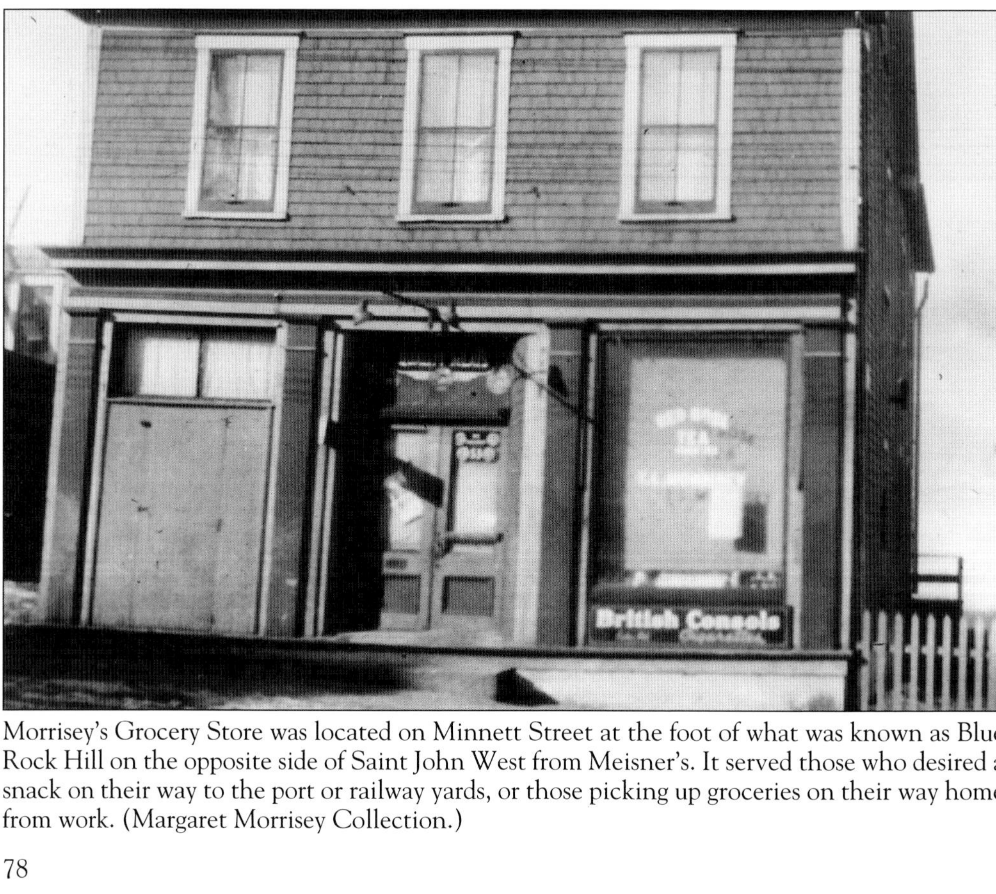

Morrisey's Grocery Store was located on Minnett Street at the foot of what was known as Blue Rock Hill on the opposite side of Saint John West from Meisner's. It served those who desired a snack on their way to the port or railway yards, or those picking up groceries on their way home from work. (Margaret Morrisey Collection.)

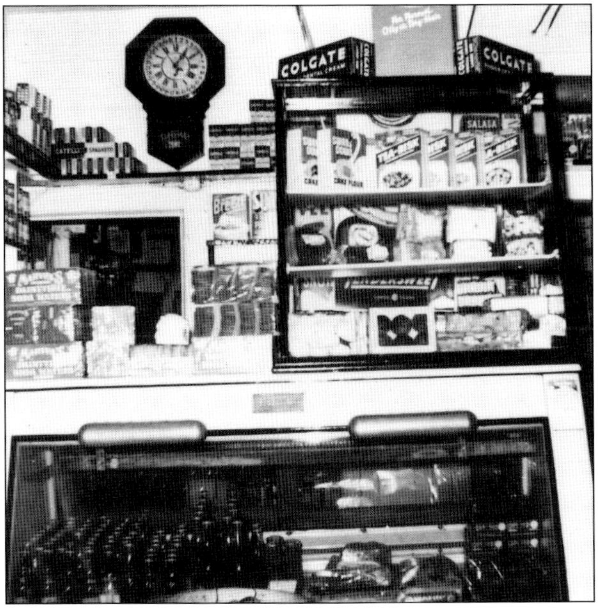

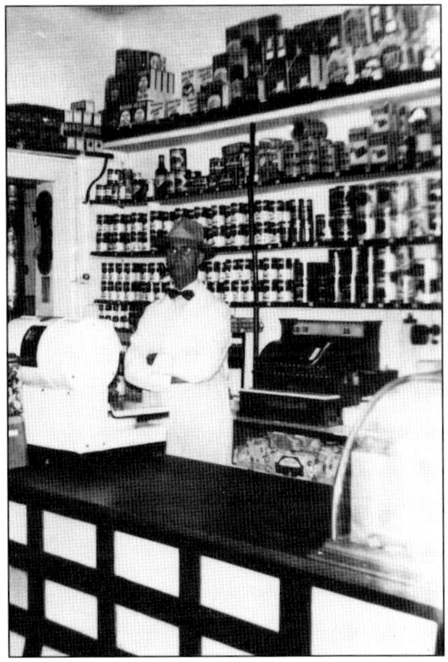

Left: Inside Morrisey's store there was hardly a nook and cranny that wasn't stuffed with some saleable item. Locally-baked Marven's Biscuits and locally-brewed Sussex Ginger Ale (the best in the land) competed with national brands like Catelli spaghetti and Colgate toothpaste for shelf space. (Margaret Morrisey Collection.)
Right: This mid-1950s photograph shows Mr. Morrisey standing ready to serve customers in a store which by this time was a peculiar mix of the old and new. Note the contrast between the up-to-the-minute bubblegum dispenser and the old-time cash register. (Margaret Morrisey Collection.)

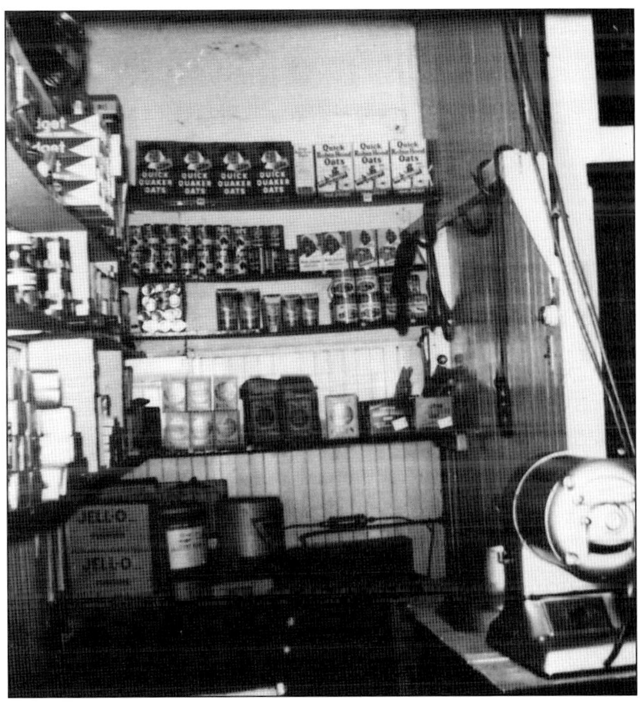

Another view of the interior of Morrisey's store. Many of the items shown here can still be bought today. (Margaret Morrisey Collection.)

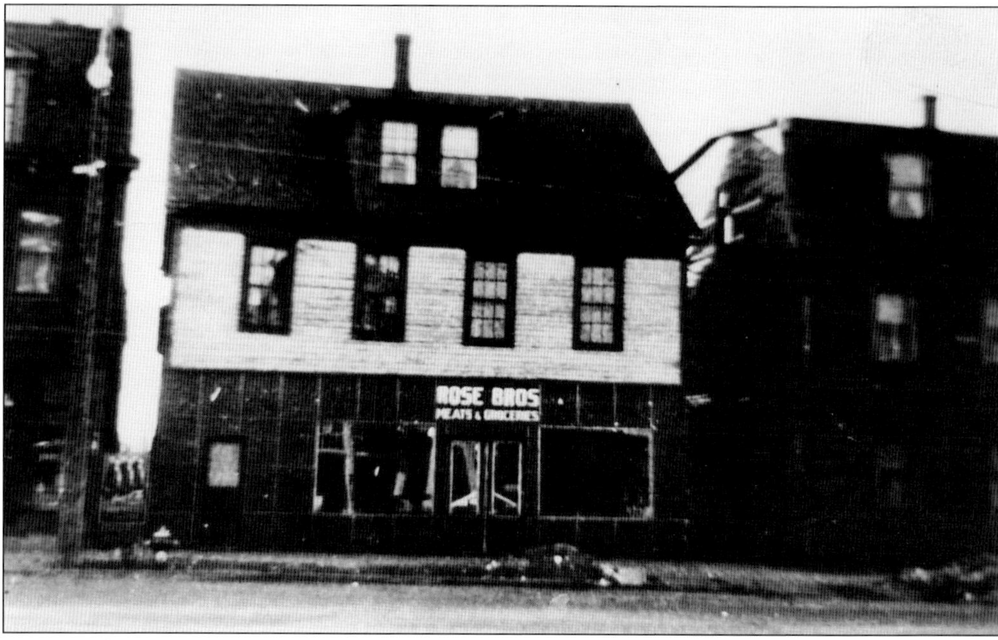

Rose Brothers Meats and Groceries on King Street in the mid-1950s. In this era, family store owners were beginning to see the first of the larger, independent chain stores like Dominion and Sobeys. This change in the retail market eventually resulted in the closure of most of the family-run operations in Saint John West. (Gerald Keith Collection.)

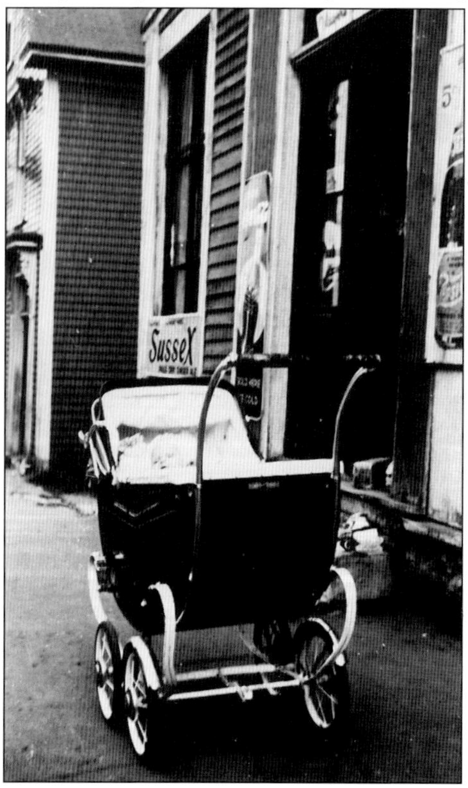

An unidentified baby waits patiently for her mom, who has stepped into Rita Quinlin's Store on Guilford Street—perhaps for the 5¢ bottle of Pepsi Cola advertised on the signboard in 1934. (Rita Craft Collection.)

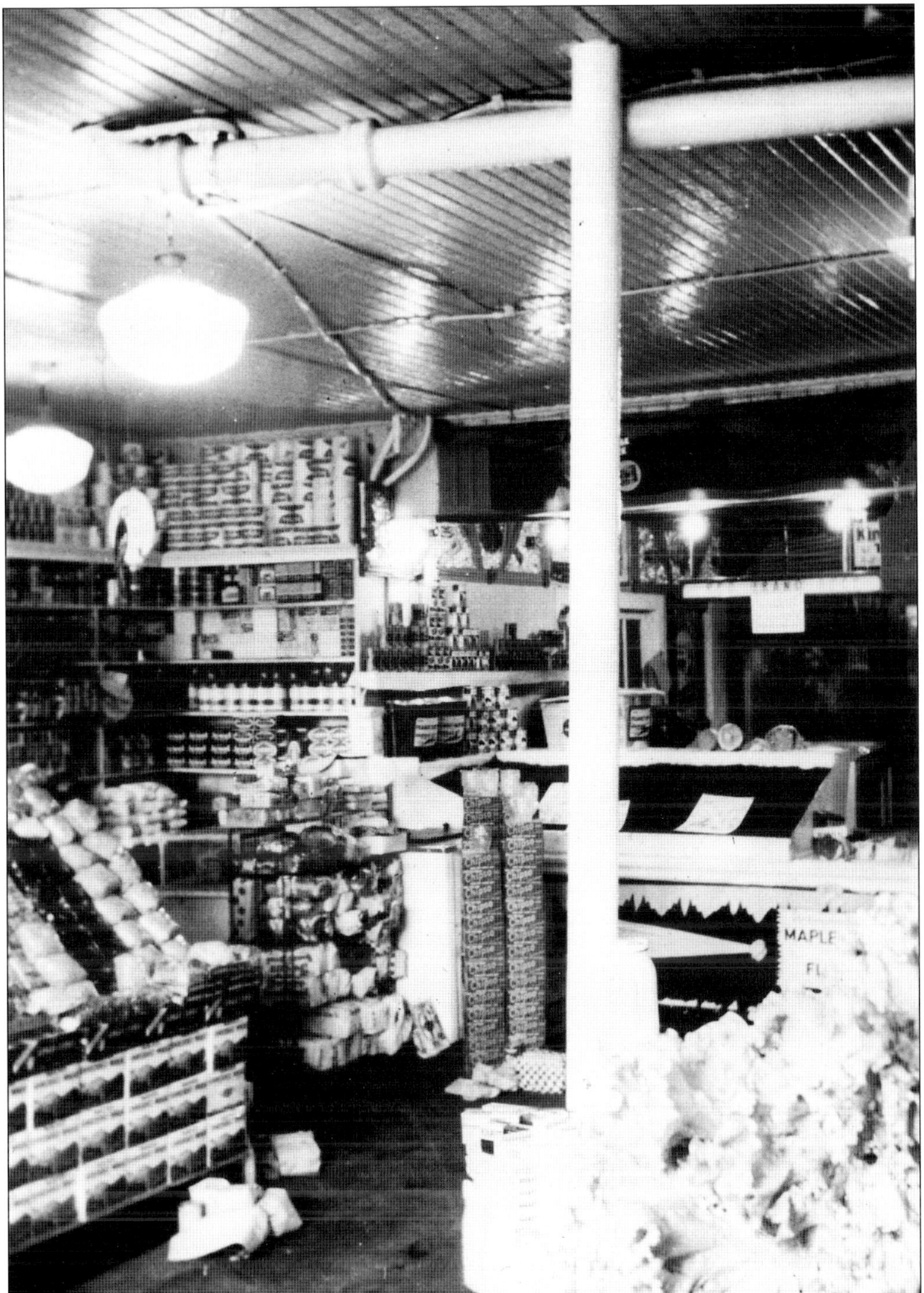

As we conclude our look at the stores in Saint John West, take a good look at this photograph of Meisner's' store and note the wide range of merchandise available in the era when most everyone shopped daily. (Shirley (Meisner) Jobe Collection.)

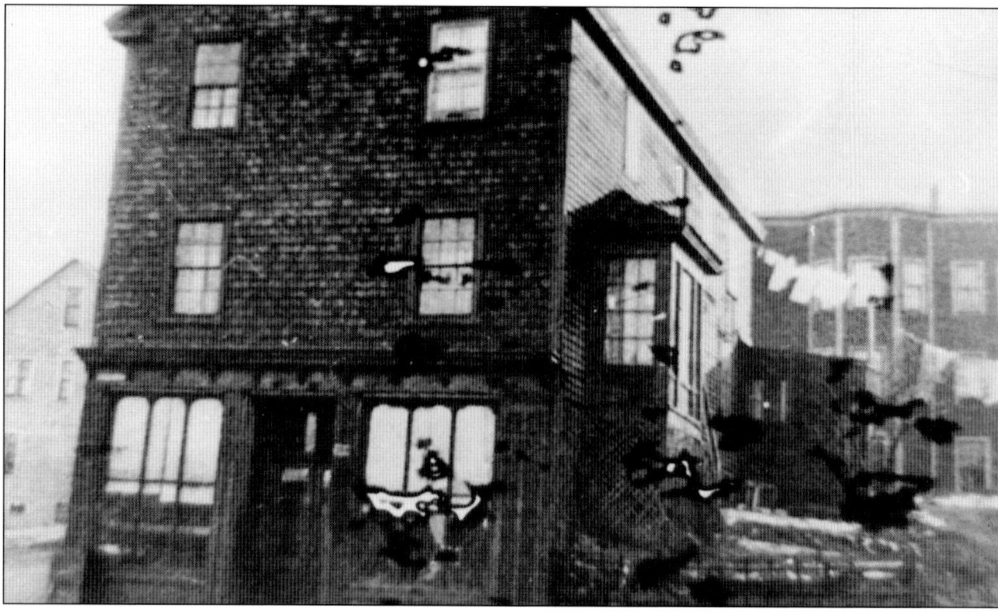

Mott's Store and Bottle Exchange on the corner of Ludlow and Guilford Street in the 1930s. Since this building was never painted it always looked much older then it really was. (Gerald Keith Collection.)

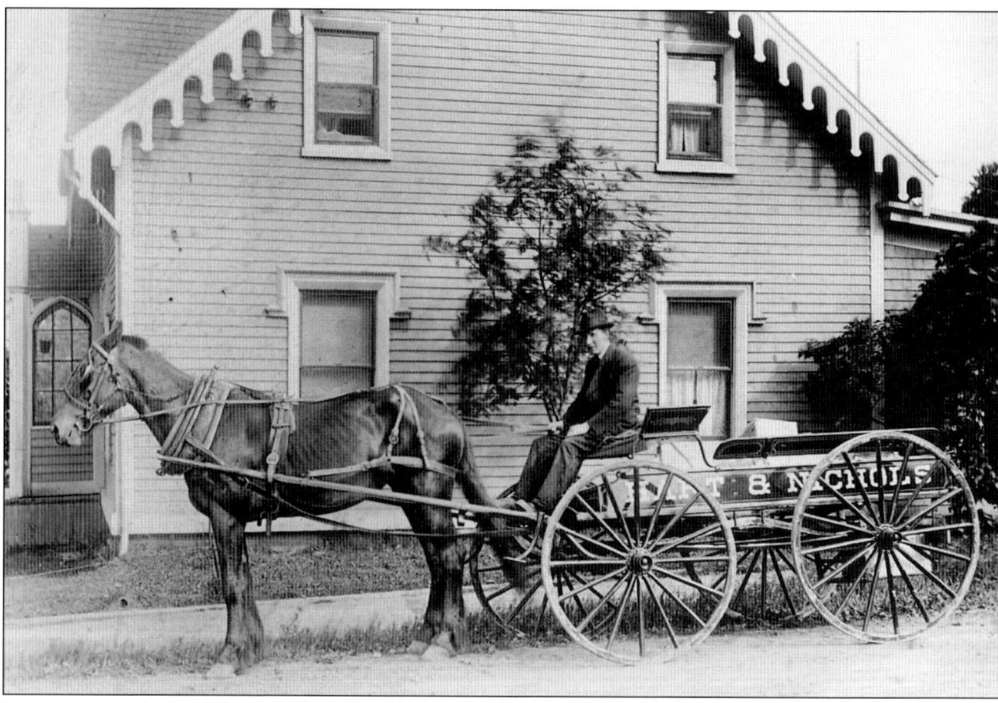

Hart and Nichol's delivery wagon in the 1920s. The horse seems to be on his last legs—perhaps he is about to be replaced by a four-wheeled transportation alternative, as it was around this time that horses were starting to be replaced by automobiles. The house, at the corner of Watson and St. John Streets, is one of the more decorative gingerbread-trimmed, gothic revival homes in Saint John West. (John Gow Collection.)

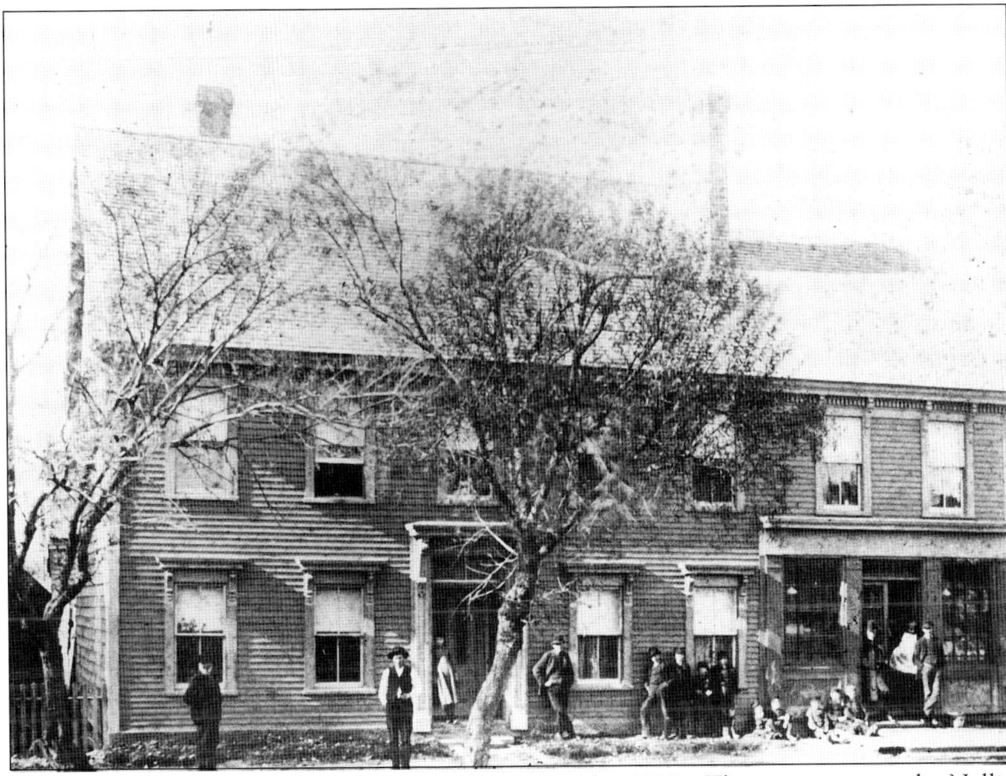

Dykeman's Corner at Prince and Watson Streets in the 1920s. This store was run by Nellie Stackhouse and known as the "Busy Bee." Later it was Lucas' Barbershop. The trees indicate that this is a spring morning being enjoyed by those gathered to take advantage of the southern exposure of this corner. (Dorothy Fair Collection.)

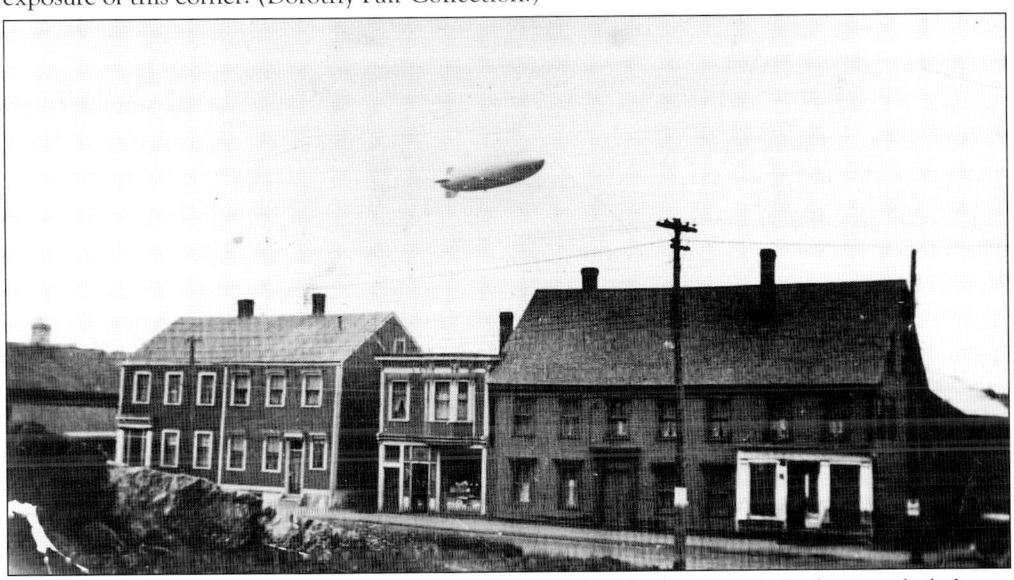

Dykeman's Corner is seen here on June 29, 1936, just days before the *Hindenburg* exploded over New Jersey. This could, however, have been on a previous tri[the ship made over Saint John. (Ann Nice Collection.)

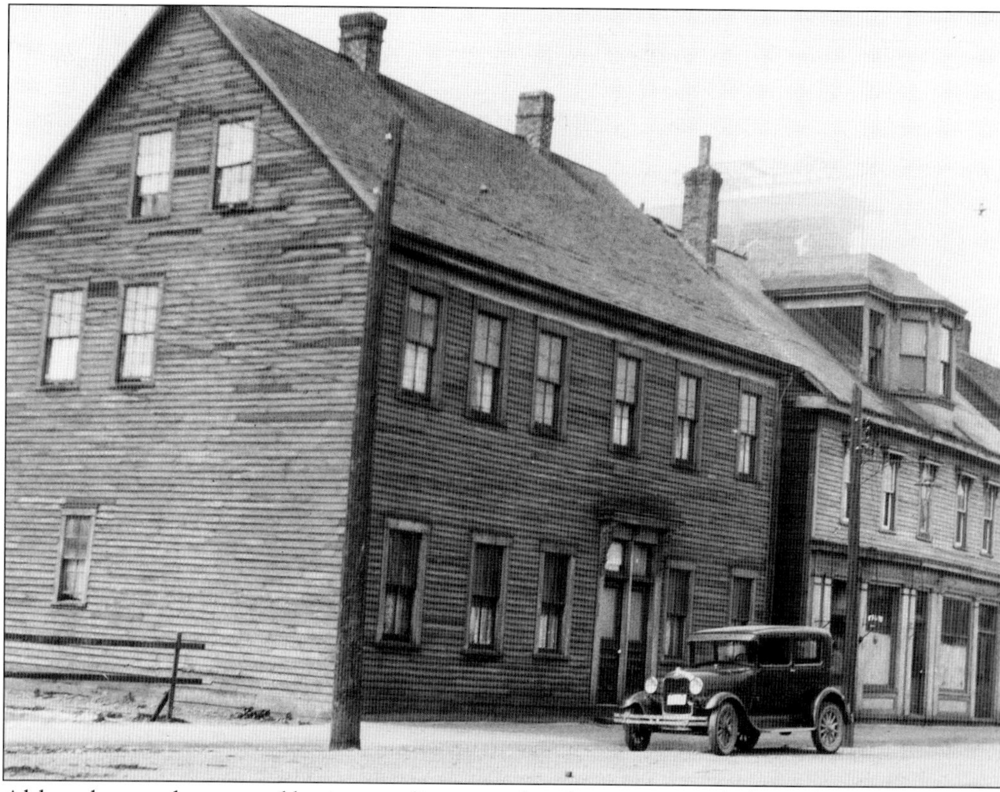

Although many houses and businesses disappeared as the port expanded—such as Milton's store shown here—it is obvious from missing shingles and the lean of the buildings that they would not have lasted to modern times in any case. (Provincial Archives.)

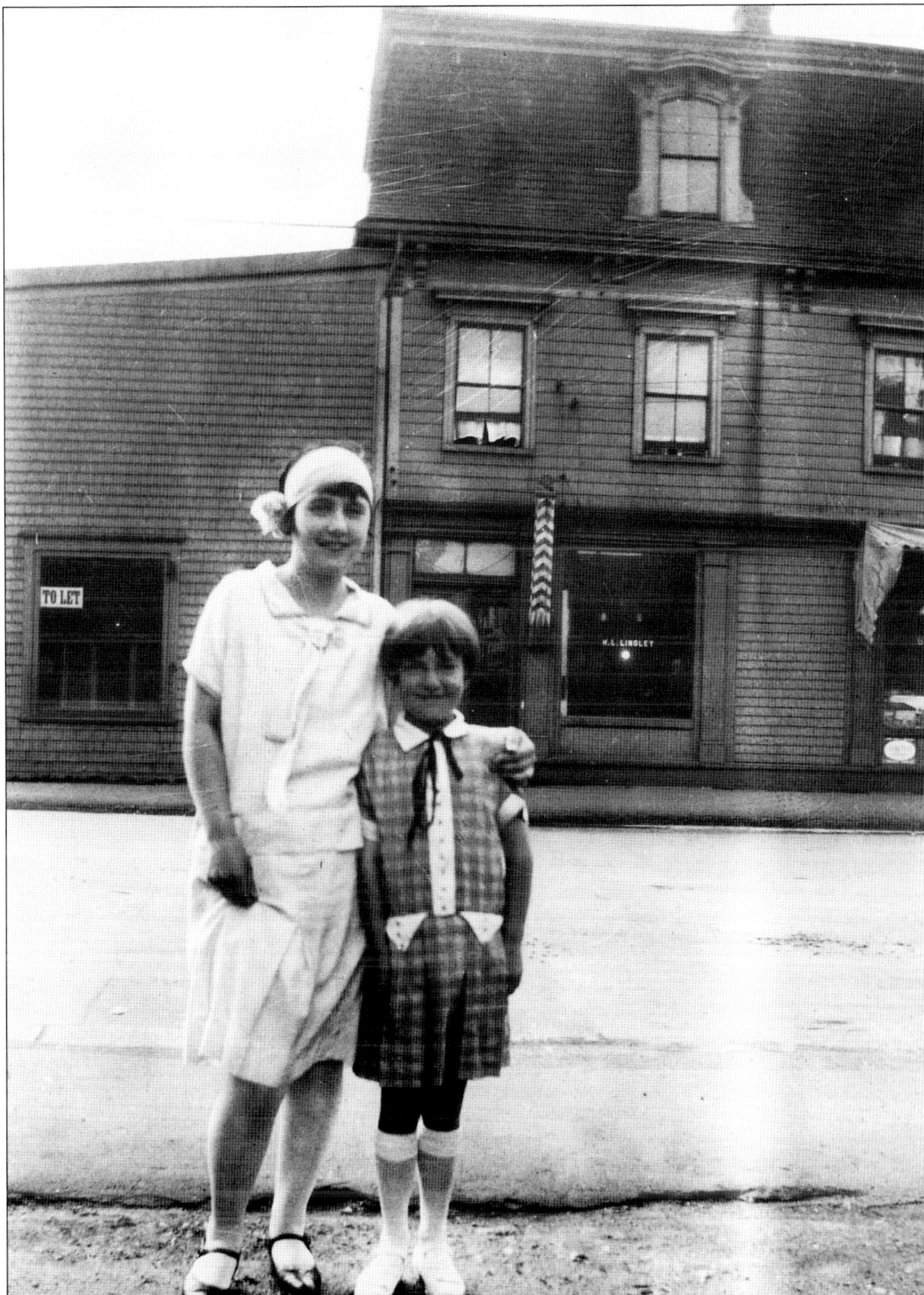

This photograph is an example of the fortuitous circumstances whereby family photographs yield information on lost history. The two young ladies were the focus of attention for the photographer, but the photograph also shows Harry Lingley's Barbershop and Goodwin's Meats, businesses that were all but forgotten. (Yvette (Daigle) Tobin Collection.)

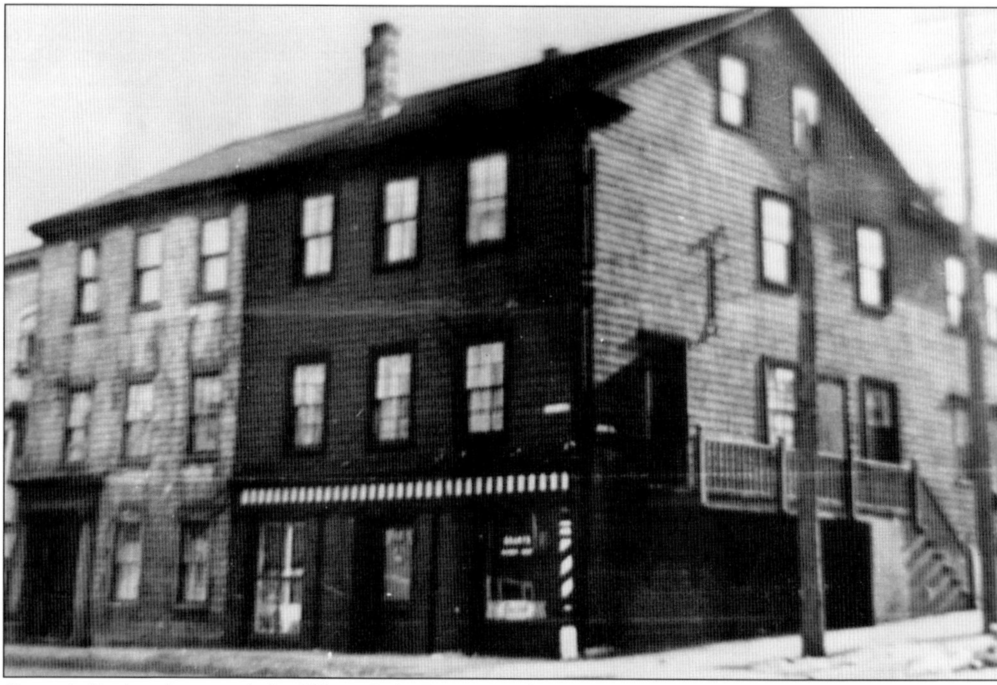

Grant's Barbershop and the West Side Beauty Salon were popular spots at the corner of Duke and Ludlow Streets until the late 1950s. (Gerald Keith Collection.)

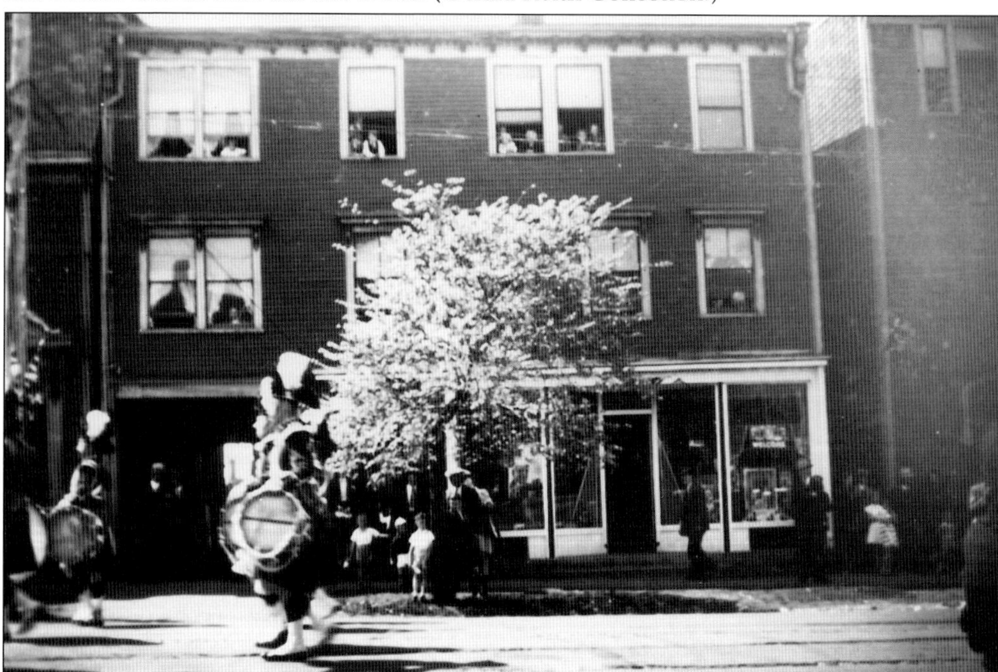

The House of Jewellers on King Street in the 1950s. Until the 1960s Saint John West residents did not have to travel to the central part of Saint John to do their shopping. Almost every conceivable product or service was available within a few blocks of their homes. (Joan (Iliffe) Galbraith Collection.)

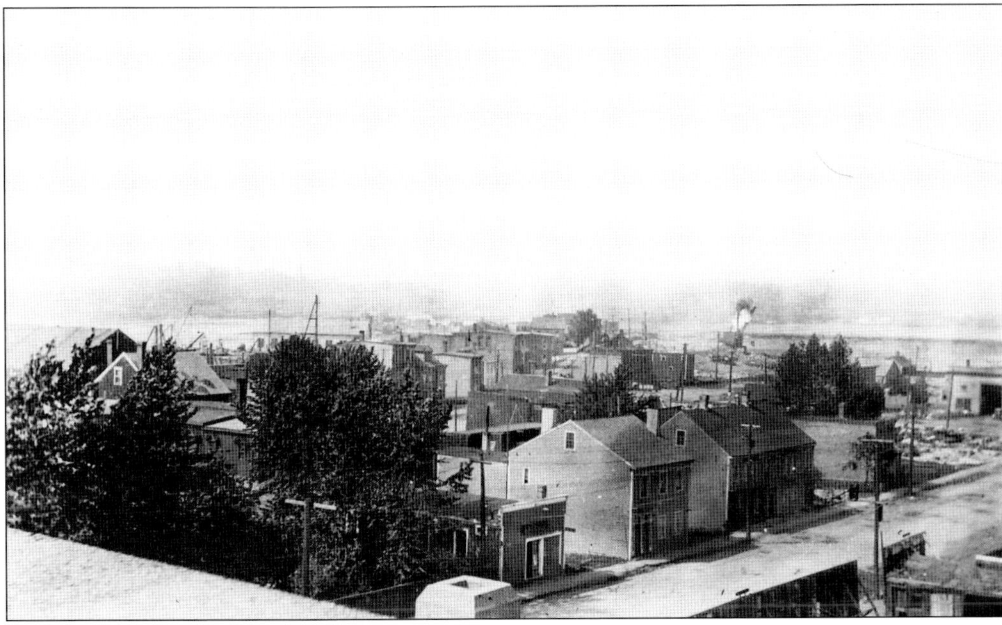

The lower end of Duke Street. The little flat-roofed building is Perry's Pool Parlour, and just down the street is Babb's Store. In the background the port expansion project is underway and the millpond is being filled in. The pool hall was later moved to Charlotte Street, and is still in operation. (Allan Family Collection.)

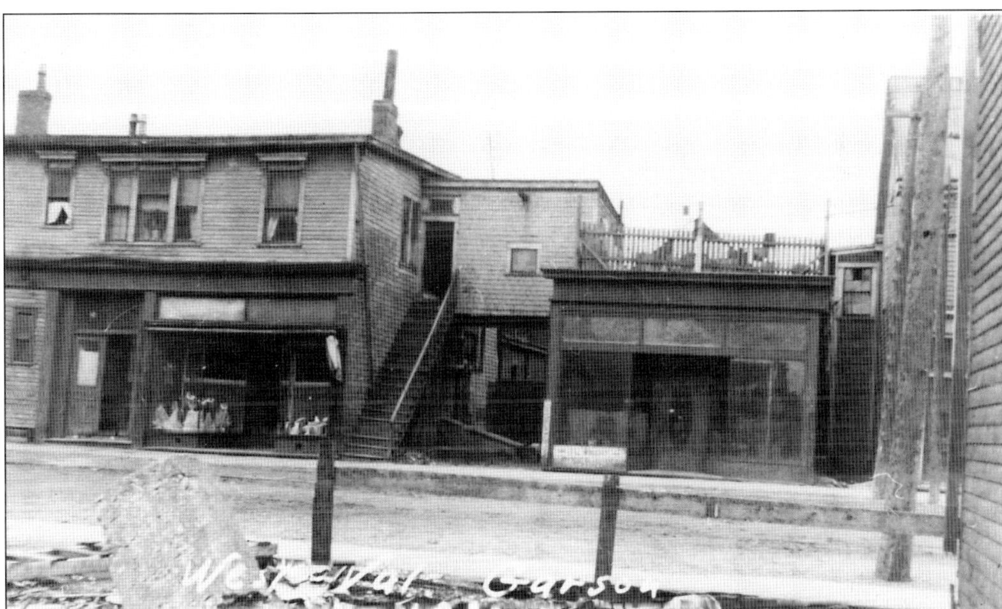

The Ideal Stores were so popular in Saint John West that they had a back as well as a front entrance, as shown in this photograph. In the centre of the picture is Wright's Shoe Store with its unusual oval glass door. (Provincial Archives.)

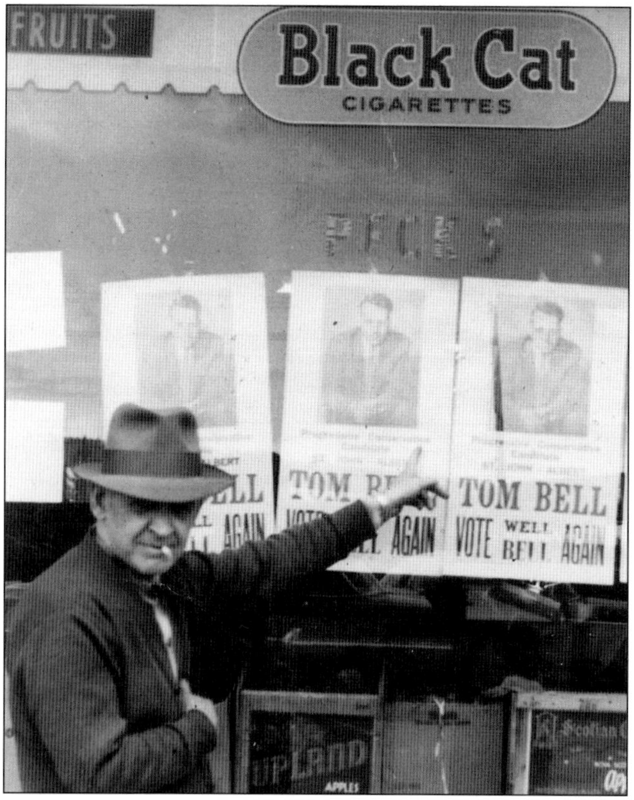

"Peck" Joyce was one of the most popular restaurant operators in the port area. He was famous for his fast foods. He continuously had a burning cigarette in his mouth, so patrons seldom got a hot dog without ashes in the mustard. Some claim that's what made them famous! (Joyce Family Collection.)

Gar Meltzer ran a combined restaurant and mercantile business at the foot of Rodney Street. It was popular with visiting seamen who could walk "the Cage," the overpass over the railway tracks from the wharves, and directly into his store. Young people also flocked there to meet the seamen and one another, especially during the wartime years. (Gar Meltzer Collection.)

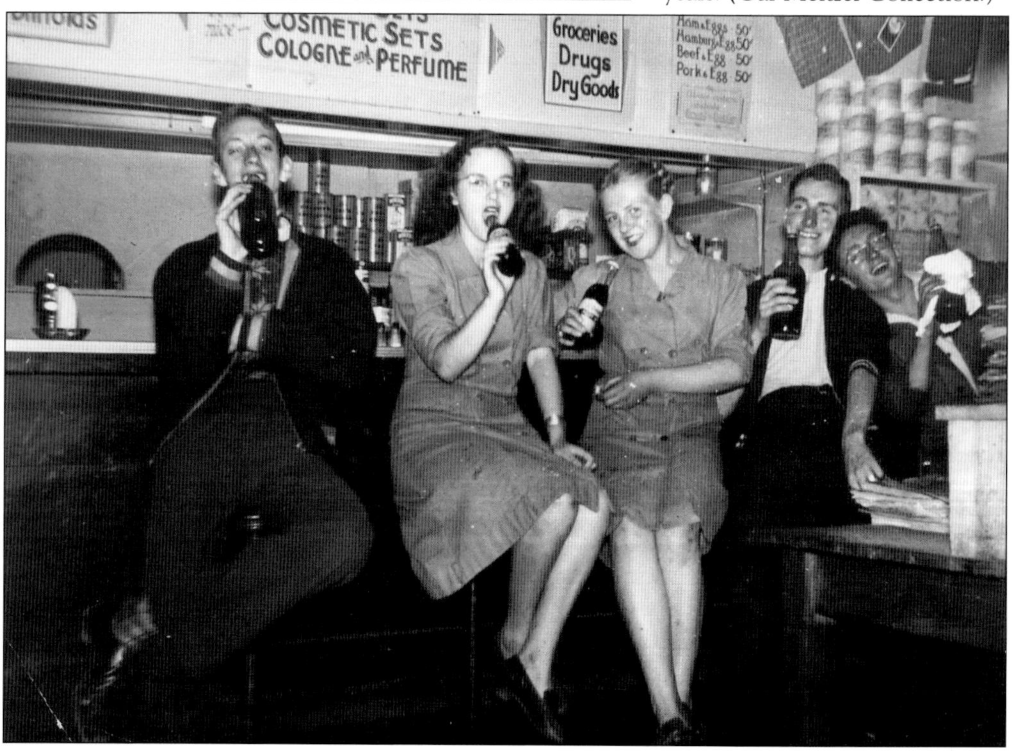

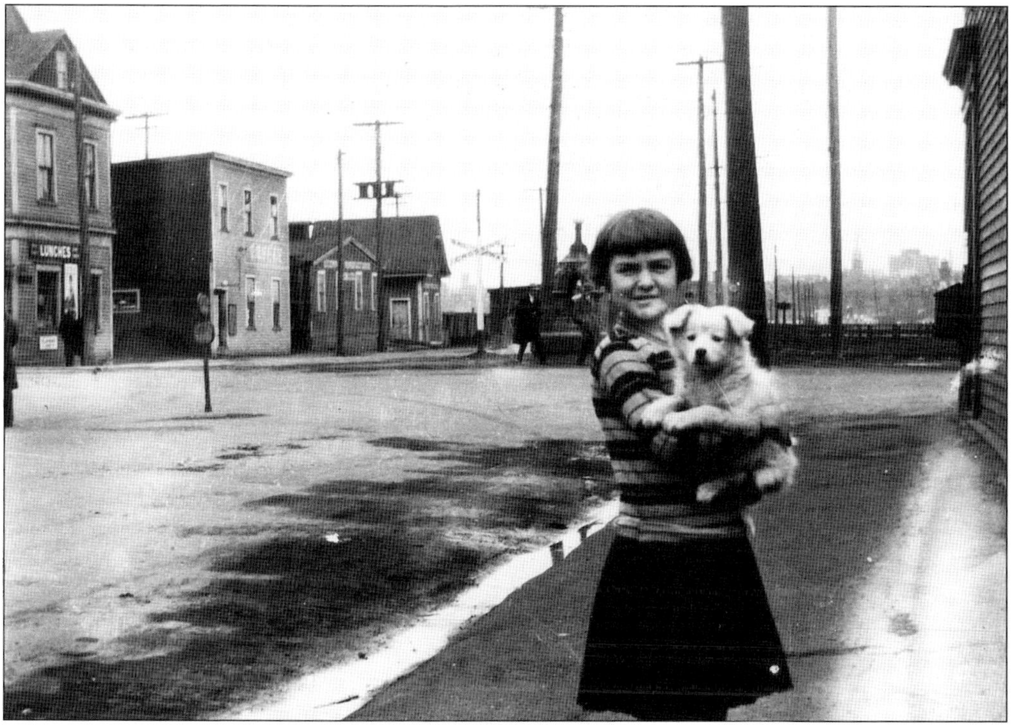

The lower end of Rodney Street with the Band of Mercy horse fountain. On the opposite side of the street is a lunch counter, a barrel factory, and a restaurant—all conveniently located adjacent to the harbour ferry to the centre of town. (Yvette (Daigle) Tobin Collection.)

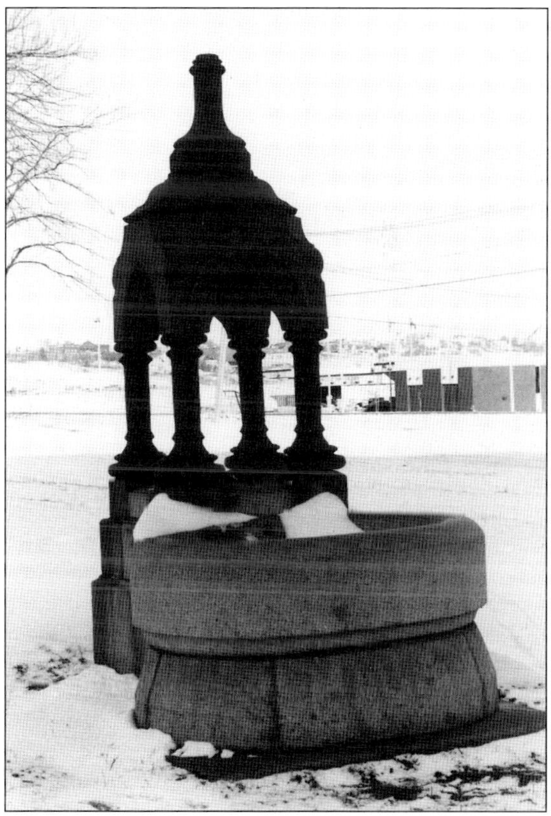

The Band of Mercy fountain still stands today. The Band of Mercy was similar to today's Society for the Prevention of Cruelty to Animals. It operated out of St. Jude's Church on Queen Square.

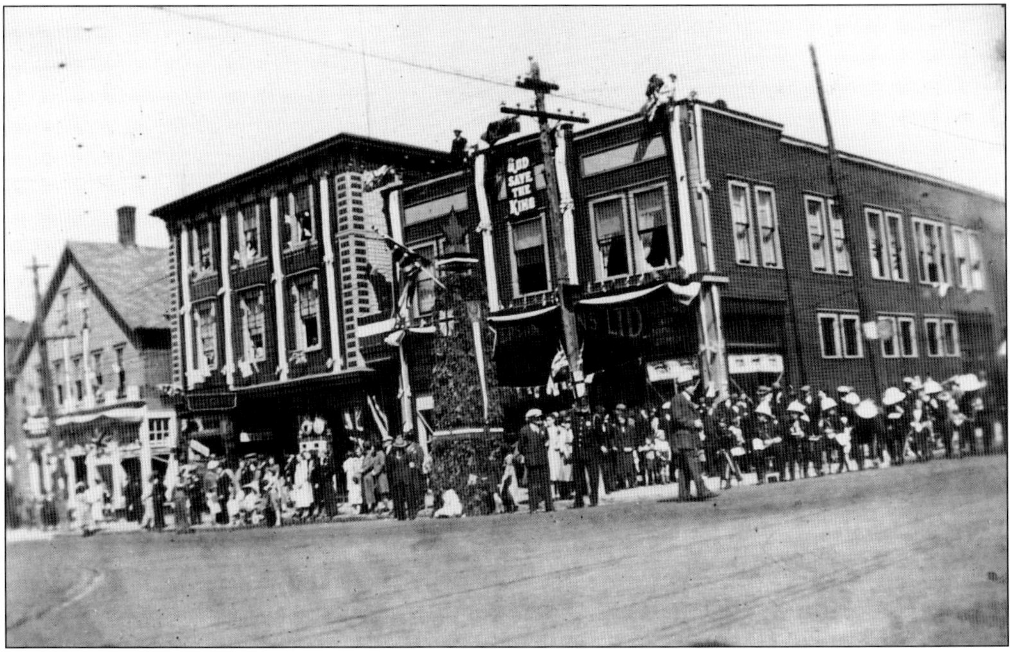

The W.E. Emerson hardware store at King and Ludlow Streets festooned for the 1939 royal visit. To the left are the Star Ice Cream Parlour and Allan's Drugstore. (Ann Nice Collection.)

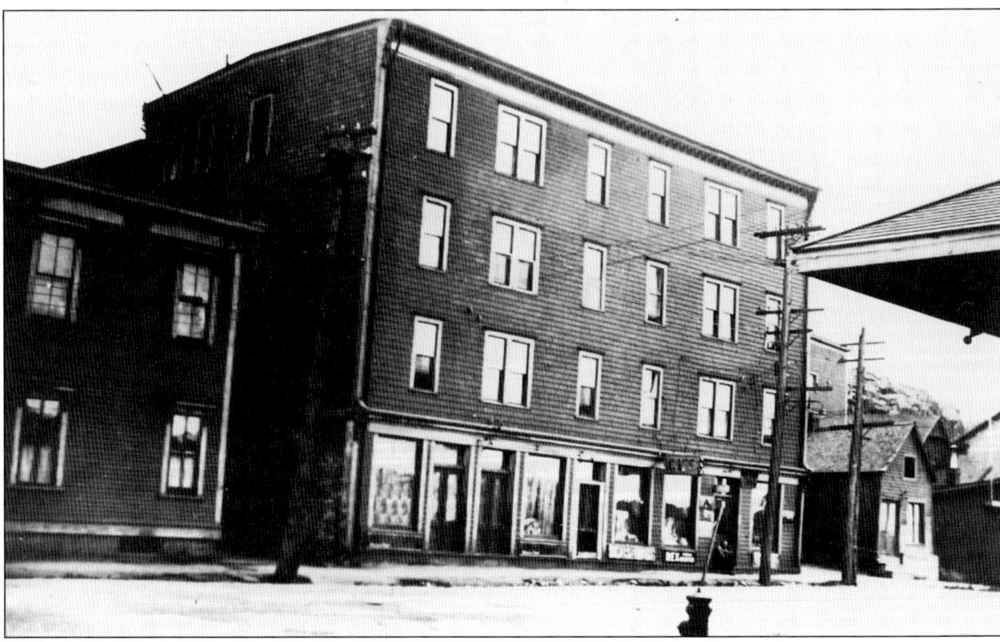

Frenette's store and restaurant on St. John Street, near Union Street. On the right is the Chinese Laundry. A portion of the Frenette Building was used as a detention centre during World War II. (National Harbours Board.)

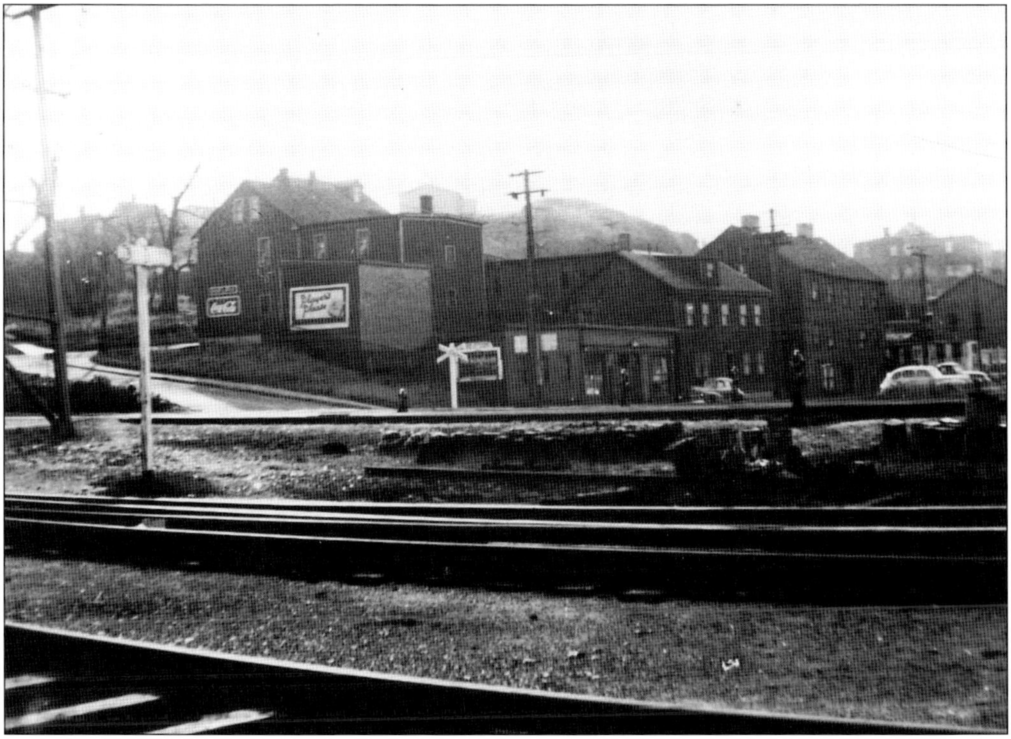

At the lower end of St. John Street port workers had to cross a half dozen sets of tracks if they wanted to get a hot lunch at one of the dog carts along the street or spend the night at the second building from the corner, the Maple Leaf Hotel. (Margaret Morrisey Collection.)

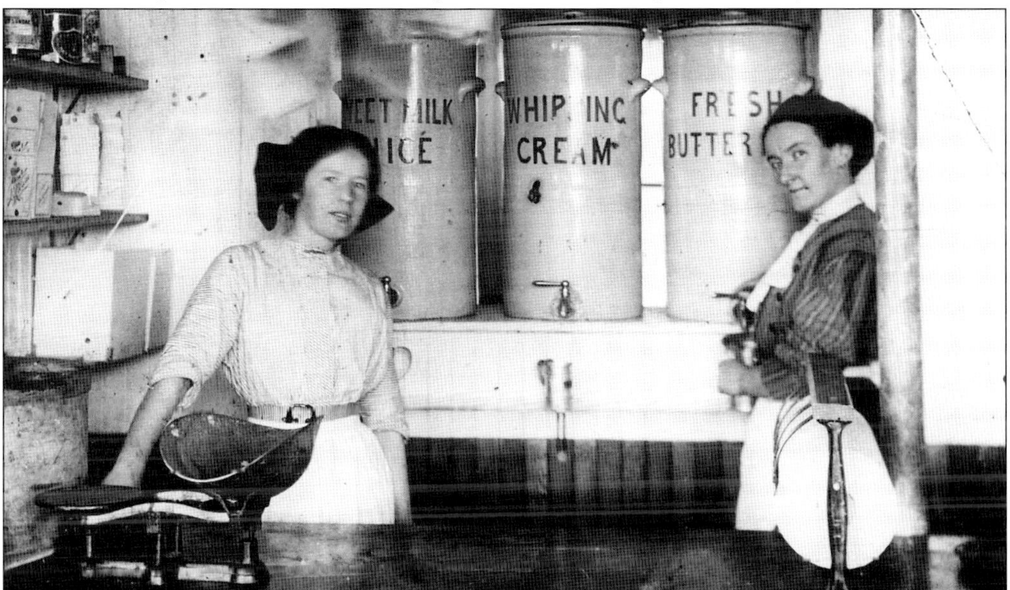

Susie Murphy (right) is shown at her Union Street lunch and ice cream parlour with the huge vats of whipping cream, milk, and fresh butter ready to be ladled out for her customers. (Murphy Family Collection.)

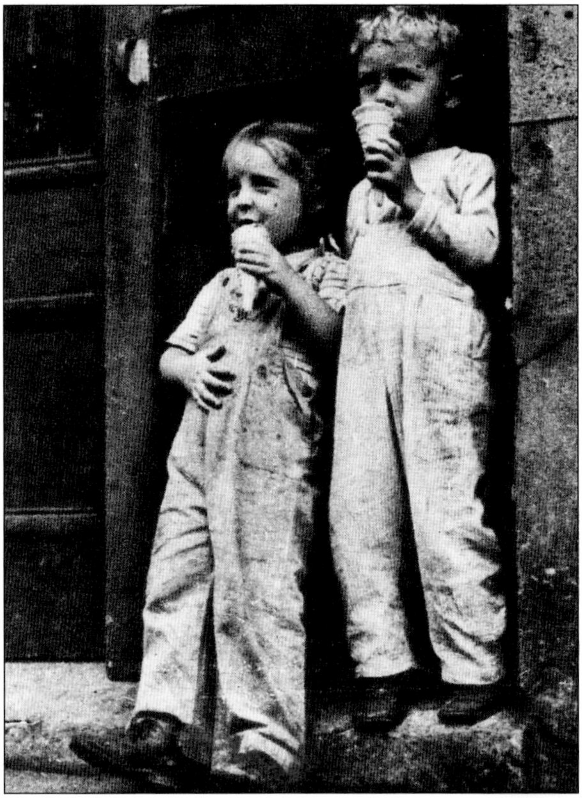

West Siders Paul Brown and Marilyn Belyea enjoy an ice cream outside McLeods Grocery on Ludlow Street. (Nina Belyea Collection.)

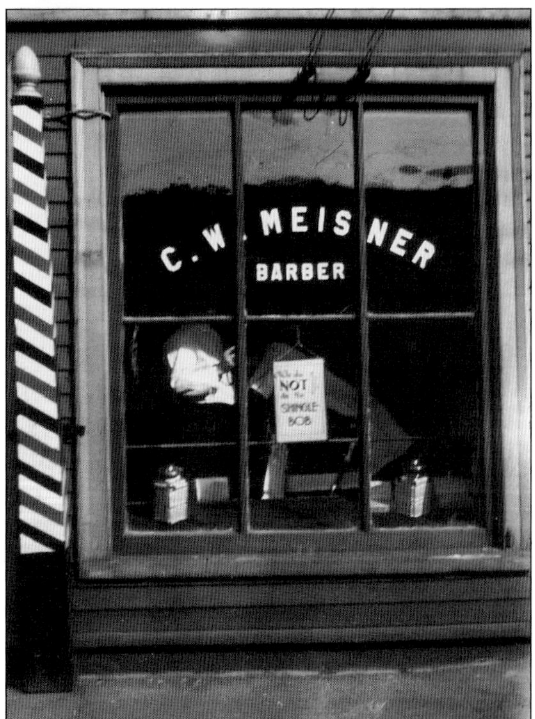

Charlie Meisner's Barbershop on King Street was a very popular spot but he made no attempt to be "fashionable," as we can tell by the sign stating: "We do not do the Shinglebob." (Joan (Iliffe) Galbraith Collection.)

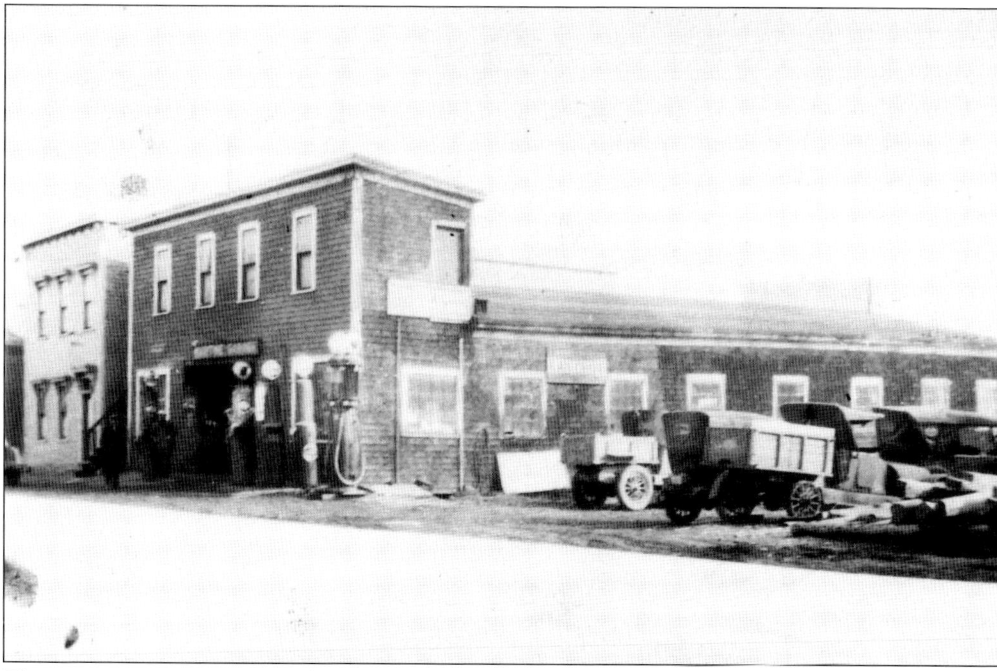

The Maritime Garage on Rodney Street likely started life as a livery stable, then added gasoline pumps and began to make vehicle repairs once Ford's Model-T made it possible for more and more people to own automobiles. (Walter Lord Collection.)

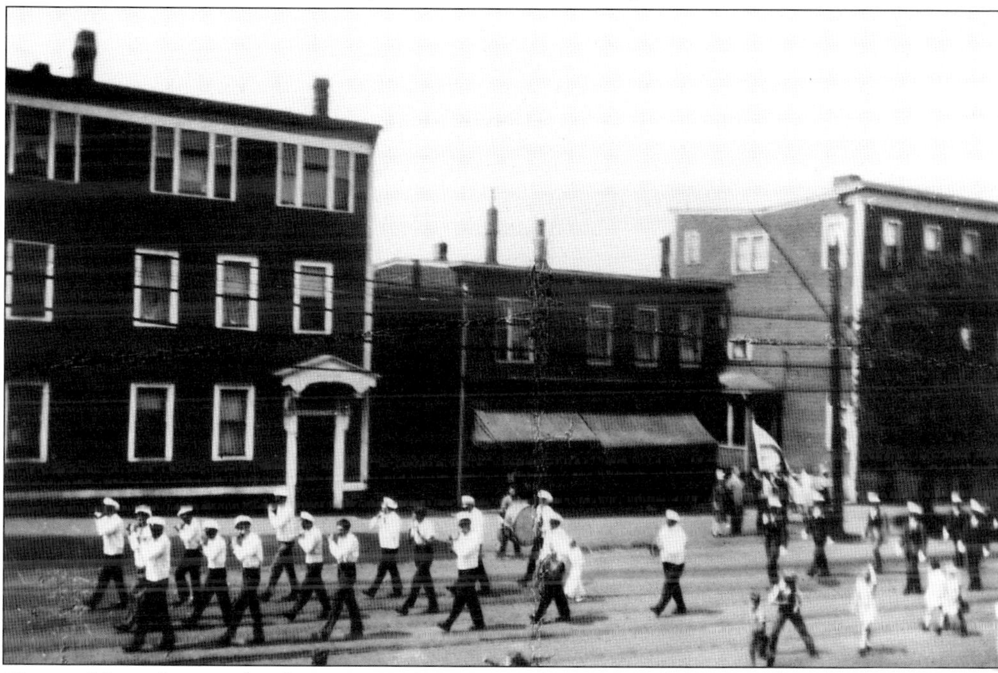

George Harned specialized in top quality men's clothing and shoes at his King Street store. His store was located just a few doors up the street from the Ideal Store where he learned the business and made his plans to open a competing store. The Ideal Store eventually moved uptown and then closed out in 1994. (Joan Iliffe (Galbraith) Collection.)

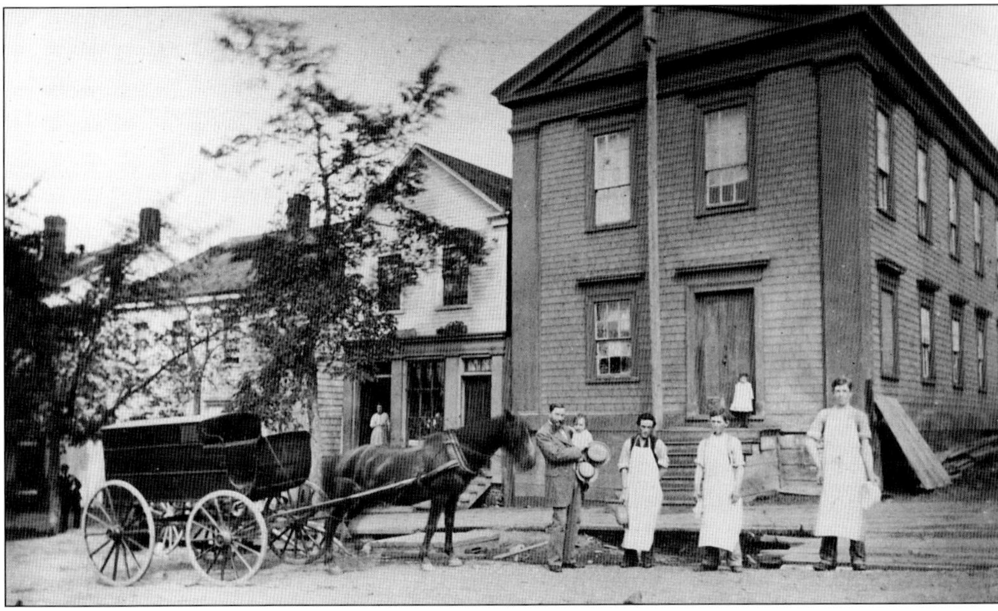

The wagon sitting outside the Cornfield Bakery is covered to prevent dust from getting onto the baked goods that would be delivered from house to house from this upper King Street shop. The Cornfield Meeting Hall is to the right. It served the Masons, and various churches and fraternal organizations before being converted to a home. It was torn down in 1992. (Ann Nice Collection.)

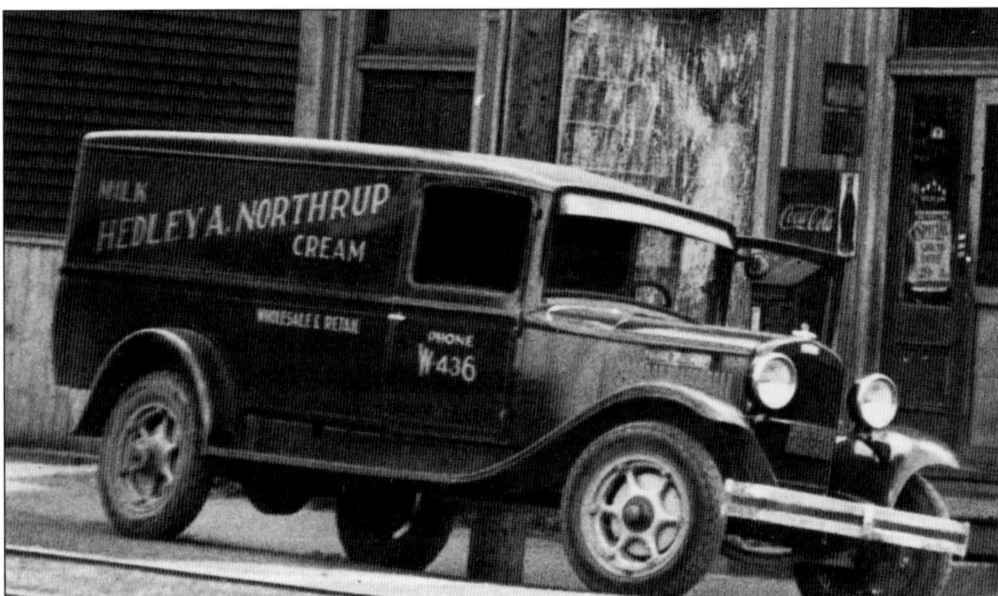

Hedley Northrup's Ice Cream Parlour on King Street was a popular spot for dating couples, for those who wanted some delicious Ganong chocolates, and for those seeking a political argument or a good backroom game of cards. Mr. Northrup was likely the first to have a delivery wagon in Saint John West. As this late 1920s photograph shows, it was a fine vehicle indeed and quite a contrast to the horse-drawn wagon shown in the Cornfield picture. (Provincial Archives.)

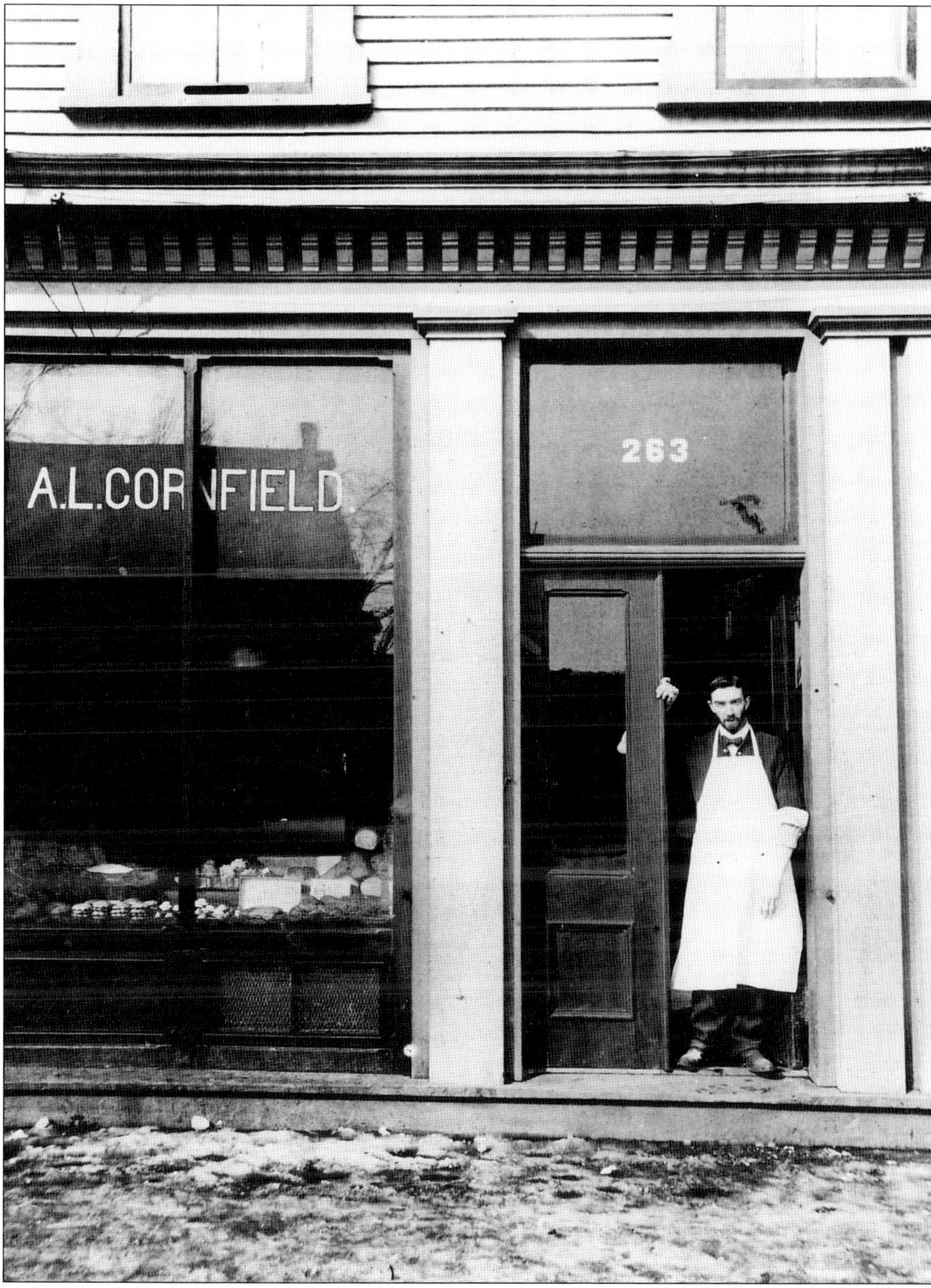

A.L. Cornfield operated a bakery at 263 King Street. He is seen here in the doorway of what later became Hedley Northrup's Ice Cream Parlour. (Ann Nice Collection.)

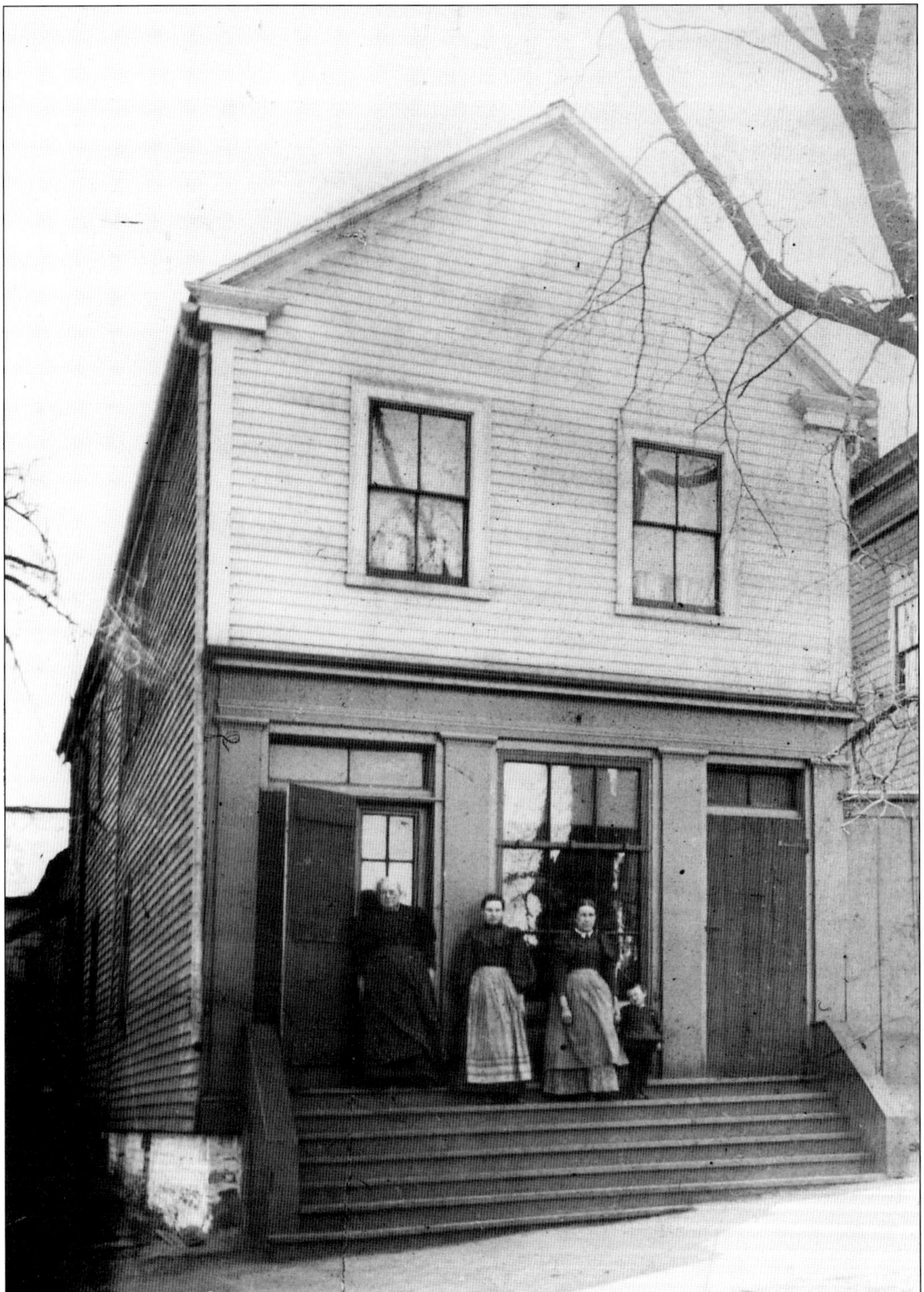

Another Cornfield bakery operated a block up King Street near Courtenay Hill. These are the bakers that were on duty when this photograph was taken in the late 1880s. (Ann Nice Collection.)

Nine

Historic and Public Buildings

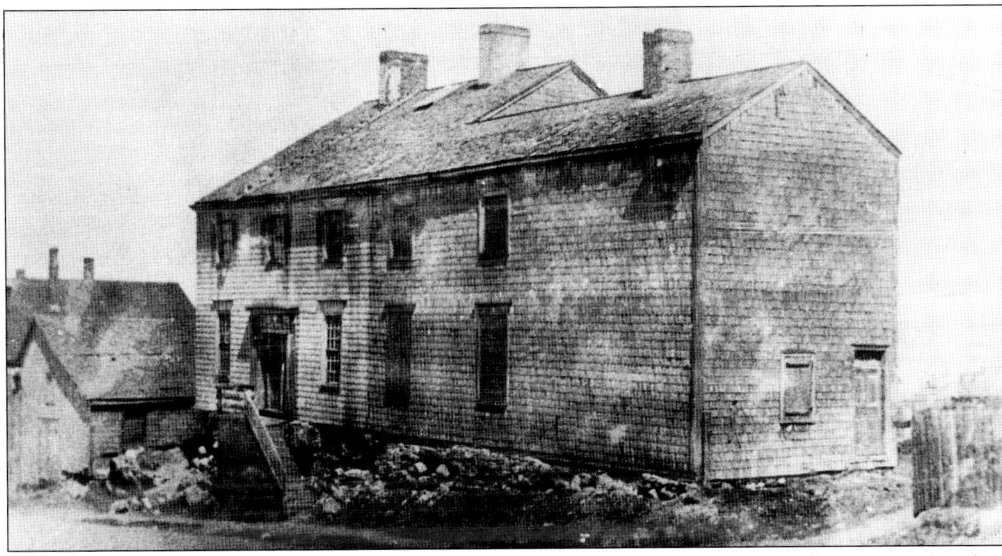

When the Loyalists arrived in Saint John Gabriel G. Ludlow was appointed as mayor. He had this home built on Duke Street on the site of the gardens of a former French settlement. Mr. Ludlow's house was torn down in the late 1880s, but his grave is still within a block of the house on Courtenay Hill. (New Brunswick Museum.)

Until the proposal was finally rejected in 1889, Saint John West, then known as Carleton, often talked of becoming a separate city from Saint John. The citizens never felt that they got their fair share of attention from the council, and their chief complaint was the lack of a convenient bridge to town. Due to the constant agitation about this issue, many public buildings were placed in Saint John West to appease the populace and to keep them happy to be a part of the city of Saint John. Among those structures was a magnificent town hall that was erected in 1863, and what is now the Carleton Community Centre is the oldest continuously used public building in Saint John. After many years of various uses with the name Carleton Public Hall, it is now a very busy community centre with about five hundred registrants of all ages taking advantage of its services. Fred Miller, a co-author of this book, is the current director of the centre. The rapport he has developed with area residents has resulted in the donation of the many photographs of old Saint John West that line his office and the walls of the centre, and that constitute the majority of the photographs that have been gathered in this book. In addition, the stories that old-time residents have shared over the years have been the basis for much of the information about the photographs that Mr. Goss has worked into the accompanying text.

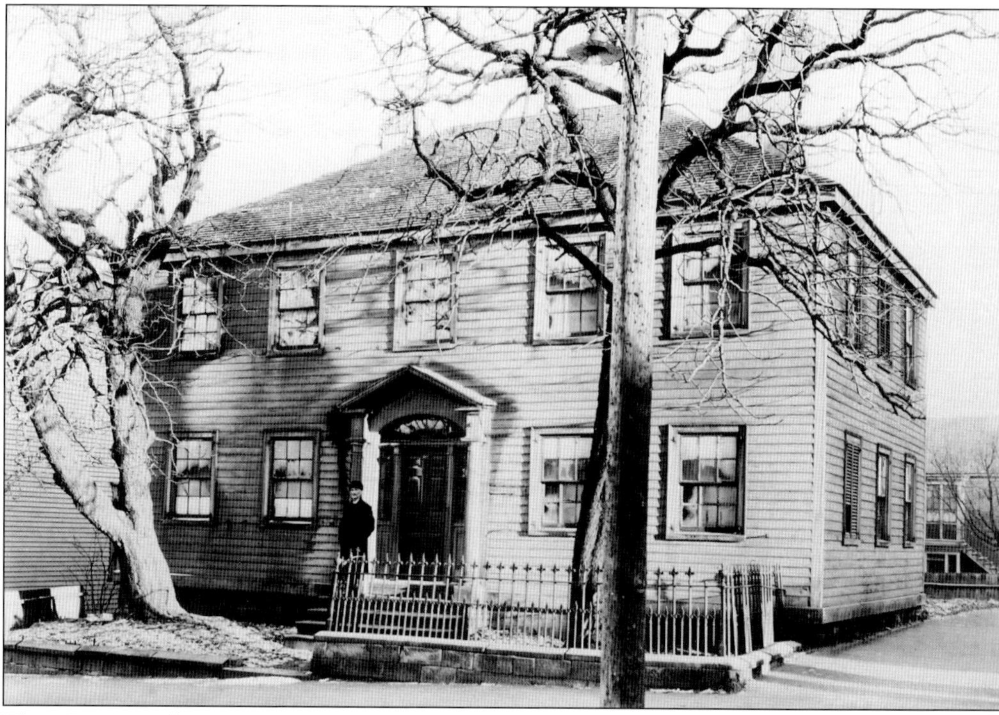

The 1791 Sewell House that still stands on Duke Street at Ludlow is just a block to the east of the site of the Ludlow house. A four-apartment seniors' home today, it is little changed outside and claims to be the oldest house in Saint John. (New Brunswick Museum.)

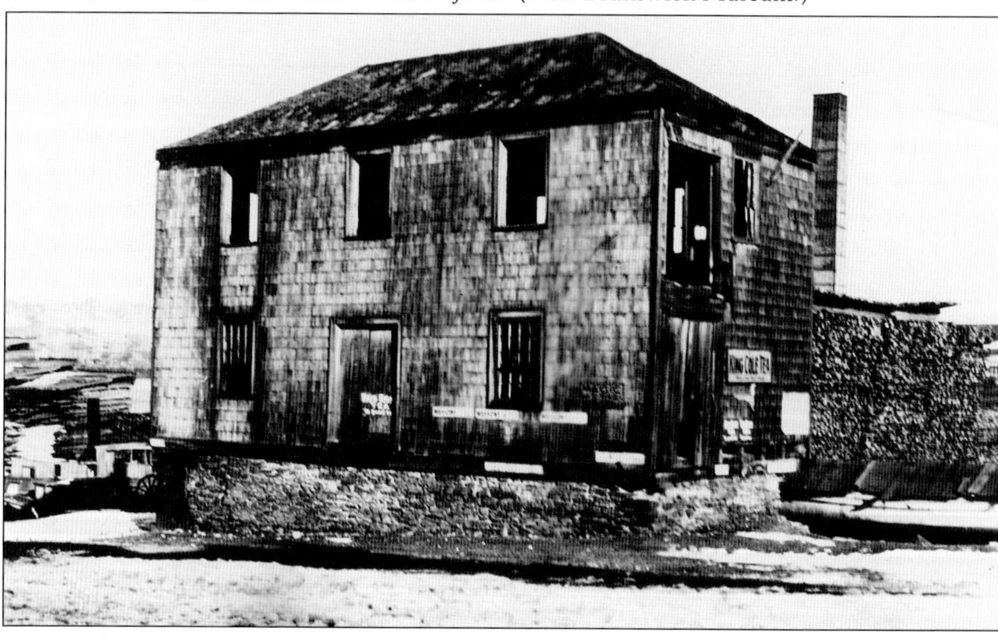

Prior to the construction of the 1863 town hall, this structure served as the market building for Saint John West. It was the first public building constructed in Saint John West and was located on the corner of Market and Shipp Streets. It was torn down in the 1880s. (New Brunswick Museum.)

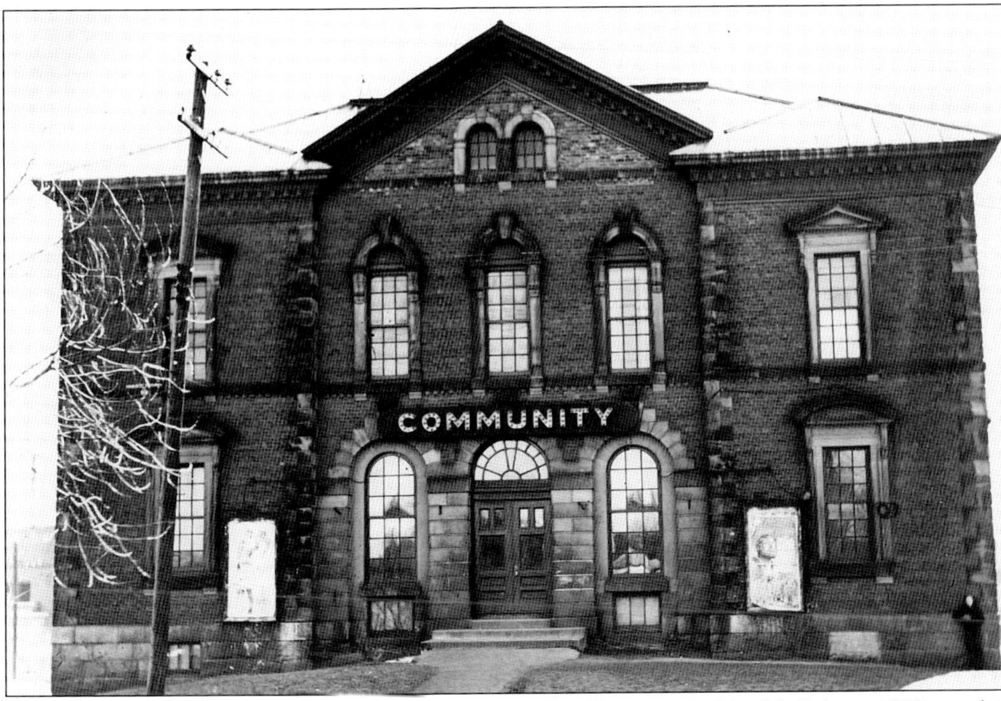

The Community Theatre was the main tenant of the Carleton Public Hall from 1925 until it was converted to a recreation centre in the late 1950s. See pp. 64 and 65 for a picture of the building prior to a fire in 1925 that destroyed the top-story auditorium. (City of Saint John Water and Sewerage Archives.)

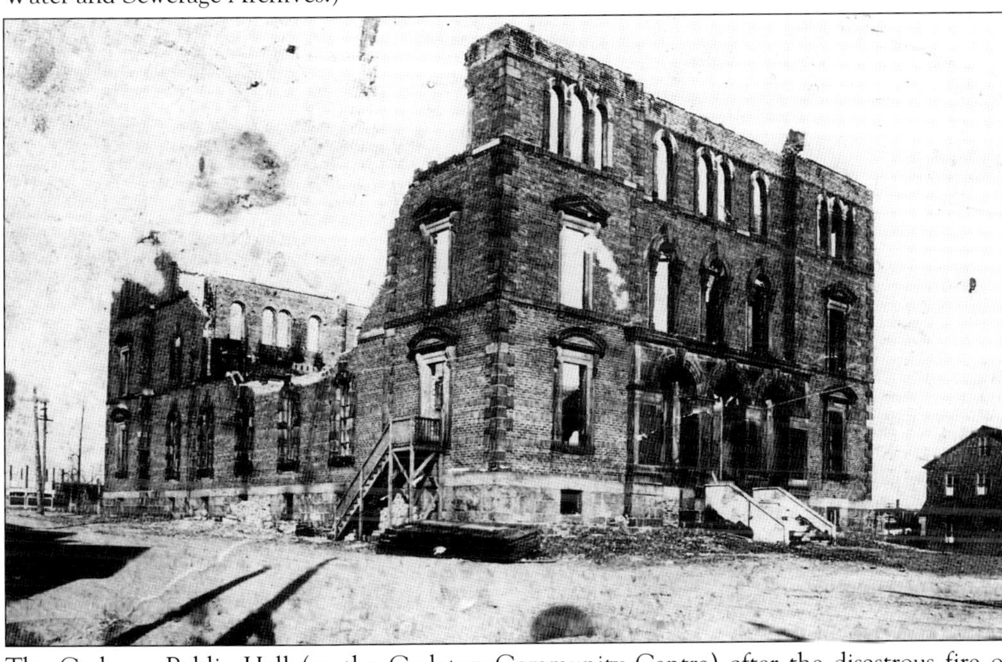

The Carleton Public Hall (or the Carleton Community Centre) after the disastrous fire of October 14, 1925. The hall was rebuilt only after public pressure from Saint John West residents as the local government was intending to collect the insurance and raze the structure.

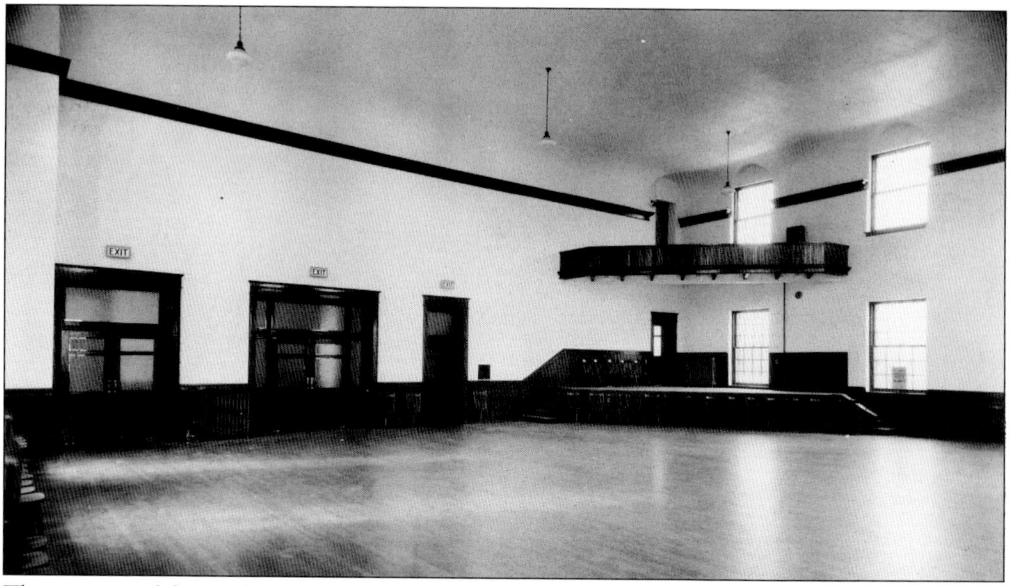

The interior of the Carleton Public Hall after being rebuilt following the 1925 fire. It originally contained a balcony for an orchestra in the huge lower floor room that was designed as a ballroom. Later, this room served as the Empress and Community Theatres and today it is a gymnasium. Before it closed in the 1950s, the theater was often called "The Bug House." (Harold Wright Collection.)

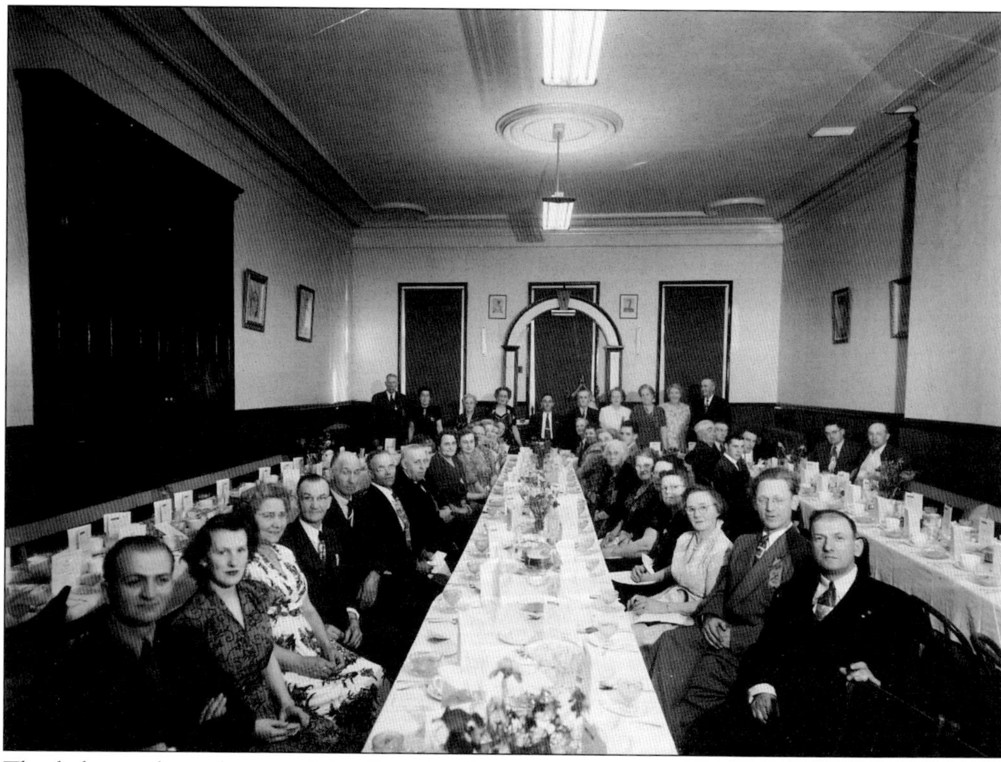

The ladies and gentlemen of the Prentice Boys organization are seated for a banquet at the Prentice Boys Hall on Guilford Street. (Fred Price Collection.)

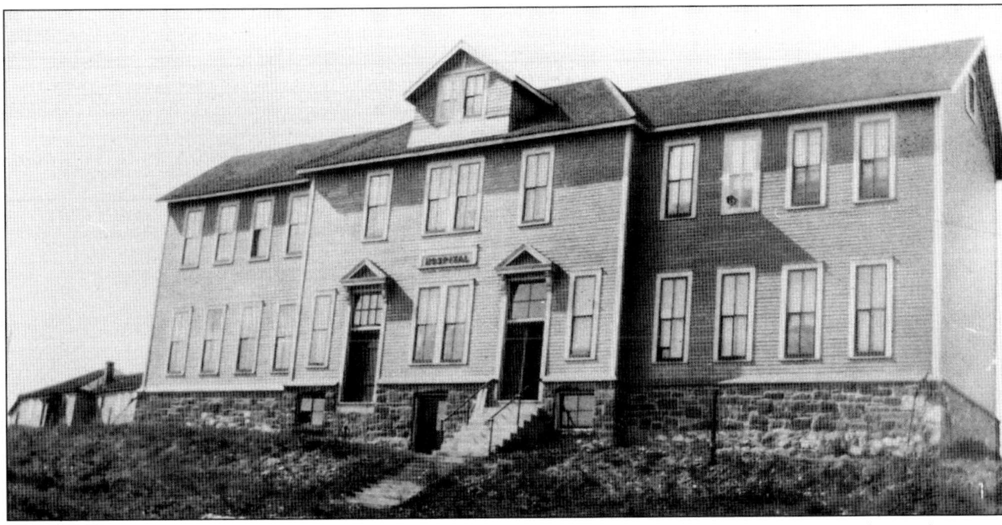

Many Carleton residents of Irish descent began their days in Canada quarantined in a hospital on Partridge Island. This is the last of the hospitals built in 1905 to handle immigrants from eastern Europe that were passing through Saint John. (Harold Wright Collection.)

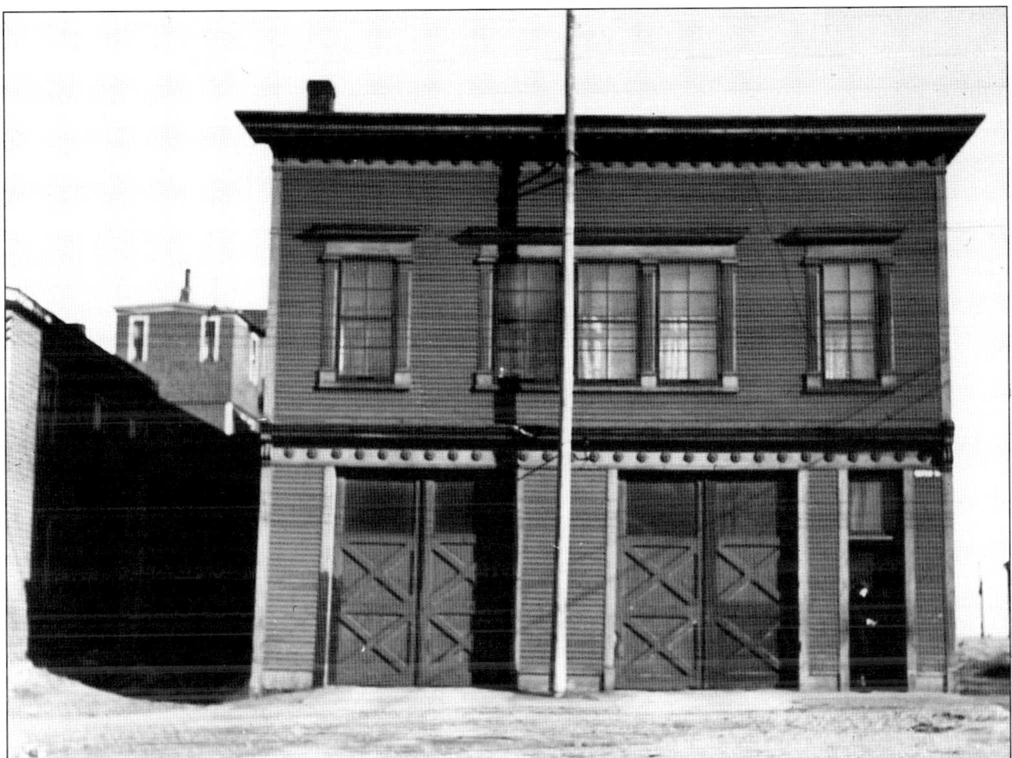

This 1859 building served as a fire hall and general city work depot for the Blue Rock Hill area of Saint John West. In its later years the Boy Scouts, Alcoholics Anonymous, and other community groups such as the PALs (Police Athletic League) met upstairs. (City of Saint John Water and Sewerage Department.)

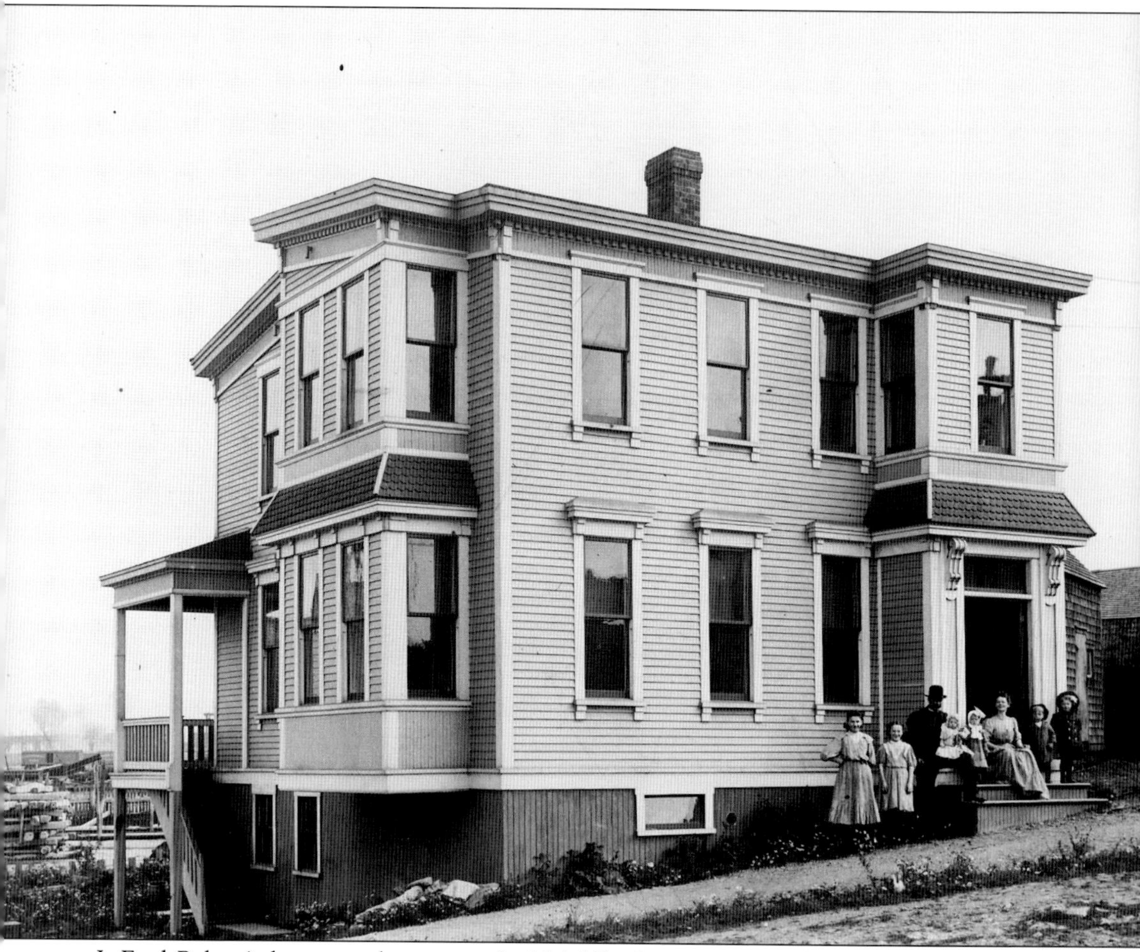

J. Fred Belyea's home at the east end of Middle Street next to the mud flats of Saint John West. Belyea was known as "Bollard" Belyea as he was a formidable member of the Common Council representing Saint John West from 1910 to 1952. It is claimed he made—and lost several—fortunes in the fishing industry. Some of the rewards of his fishing career were no doubt spent on this fine house, and on the family that appear with him. (Margaret (Belyea) Brown Collection.)

Ten

Almost Surrounded by Water

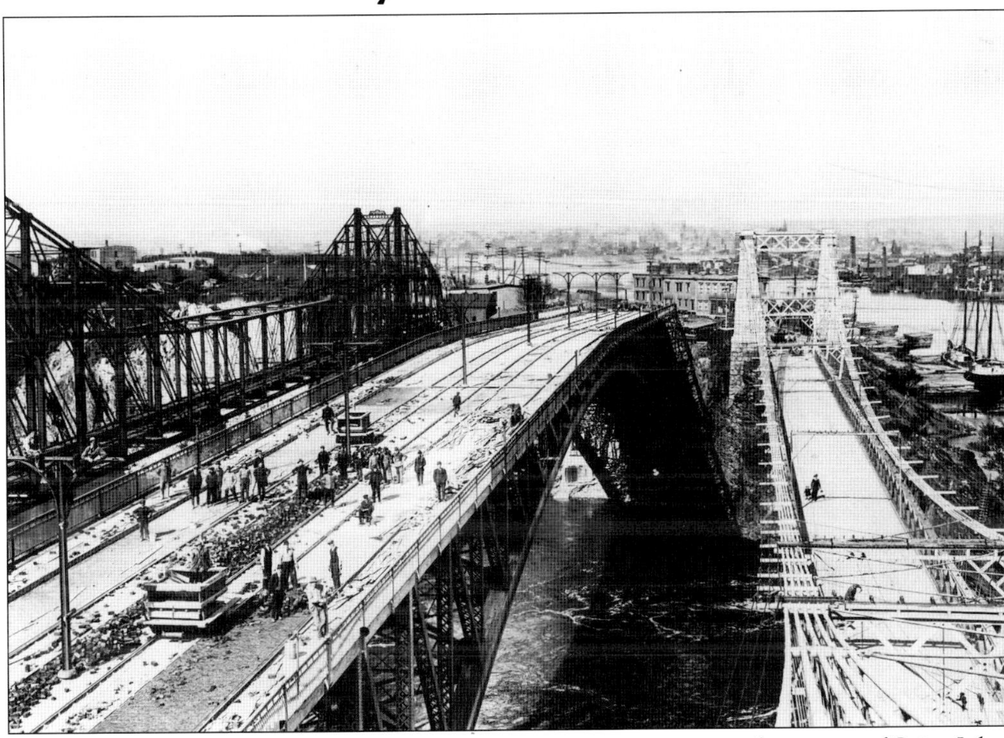

Of constant concern to Saint John West residents was easy access to the centre of Saint John. From the earliest times, a ferry service was run for this purpose and it was maintained until 1953. As there were often times when this service was not adequate, there was always agitation for a bridge from Saint John West to the centre of town. Harbour tides and the necessity of passage for vessels steaming up the St. John River made construction of a low bridge impossible, and the technology to build long, high, unsupported arches for a high bridge had not yet been developed. In 1837 a suspension bridge was built across the shortest point at Straight Shore, from Watson to Merritt Street, but, when almost complete, it collapsed due to weak cables and seven men died in the tragedy. The next attempt was made in 1853 when the bridge shown on the right of the picture was constructed by Kilby Reynolds. It was torn down in 1916 when the bridge in the centre (which still stands today) was built across the 600-foot chasm. The bridge to the extreme left is the original railway bridge. Though other attempts were made to build a bridge from lower Saint John West, it was not till 1968 that a high-arched bridge was built out over the remainder of Navy Island to the centre of the city. (Harold Wright Collection.)

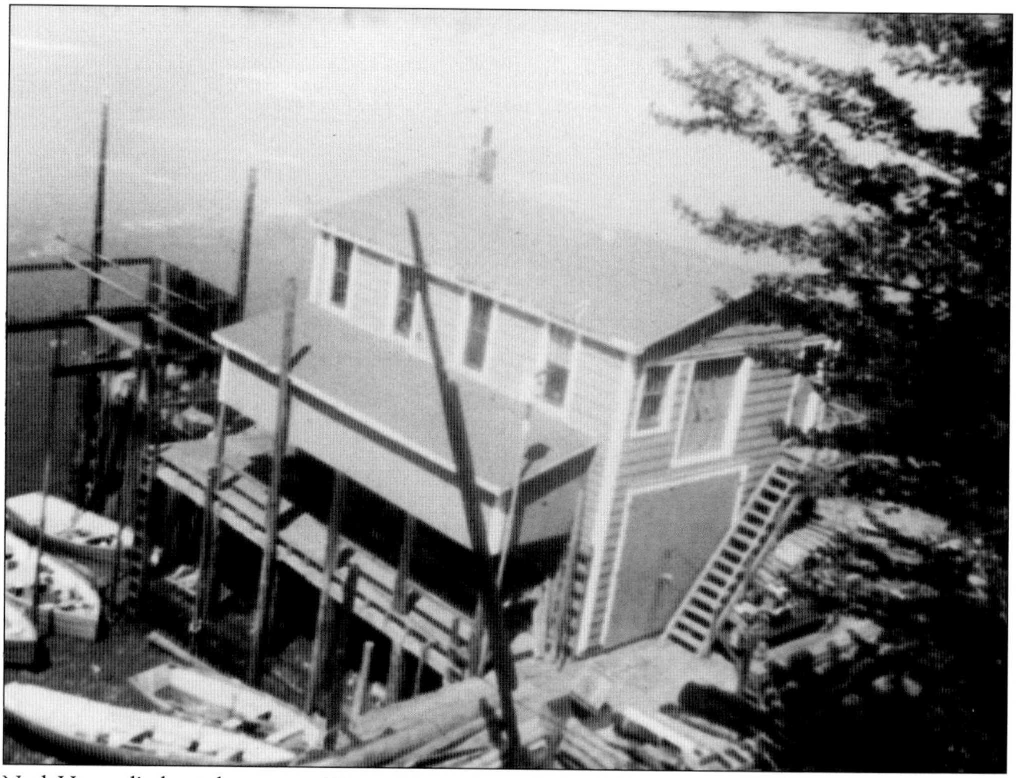

Ned Harned's boat house on Water Street is typical of the structures that were built up on poles to compensate for the tidal variations in the Bay of Fundy and Saint John Harbour of up to 26 feet. Little fishing is done now, but in times past, spring meant that gaspereau, shad, and salmon would be swimming upriver and could be caught in great quantities. (Malcolm Harned Collection.)

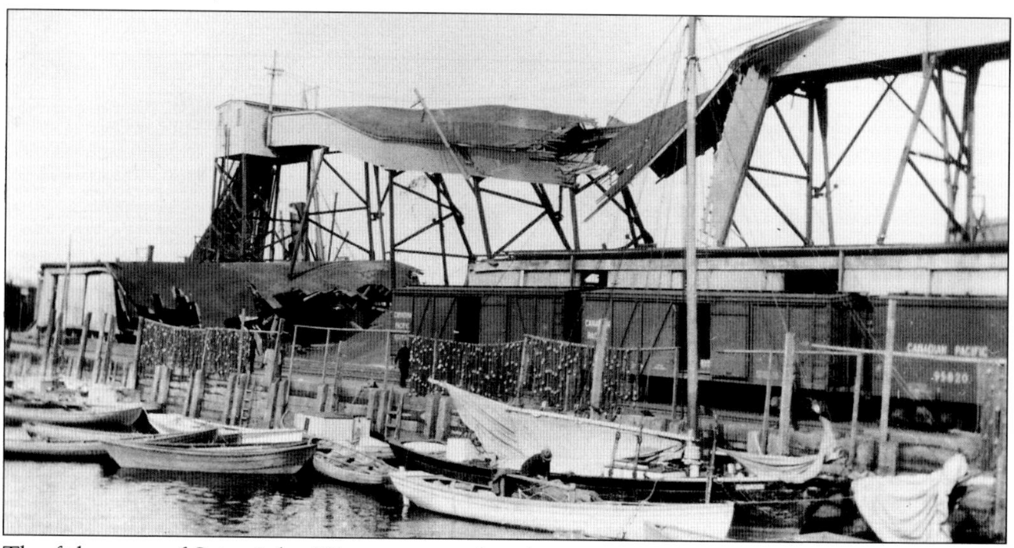

The fishermen of Saint John West co-existed with activity at the port. Nets were hung to dry on wharves that also held boxcars unloading freight. This photograph was taken in 1917 when a collapse in one of the grain elevators occurred.

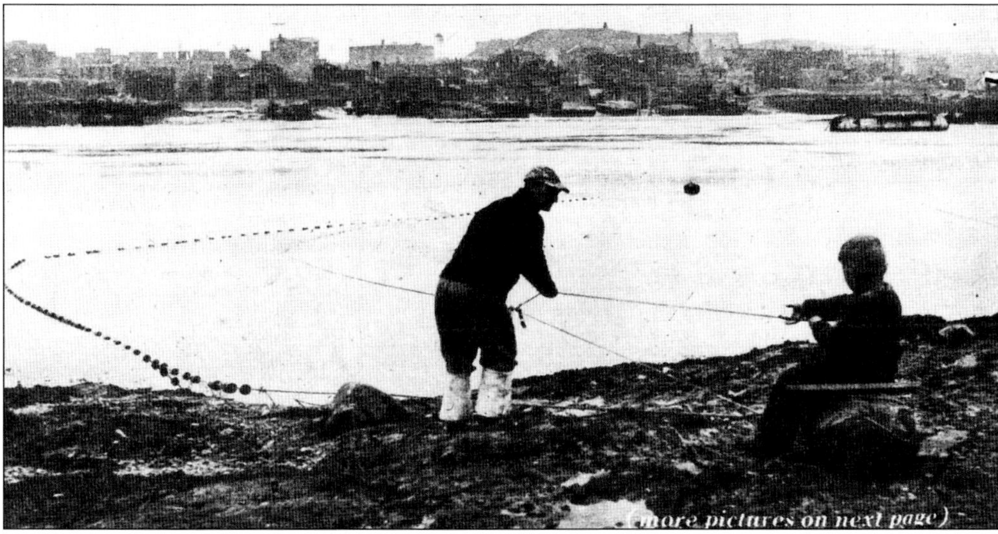
(more pictures on next page)

Anthony Belyea and his son Richard are pictured in 1946 with a set net designed to catch the salmon off Navy Island. (Nina Belyea Collection.)

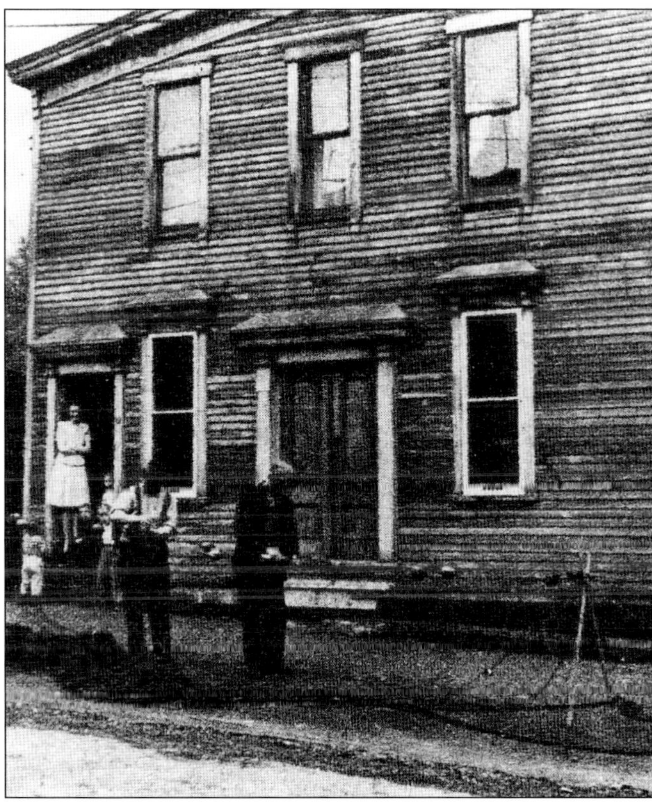

Anthony Belyea's home at 105 Ludlow Street. The downstairs portion of the house was used for the fishing operation while the family lived upstairs. In a very good example of practical utilization of space, in this photograph they are simming the nets on the street outside the home. (Nina Belyea Collection.)

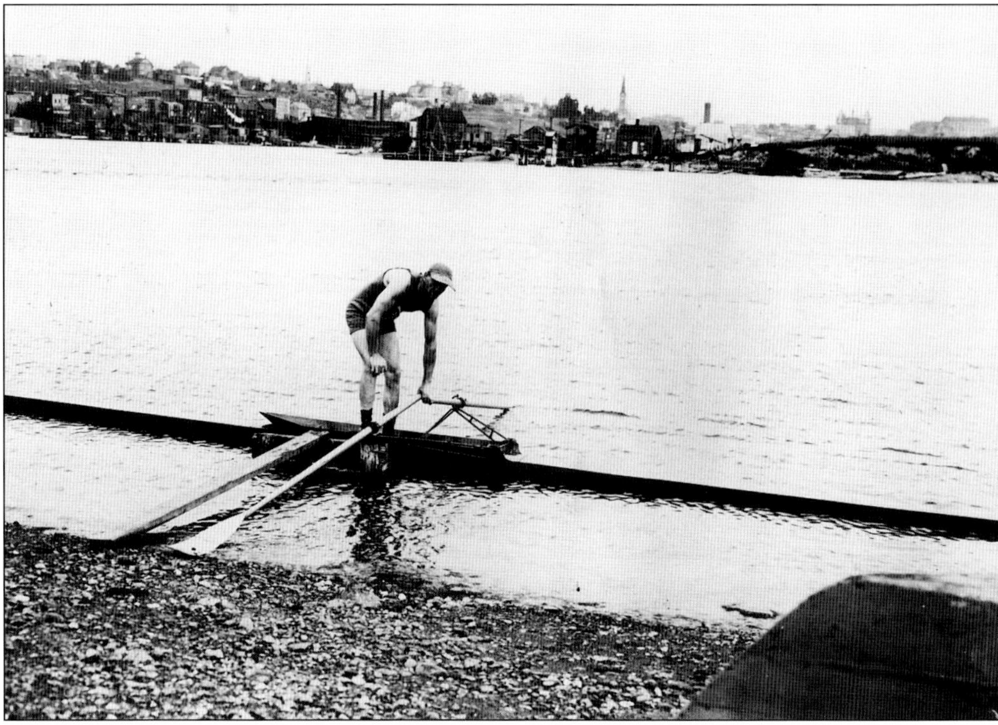

Fisherman Hilton Belyea was a champion sculler. He built his muscles rowing small boats about the harbour, and for recreation he took part in sculling races. This is Buttermilk Channel from Saint John West with Navy Island (behind Belyea), and Saint Luke's Church spire in the North End of Saint John (on the horizon). (Margaret (Belyea) Brown Collection.)

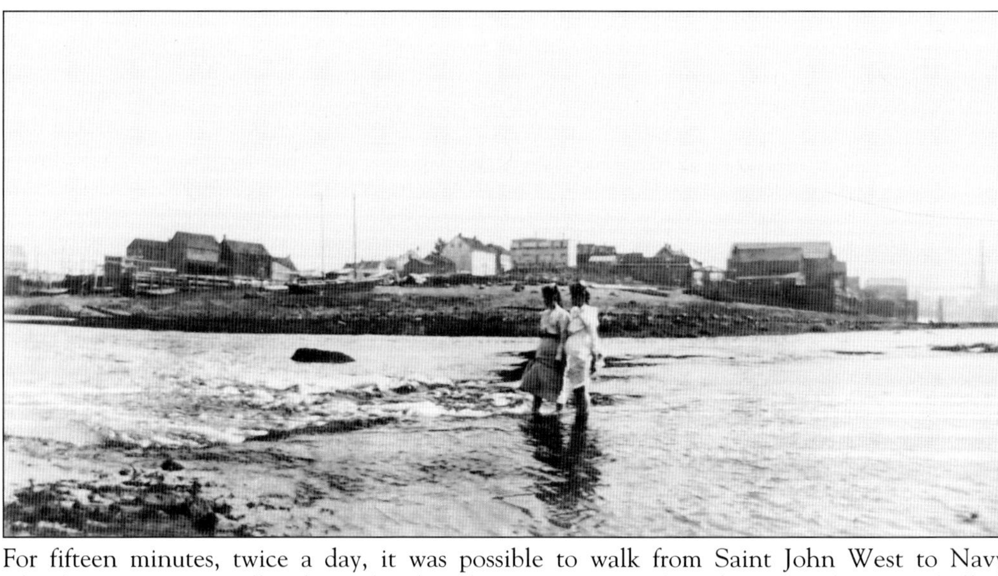

For fifteen minutes, twice a day, it was possible to walk from Saint John West to Navy Island across Buttermilk Channel. Though it was never dry, the water became shallow enough to cross to the homes of a dozen fishermen who called the island their home. (Terry Keleher Collection.)

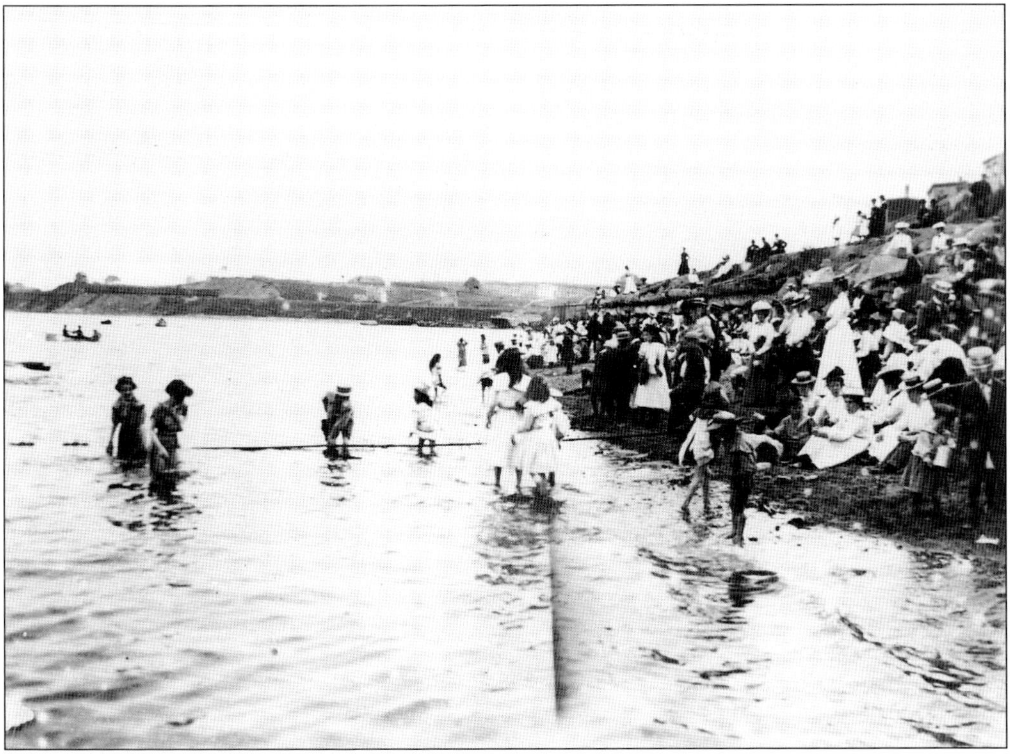

At Beatteay's or Blue Rock Beach, bathing was considered beneficial to the health, and on hot days folks would travel 30 to 40 miles from inland locations to dip their feet in the 50 degree Bay—but few swam in the chilly water at Beatteay's beach, shown here. (Erb Collection.)

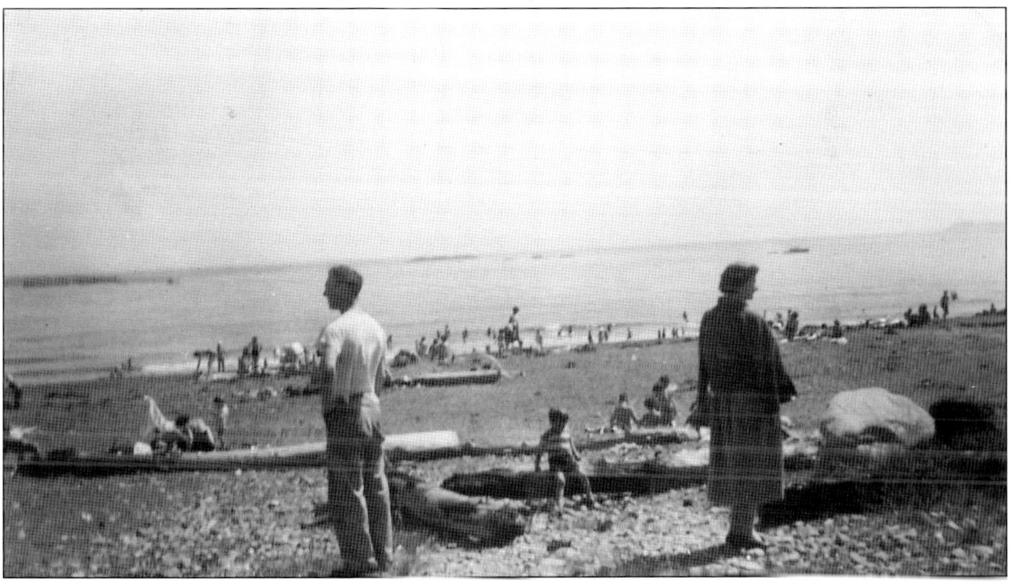

When Beatteay's Beach was gradually filled in by port and railway operations folks moved West along the coast to Bay Shore Beach. Until the early 1960s this was the popular place for Saint John West residents despite the fact that there were no facilities available. (Art Cormier Collection.)

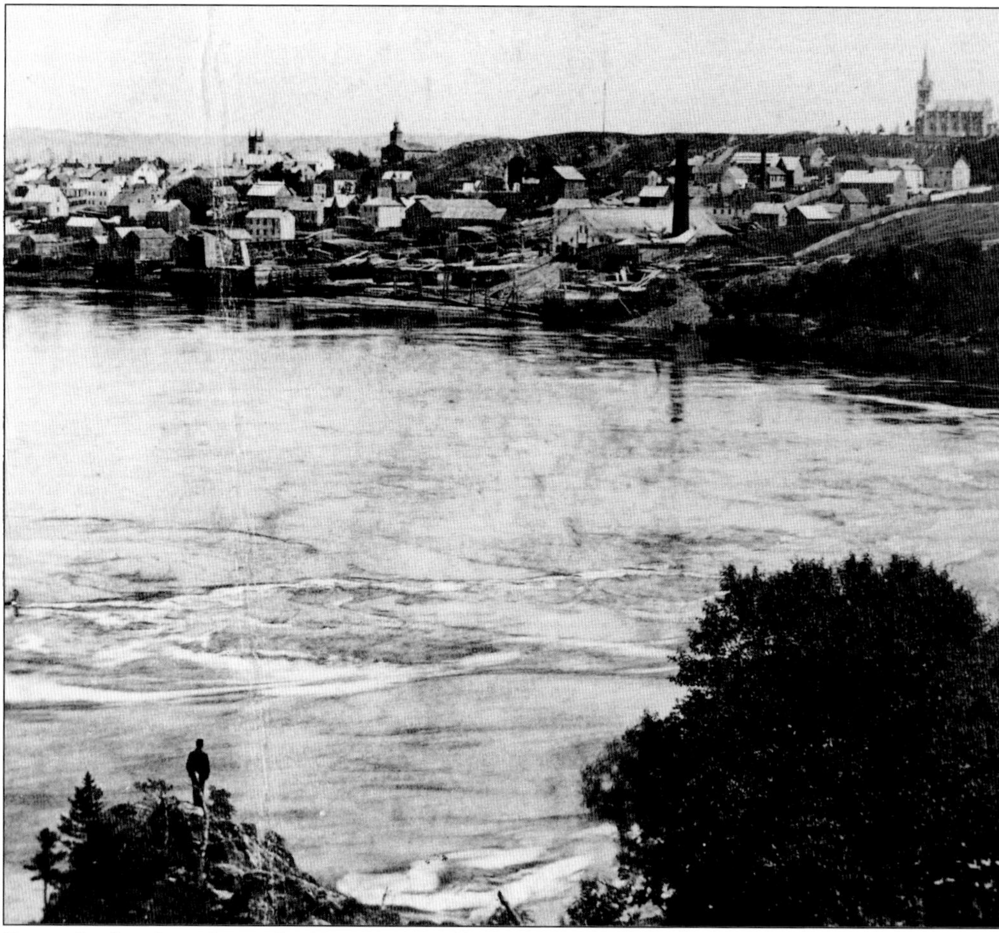

From the heights above the Reversing Falls it is easy to see how much of Saint John West is shaped by the water that surrounds it, and also how work and recreation has always been influenced by the area's position. (New Brunswick Museum.)

Eleven

Churches and Schools

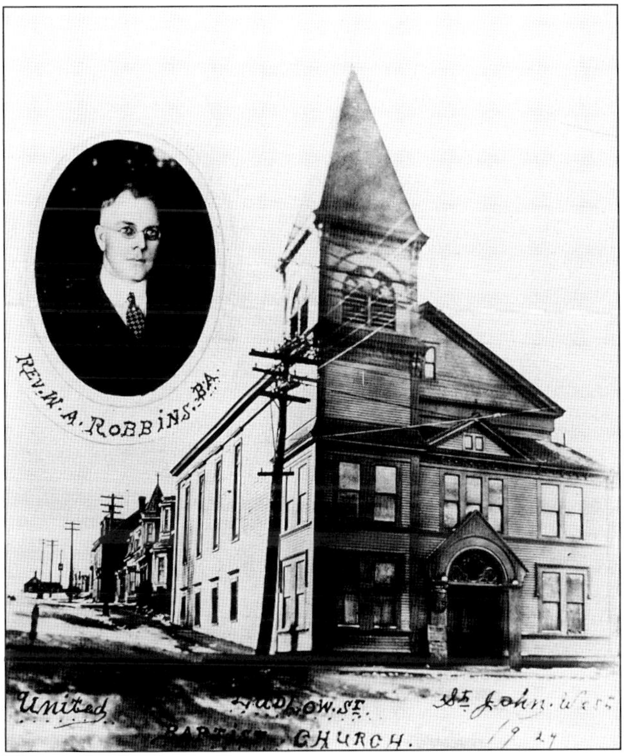

The Ludlow Street Baptist Church in 1924. It was one of two Baptist churches in lower Saint John West. This church was located at the corner of Ludlow and Duke Streets about halfway up the hill between the business district and wilds of Courtenay Hill. (Harold Wright Collection.)

The churches and schools of Saint John West have played an important part in the development of the community. It is surprising that there were so many of them in such a small area. There were churches of most denominations, and both Catholic and Protestant schools in the era when both had separate, private schools. In addition there were temperance halls and missions, such as the Blue Rock Mission that served the people of St. James Street and the Seaman's Mission which served the sailors who came to the port. Long before free and compulsory schools were widespread, the Anglican Church established the Madras School in a building which still stands on Ludlow Street, and there were other private schools such as the Mechanics Institute, the Bond Meeting House, the Tilton building on King Street, and a school in the Carleton Public Hall. While the oldest school in Saint John West only dates back to 1922, the oldest church dates from 1821 and is still a lively branch of the Christian faith.

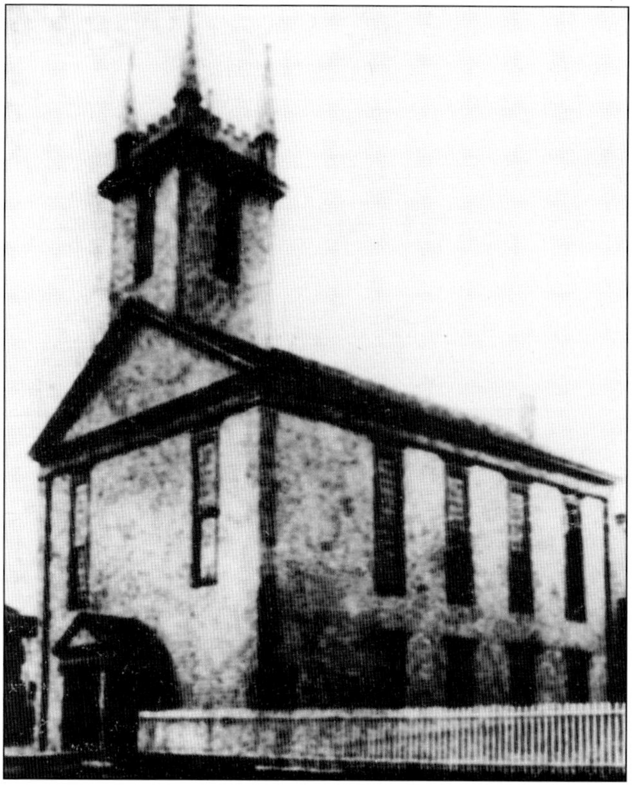

This very early photograph of the Ludlow Street Baptist Church with its tall windows shows that it was a substantial structure for the times. It was built to a primitive four-square design which stood the test of time. (Doug Carter Collection.)

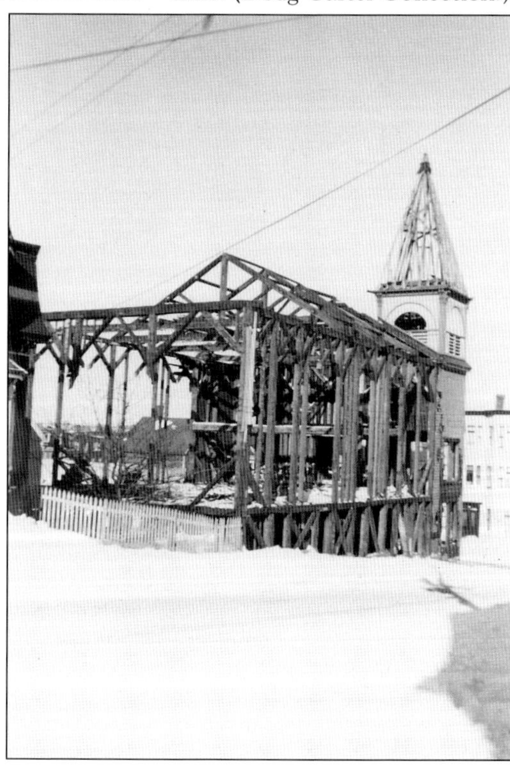

The Ludlow Street Baptist Church was amalgamated with the Charlotte Street Baptist Church to form the Hillcrest Baptist Church. When it was torn down in 1961, the huge square timbers of the Ludlow Street church showed it was much like a ship turned upside down, which shows the level of technology in architecture and construction at the time it was built. (Roy H. Makenney Collection.)

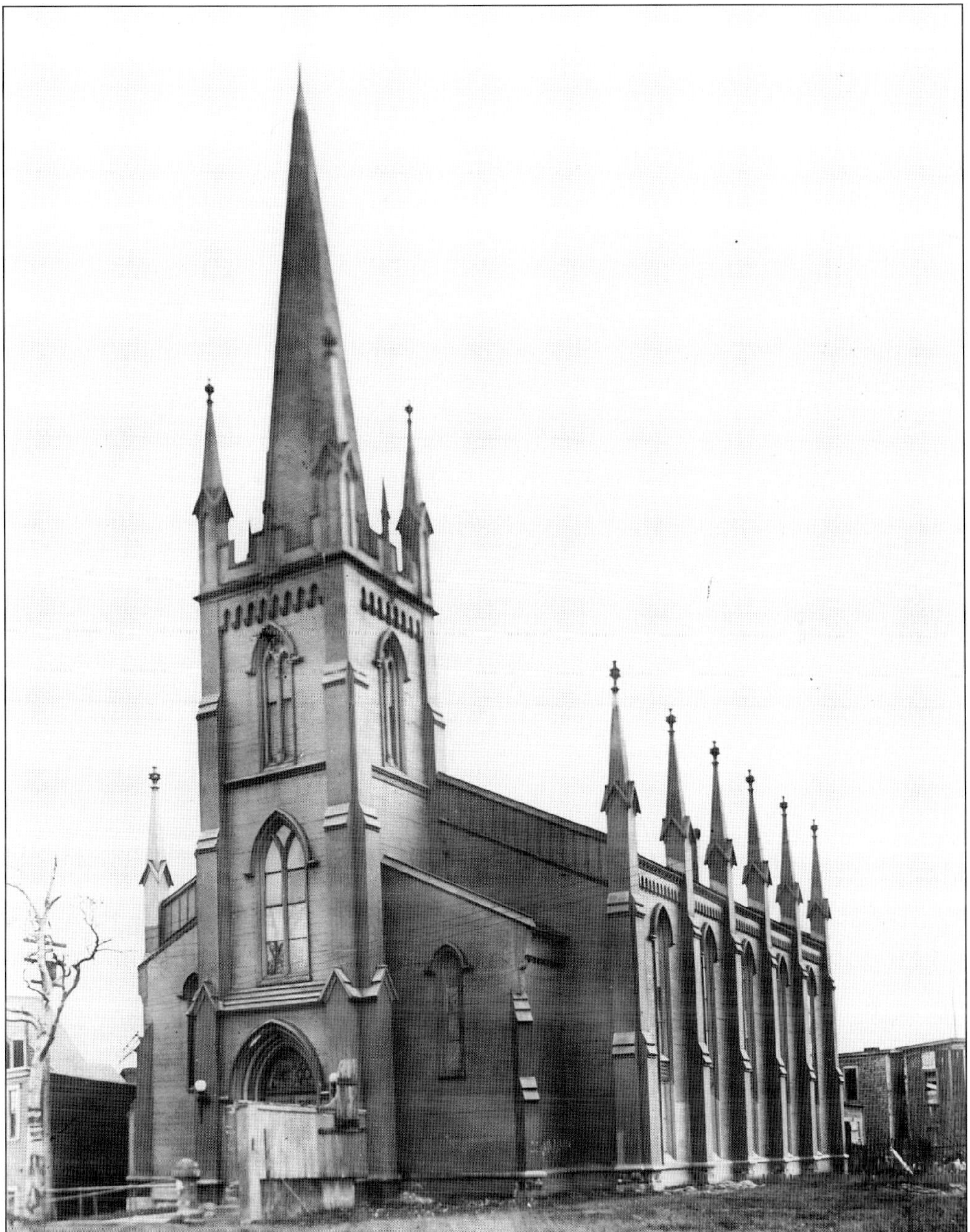

The Presbyterians established their kirk in 1857 adjacent to the first cemetery established in Saint John West. It was built atop Courtenay Hill in 1857, and it prospered until a fire on April 13, 1973, destroyed the structure. Gabriel G. Ludlow, Saint John's first mayor, and his wife Ann are buried in the cemetery in the church courtyard. They lived only a block away on Duke Street. (Carleton Kirk United Church Collection.)

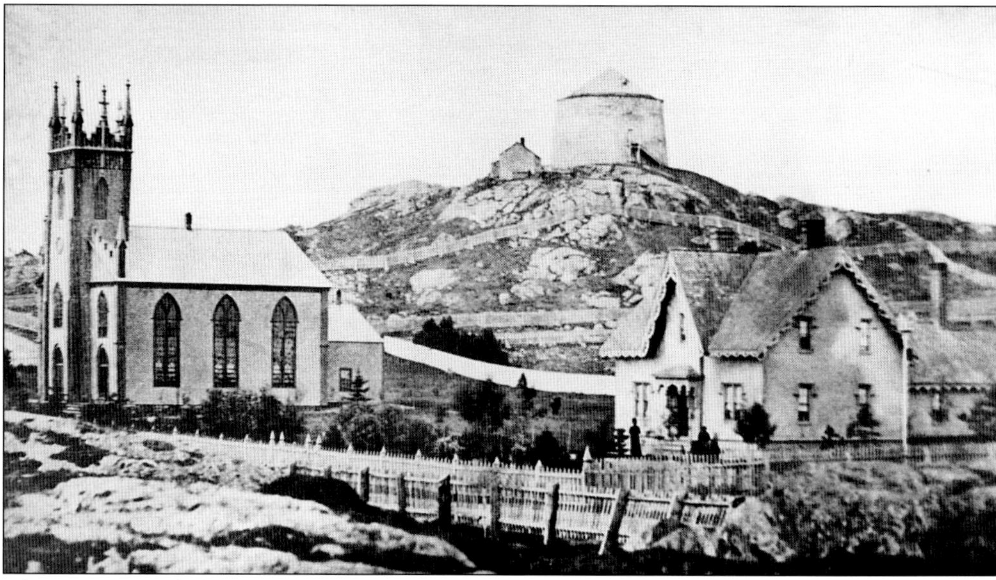

The Roman Catholic Church established a chapel in 1849 on land that at that time constituted the outskirts of the city. Martello Tower, built in 1812, stands high above the chapel. The fences around the two show that this area was still farmland at the time. The rectory to the right is a well-decorated carpenter gothic house—a design that was popular in the mid-1800s. (Harold Wright Collection.)

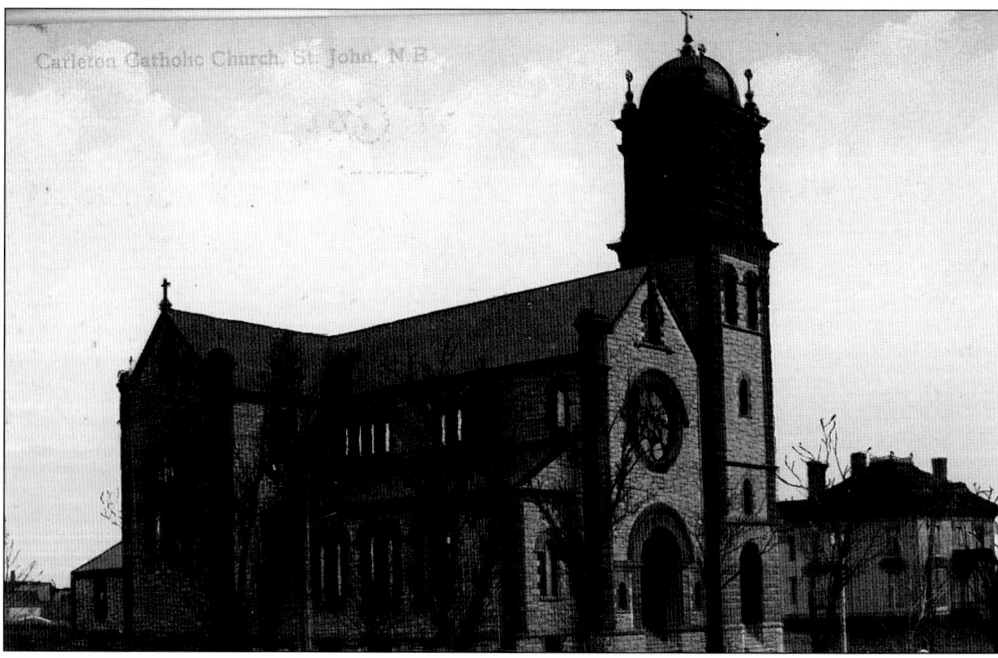

The first Catholic church, a wooden structure, burned. The second church was hit by lightning and burned in 1905. When the third church was built, a Byzantine design was chosen, and a fine brick building with many lightning rods was erected. It stands today at the corner of Lancaster Avenue and Dufferin Row as testimony to the old adage: "If at first you don't succeed . . ." (Erb Collection.)

The Methodists were known for their unadorned church buildings, and this church, built on Guilford Street in 1841, is no exception. Carleton Methodist Church was in the process of merging with the West Side Kirk on Courtenay Hill when fire struck the kirk in 1973, so, to meet the needs of the area, the Methodist church remained in service a bit longer until the modern Carleton Kirk United Church was opened on Easter Sunday, April 10, 1977. (Carleton Kirk United Church Collection.)

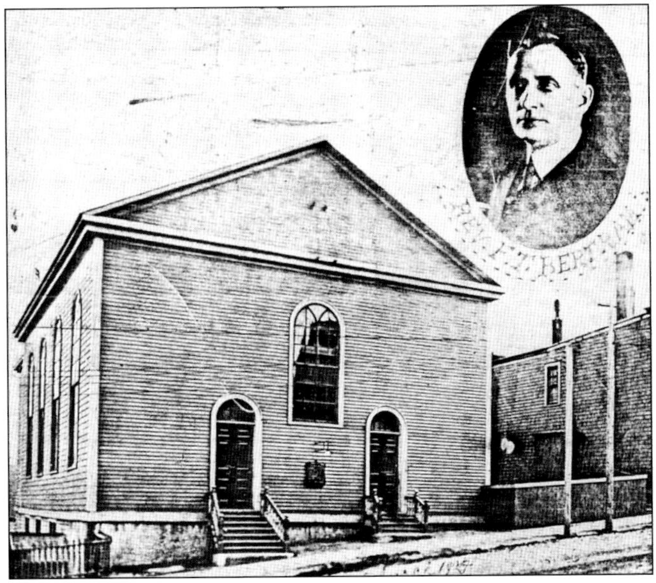

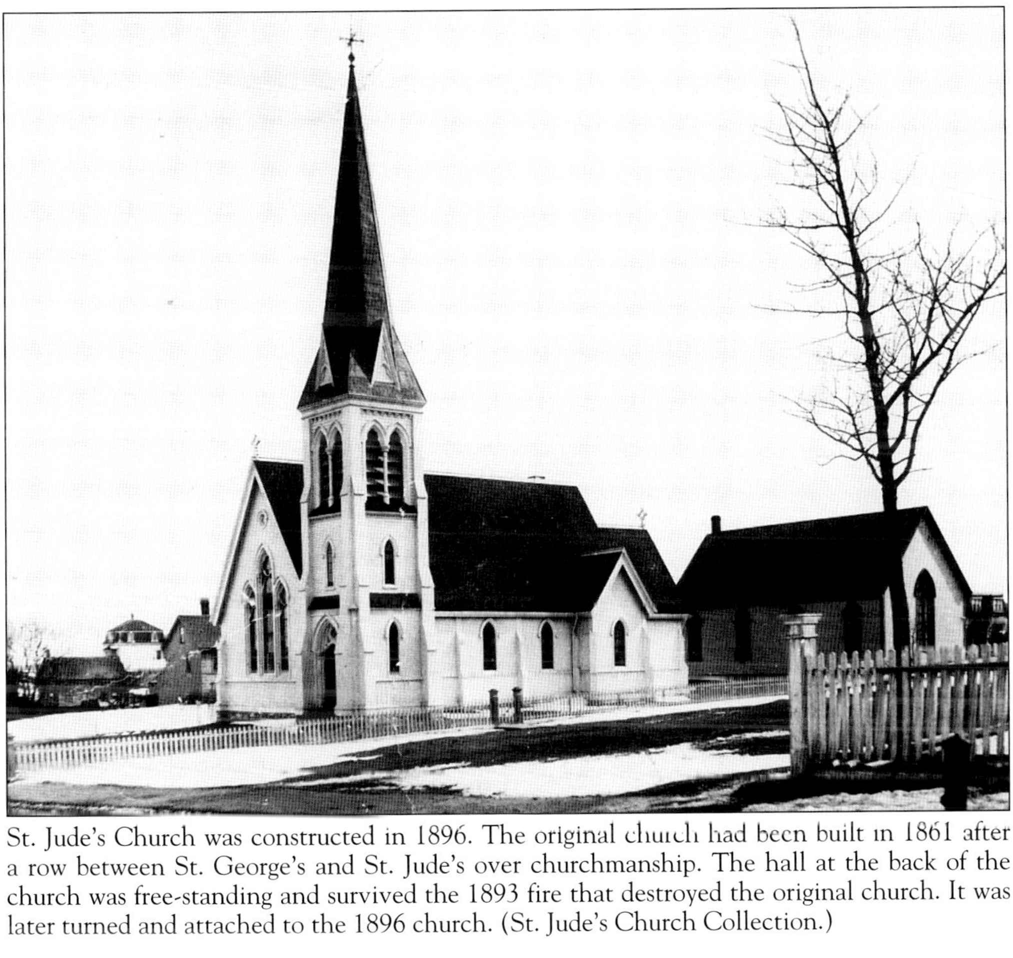

St. Jude's Church was constructed in 1896. The original church had been built in 1861 after a row between St. George's and St. Jude's over churchmanship. The hall at the back of the church was free-standing and survived the 1893 fire that destroyed the original church. It was later turned and attached to the 1896 church. (St. Jude's Church Collection.)

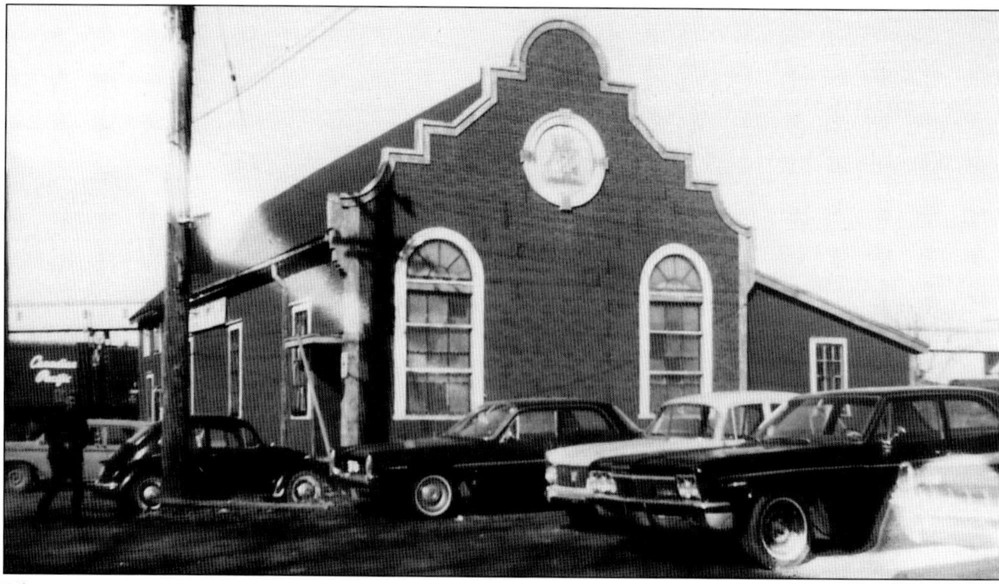

The seamen coming into Saint John were ministered to from this building which stood at the foot of Rodney Street near "the Cage." A newly-built Seaman's Mission building is still in active use near the Carleton Community Centre. (Yvette (Daigle) Tobin Collection.)

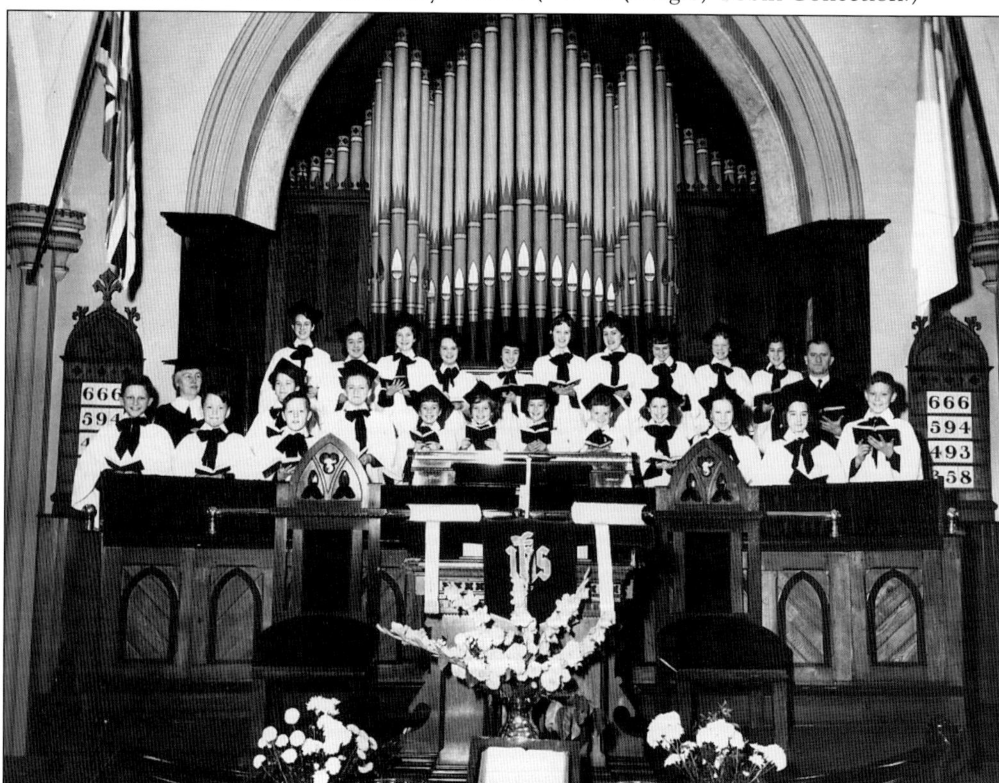

The junior choristers of the Kirk Church in March 1957 as they celebrated the 100th birthday of their church. (Carleton Kirk United Church Collection.)

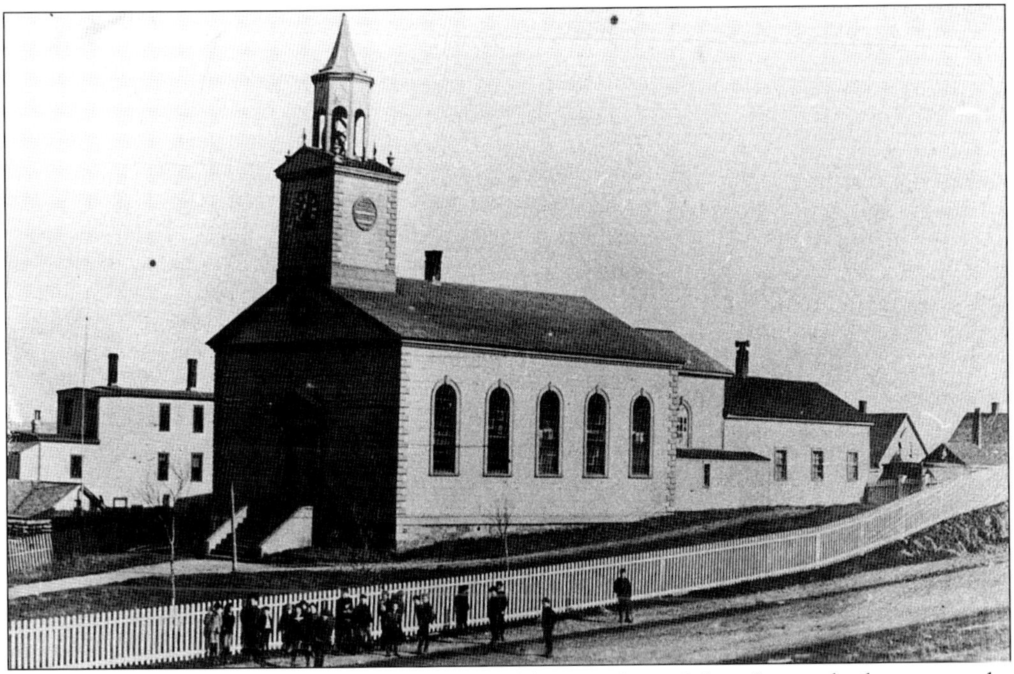

St. George's Church is the oldest church building in Saint John. It was built on a rocky outcropping by Courtenay Hill, and opened on November 6, 1821. It has undergone many changes and expansions since this 1880s photograph was taken. (St. George's Church Collection.)

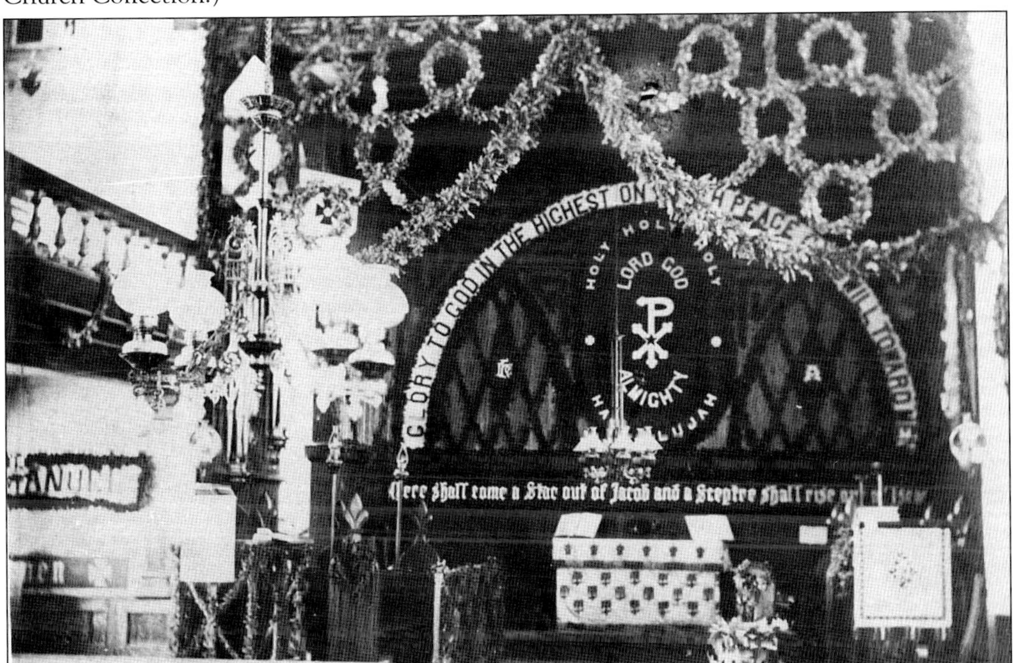

The Anglican churches of Saint John competed vigorously to see which could decorate the most lavishly during the festive season. St. George's often took first place. Sometimes it would take a week to get the greens and mottos in place. (St. George's Church Collection.)

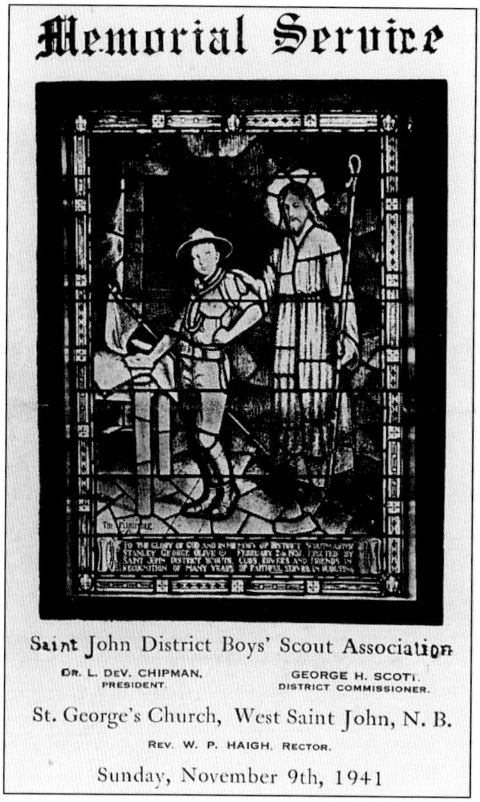

Memorial Service

Saint John District Boys' Scout Association

DR. L. DEV. CHIPMAN, PRESIDENT

GEORGE H. SCOTT, DISTRICT COMMISSIONER.

St. George's Church, West Saint John, N. B.

REV. W. P. HAIGH, RECTOR.

Sunday, November 9th, 1941

The Boy Scout "Pathfinder" window in St. George's Church is the only authorized copy in North America of a painting called *The Pathfinder* by English painter Ernest S. Carlos. It was dedicated in 1941 to Scoutmaster Stanley Olive, who founded the earliest Scout troop in Saint John West at Saint Jude's about 1912, and twelve years later (when in his sixties) served as a scoutmaster at St. George's.

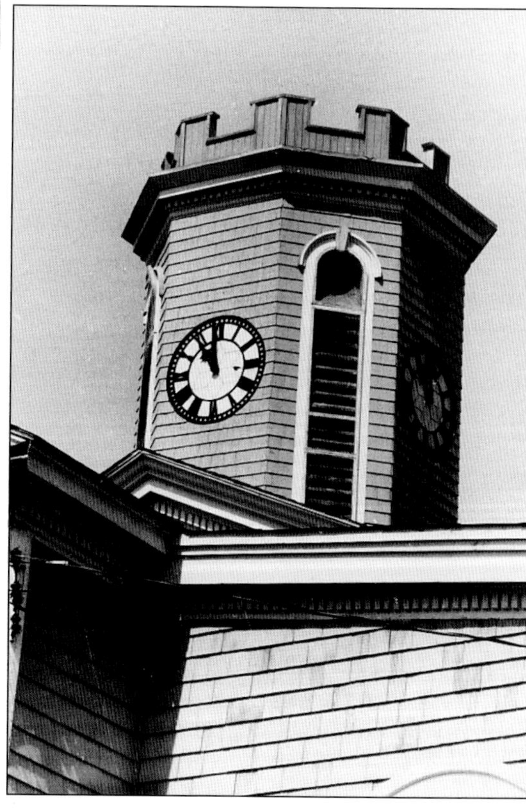

The clock in St. George's tower was given as a gift from the post office when the Union Street post office was torn down in 1932. As it is a public clock, the City of Saint John contributes $150 per year to the cost of keeping the mechanical works of this clock ticking in the 1890 belfry. See p. 33 for more information on the earlier clock. Today, this clock is the only mechanical clock remaining in Saint John, as all of the others have been electrified.

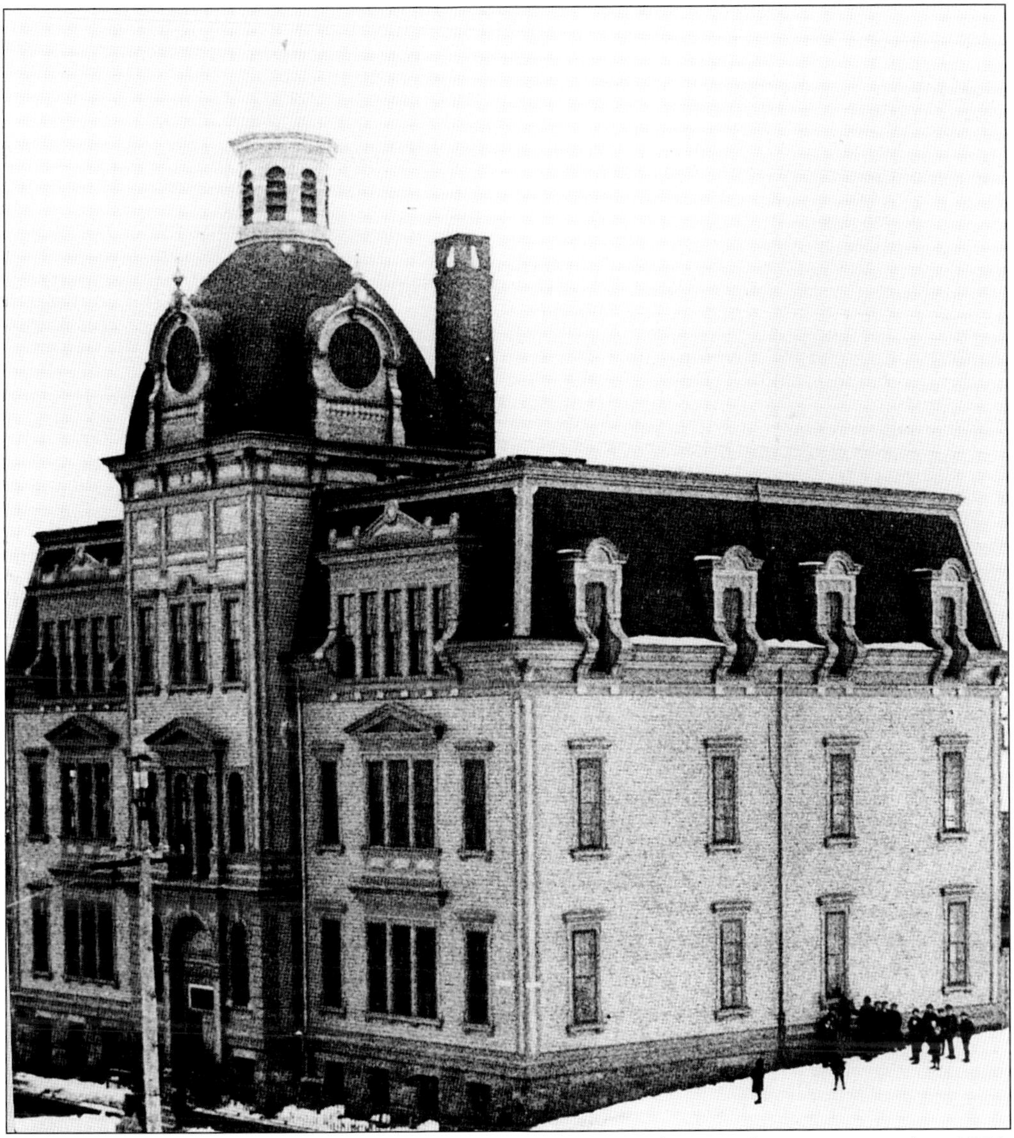

The old Albert School—a magnificent wooden structure in classic style—was opened in 1876. Sadly, it burned to the ground in May 1928. The group of children throwing snowballs in this photograph are all male. The girls would have been on the other side of the building as they had separate entrances and classrooms. At this time, there were as many as forty-nine students per room. (Board of School District 8 Collection.)

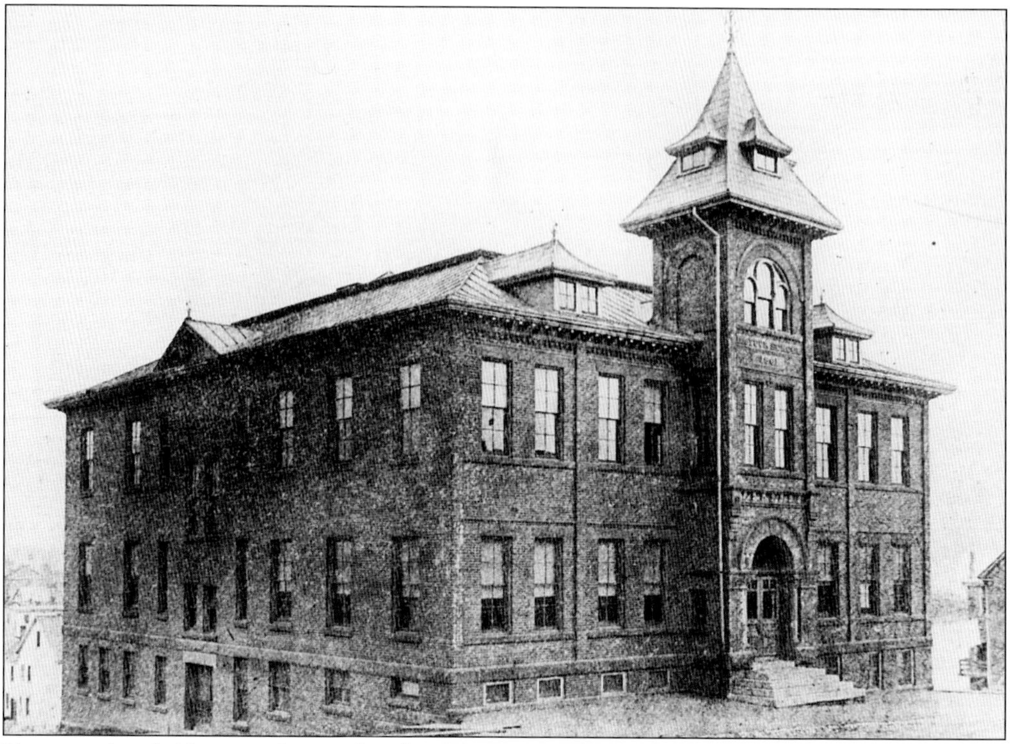

To serve the children on the south side of the peninsula, a school was constructed on St. John Street in 1901 and opened in 1902. LaTour School was named after the heroine Lady LaTour who died in her fortress after it fell to d'Aulnay on April 6, 1645. In 1900 it was believed the fort had been on the West Side near Navy Island, but it has now been proven to have been on the other side of the harbour.

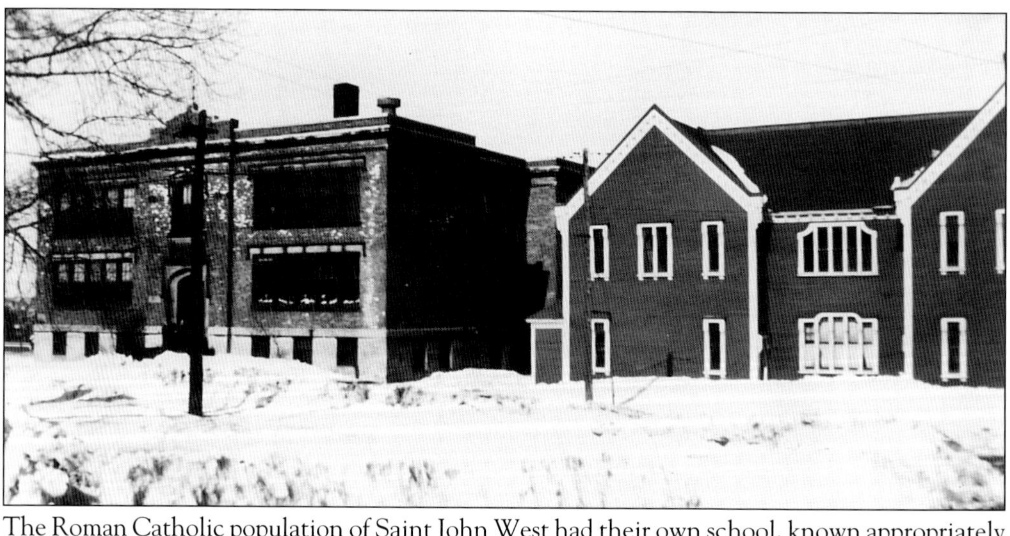

The Roman Catholic population of Saint John West had their own school, known appropriately as Saint Patrick's. Lots were purchased on St. John Street in 1855 for the construction of the first school. It was a wooden structure, and is shown on the right in this photograph. In 1931 the brick structure to the left was built and the older building became an auditorium. (Mary Cobham Collection.)

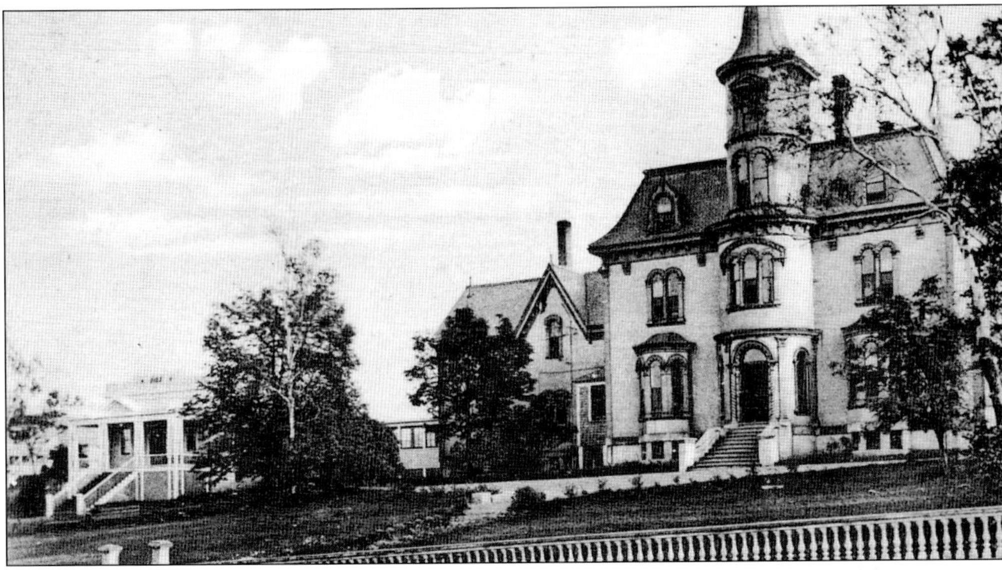

Jewett's Castle stood on Prince Street at Lancaster and had a magnificent view of the Reversing Falls and the lumbermill that the Jewett family had owned. It became a "Deaf and Dumb School" around the turn of the century. During World War I, it served as a soldier's hospital and recreation centre. After World War II, it was incorporated into a military hospital, which was torn down in the summer of 1994. (Erb Collection.)

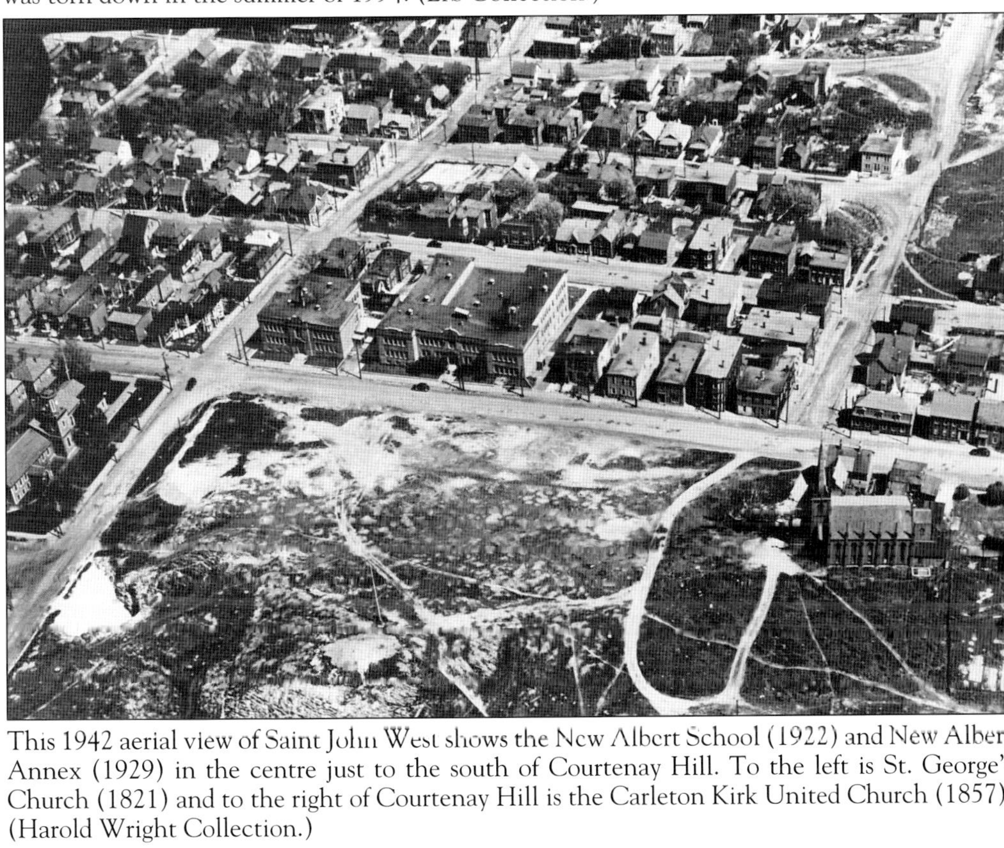

This 1942 aerial view of Saint John West shows the New Albert School (1922) and New Albert Annex (1929) in the centre just to the south of Courtenay Hill. To the left is St. George's Church (1821) and to the right of Courtenay Hill is the Carleton Kirk United Church (1857). (Harold Wright Collection.)

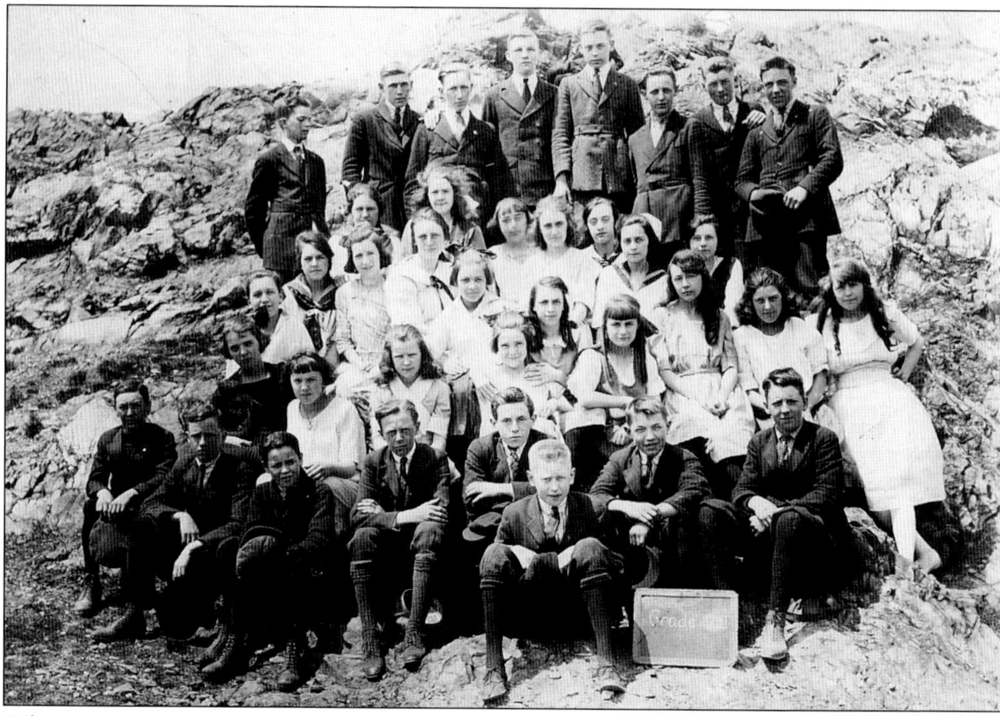

When it was time to take school photographs in 1922, George Cameron, shown to the left of the grade eight slate board, was one of those who posed on the rocks of Courtenay Hill just north of the New Albert School. (George Cameron Collection.)

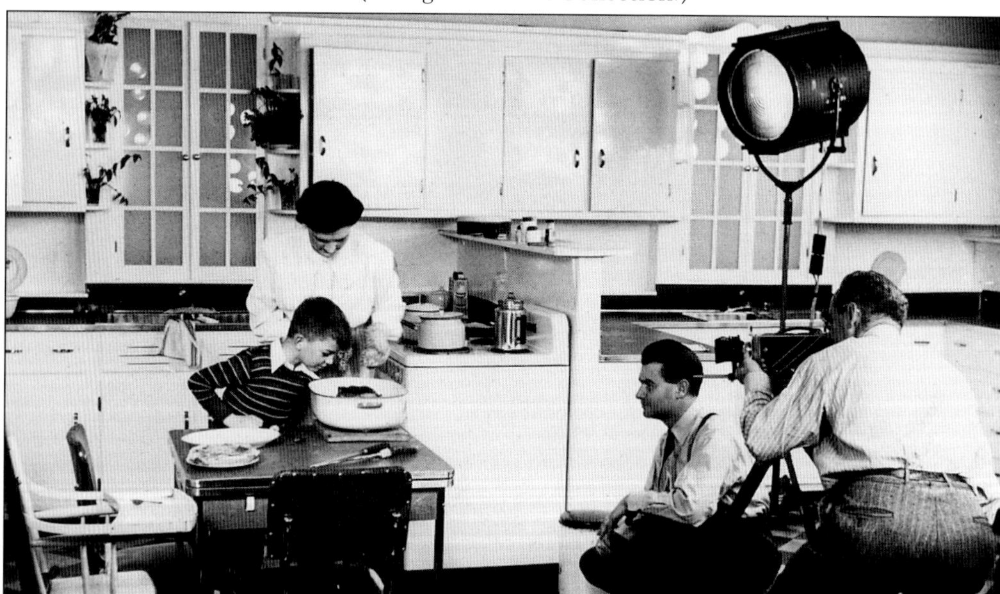

In the early 1950s the New Albert School received national recognition for its innovative home economics programs. The National Film Board made a film which was shown across Canada in recognition of their leadership in this field. (New Albert School, Margaret Kindred Scrapbook.)

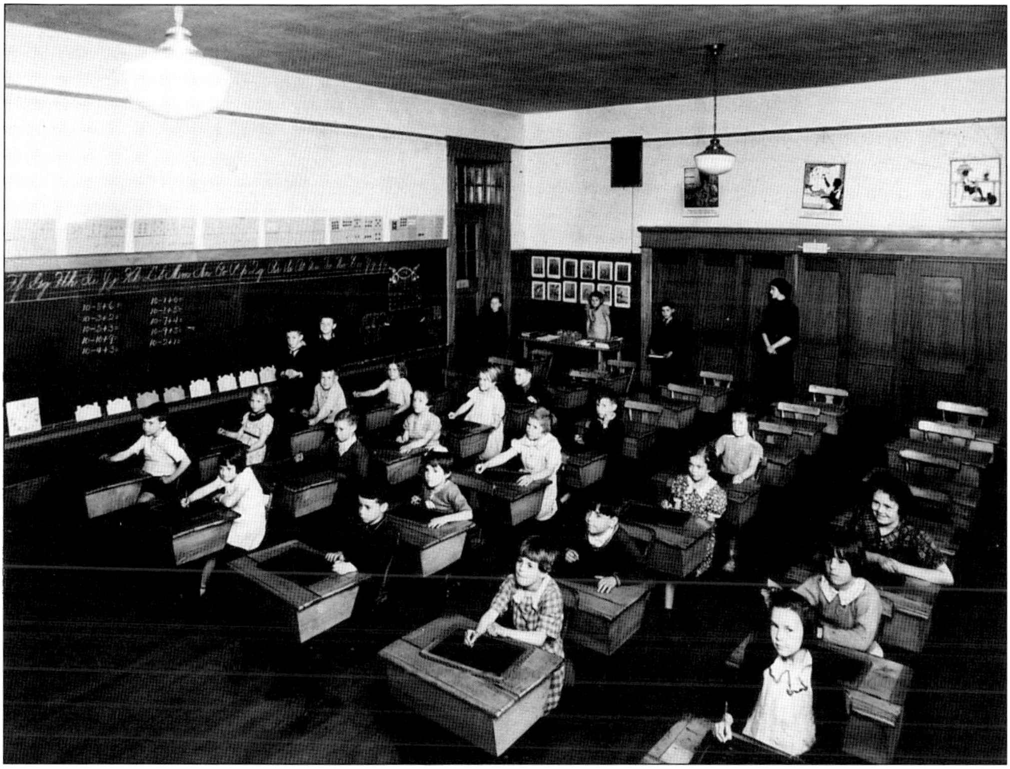

Miss Napier's classroom in the New Albert School in 1938 was fairly typical of classroom situations of the era. (Walter Lord Collection.)

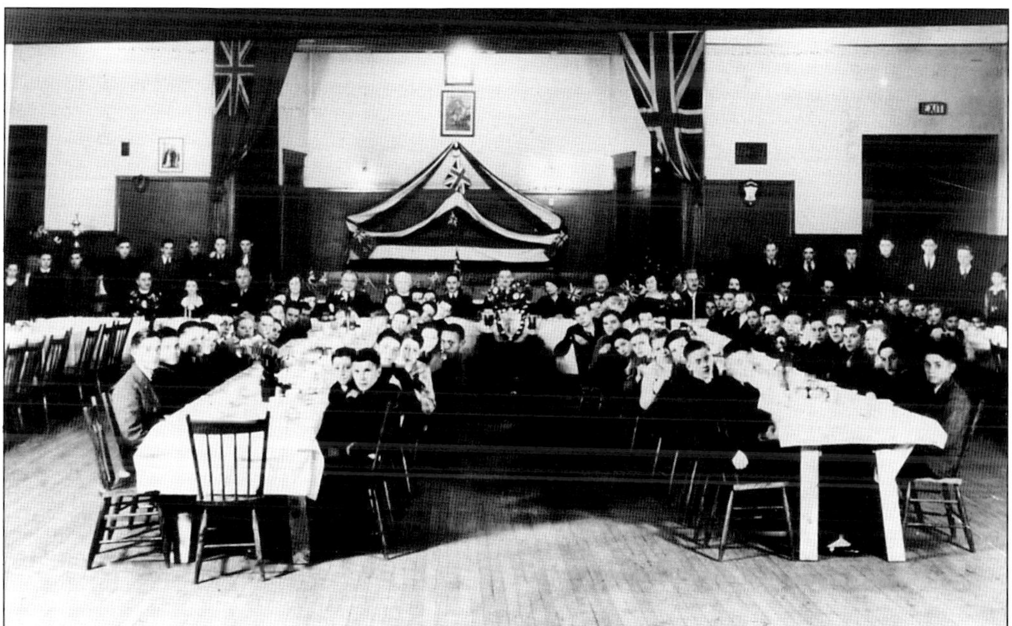

A gathering in the auditorium of the New Albert School for a banquet and awards presentation in 1948. (New Albert School, Margaret Kindred Scrapbook.)

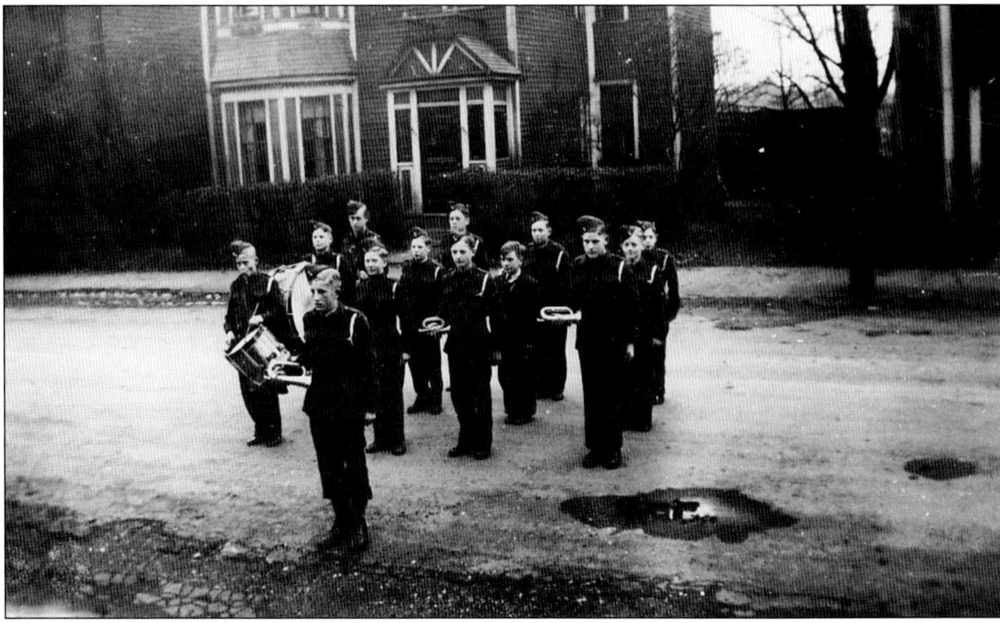

The New Albert Cadet Marching Band Troop #1 carrying out their drills on Guilford Street in preparation for a competition. This successful marching band received top marks for Maritime Canada on numerous occasions. (Malcolm Harned Collection.)

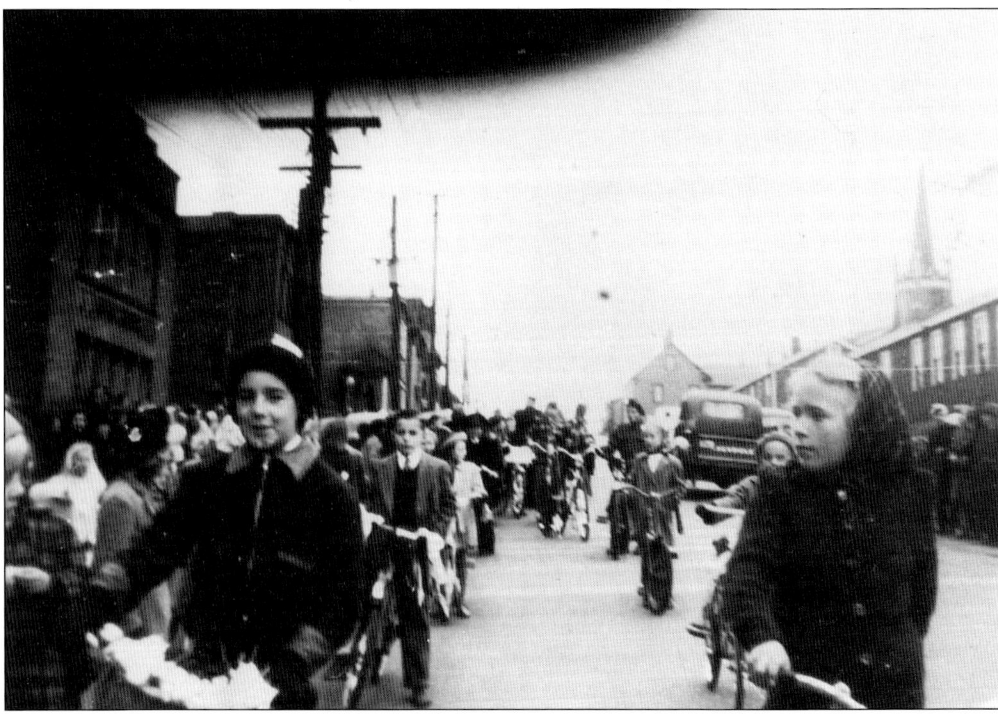

A children's parade opposite the New Albert School in 1949. At that time the World War II army huts shown at the right were still standing and were being used as temporary housing for veterans. The spire in the background is the Carleton Kirk Church which burned to the ground in 1973. (New Albert School, Margaret Kindred Scrapbook.)

Twelve

Saint John West and Its Neighbours

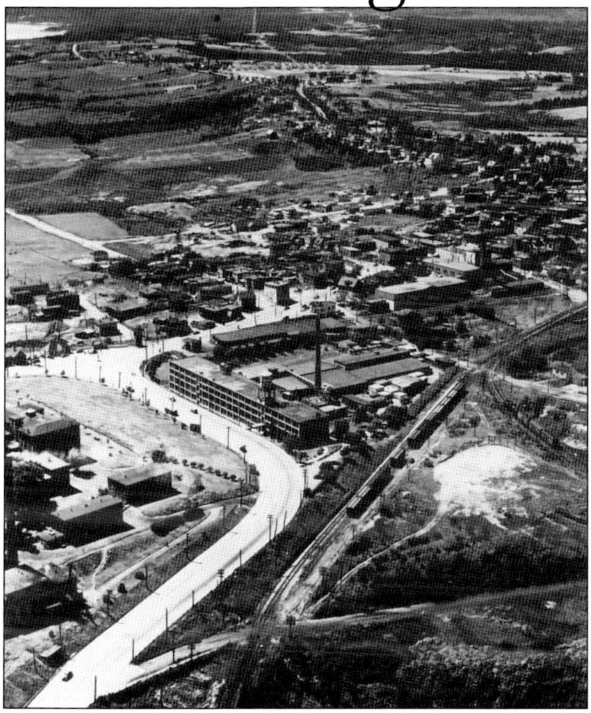

T.S. Simms built a huge brush-making operation on Bridge Road in Fairville in 1912. This factory is the one with twenty-five thousand windows on the right side of the road. On the left of the picture is the Provincial Asylum, now known as Centracare. Beyond the Simms Factory stretches Main Street, and the scattered settlements of the parish of Lancaster immediately west of Carleton, where many of the workers came to keep business humming. (Terry Keleher Collection.)

The foundries, lumberyards, railway lines, gravel pits, quarries, port facilities, and mercantile concerns of Saint John West all needed workers . . . many workers in the days before automation. There were not enough able-bodied men in Saint John West to fill all the positions that were needed, so men moved in from other communities as far away as Montreal in order to do the work, some permanently and some on a seasonal basis. The port also attracted those in outlying areas such as Beaconsfield, Fairville, Milford, Randolph, and Lorneville. Some workers moved into Saint John West for the winter, taking a flat near their work for four or five months, and then moved back to their homes and summer occupations such as fishing, lumbering, or quarrying.

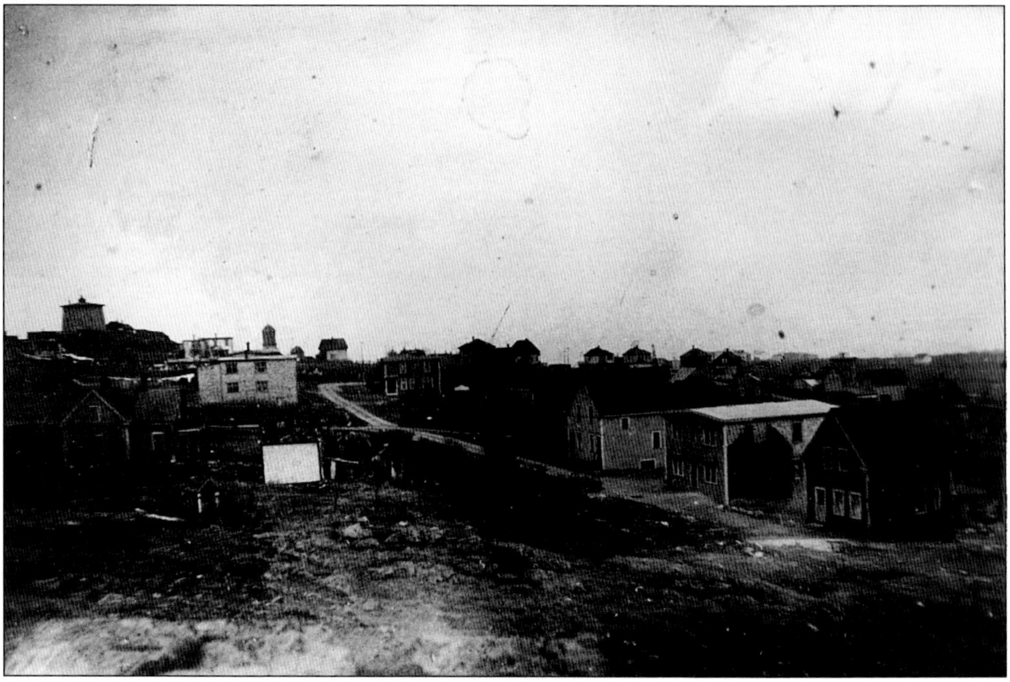

Pleasant Street (seen here) connected to Sea Street, which led from Martello Tower on the top of Tower Hill down to the ocean at Bay Shore where there were sand and pit operations that provided work for West Siders.

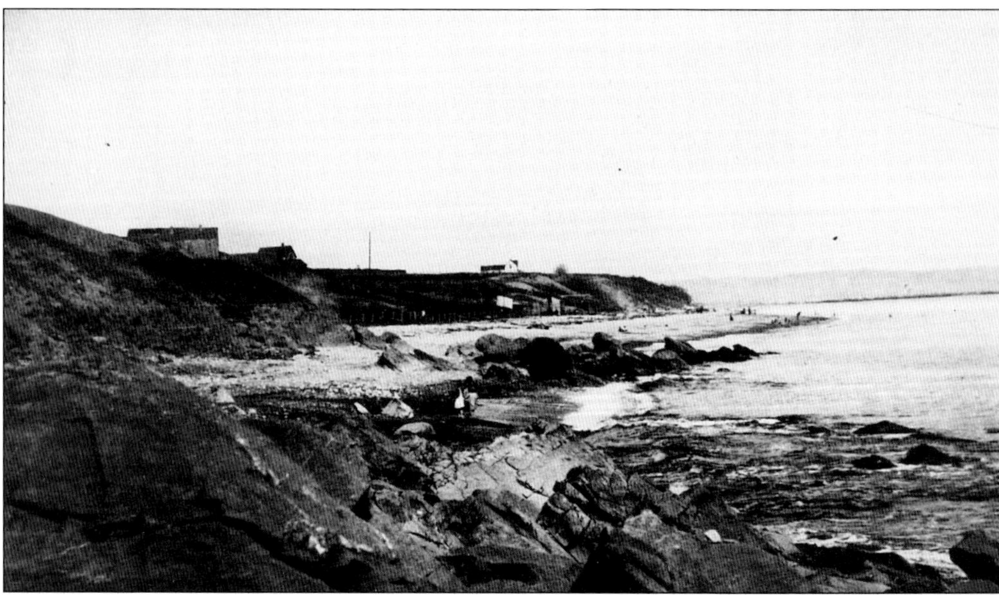

On the ridge behind Bay Shore Beach there were cottages and hotel accommodations, dance halls, and restaurants operated by enterprising local people for those who came to enjoy the beach in the early part of this century. (Erb Collection.)

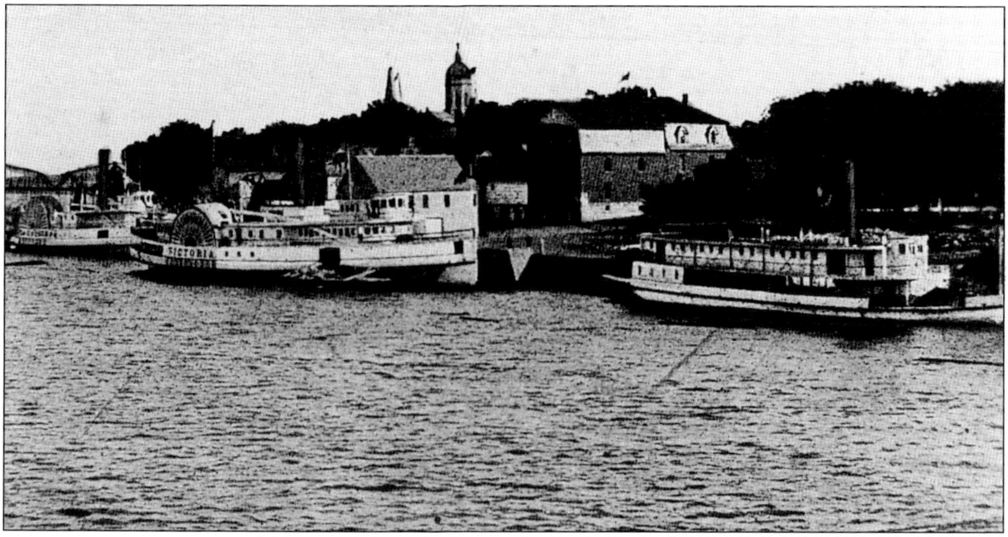

The riverboat *Victoria* is seen here at Fredericton. Today, Fredericton is about an hour's drive from Saint John, but when this photograph was taken about 1900 it would have taken two days by stagecoach. However, it could be reached by steamboat in six hours during the summer, so many West Siders would take the boat as a special outing. (Erb Collection.)

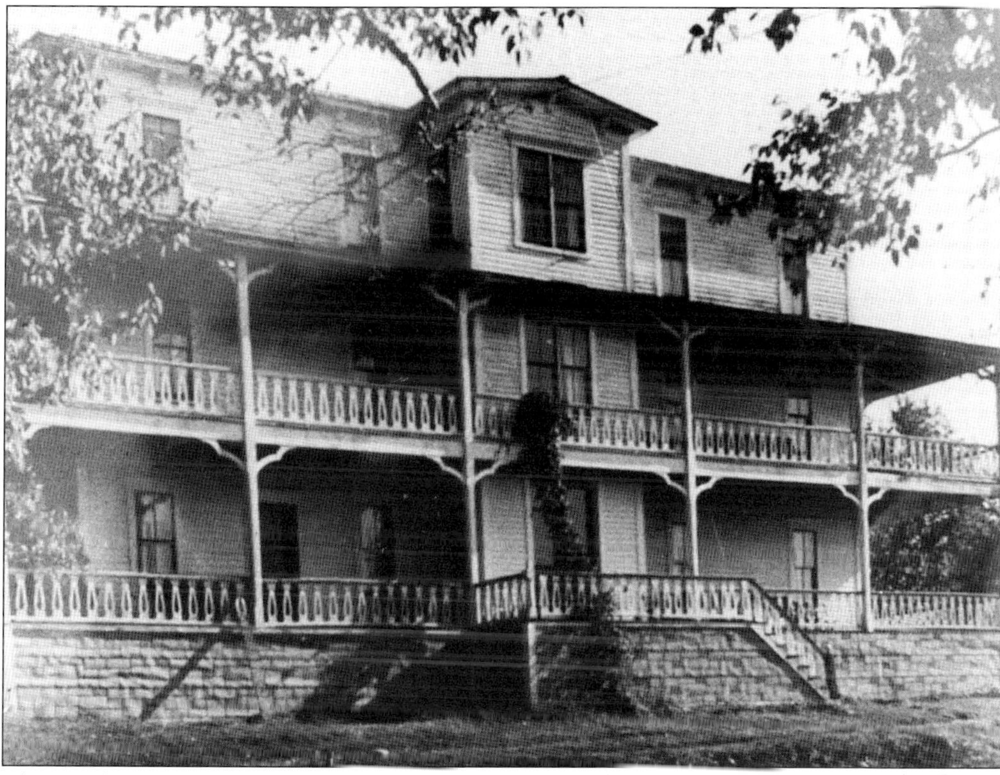

The riverboat would also take folks up the river to popular riverside hotels such as the Cedars which was on the Long Reach on the Kingston Peninsula, about an hour and a half from Saint John. Cyclists from Carleton liked to bike to the hotel, too, and take the riverboat home. (Saint John Regional Library Collection.)

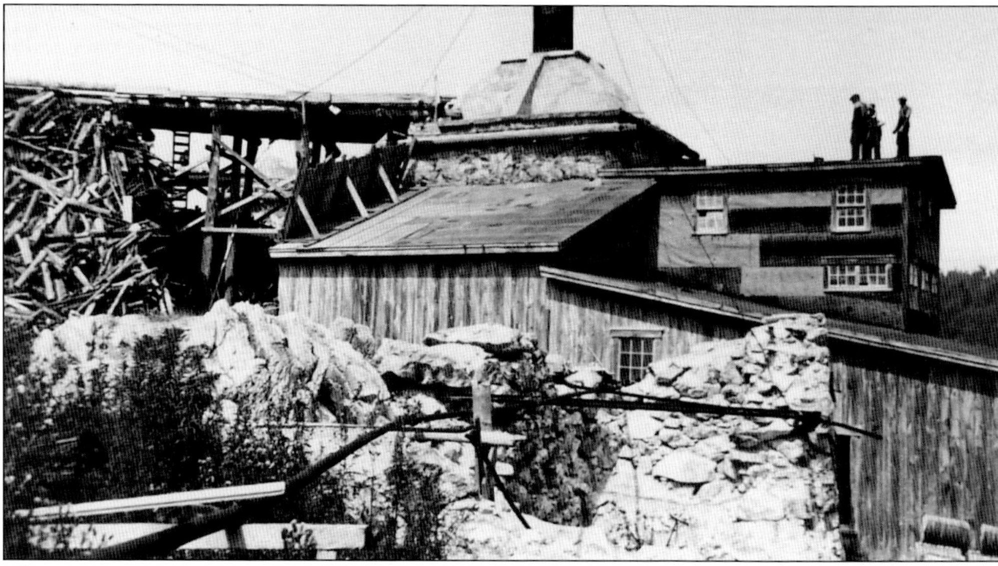

The quarrying operations in the Randolph area were an important source of income for men in the Saint John area during the summer months. Saint John West men would find work here if not enough men could be found in the Randolph area. The operation shown was part of the crushing and burning process that made the Greenhead limestone usable for cement. Much of it was exported to the eastern United States. (Saint John Regional Library Collection.)

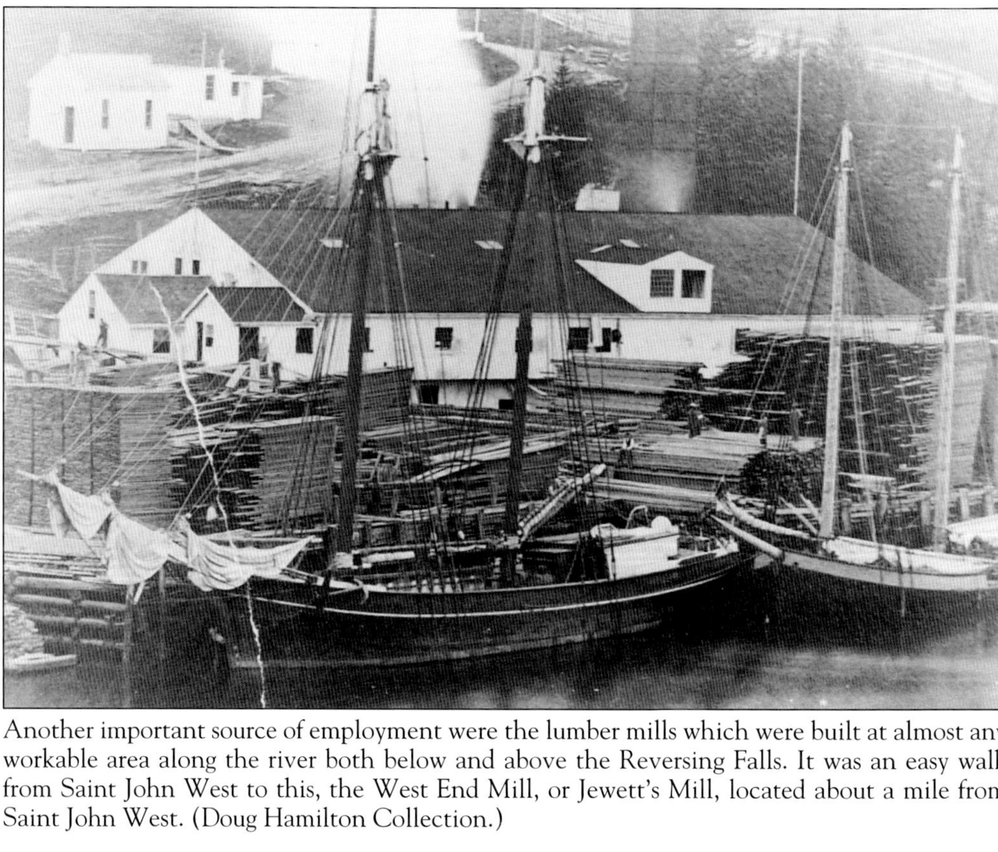

Another important source of employment were the lumber mills which were built at almost any workable area along the river both below and above the Reversing Falls. It was an easy walk from Saint John West to this, the West End Mill, or Jewett's Mill, located about a mile from Saint John West. (Doug Hamilton Collection.)

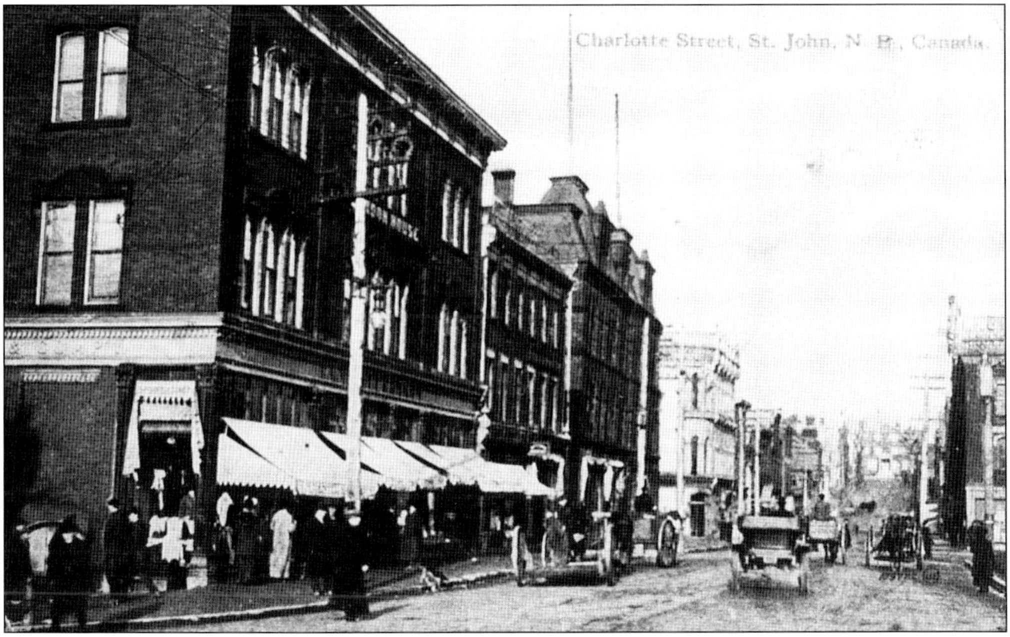

Uptown Saint John was easily reached by residents of Carleton by taking the ferry from Sand Point across the harbour to the foot of Princess Street and then walking up the steep hills of the central part of the city. This view shows Charlotte Street, which was one of the main business streets in the district. This turn-of-the-century postcard shows what were then relatively new buildings—uptown Saint John was completely rebuilt after the Great Port Fire of 1877. (Erb Collection.)

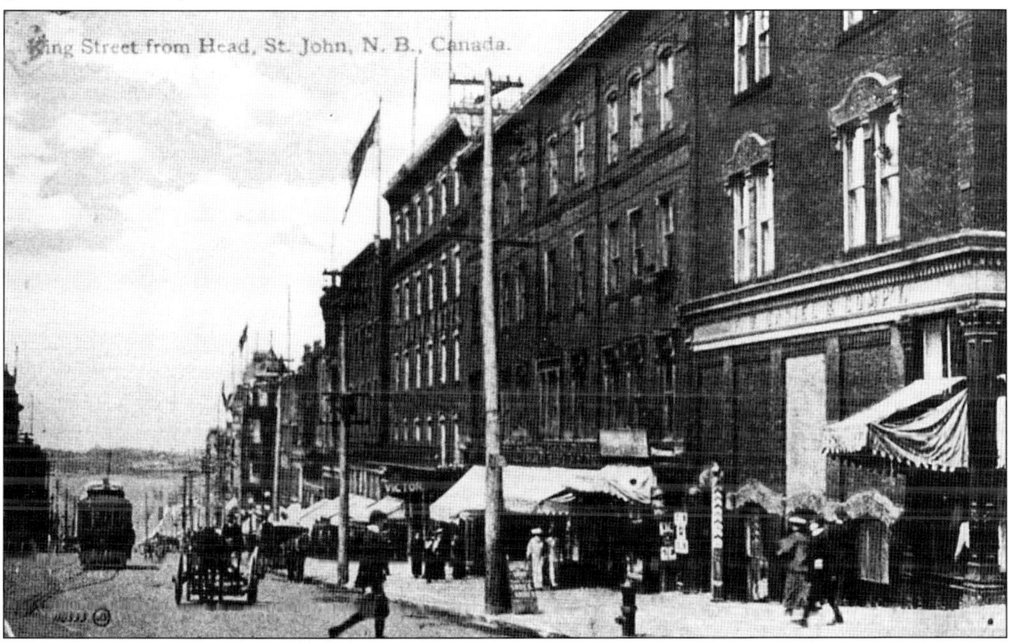

King Street is the shortest, steepest, widest Main Street in all of Canada. Note that traffic in this photograph is on the left side of the road. This didn't change to the right until December of 1922 in New Brunswick. (Erb Collection.)

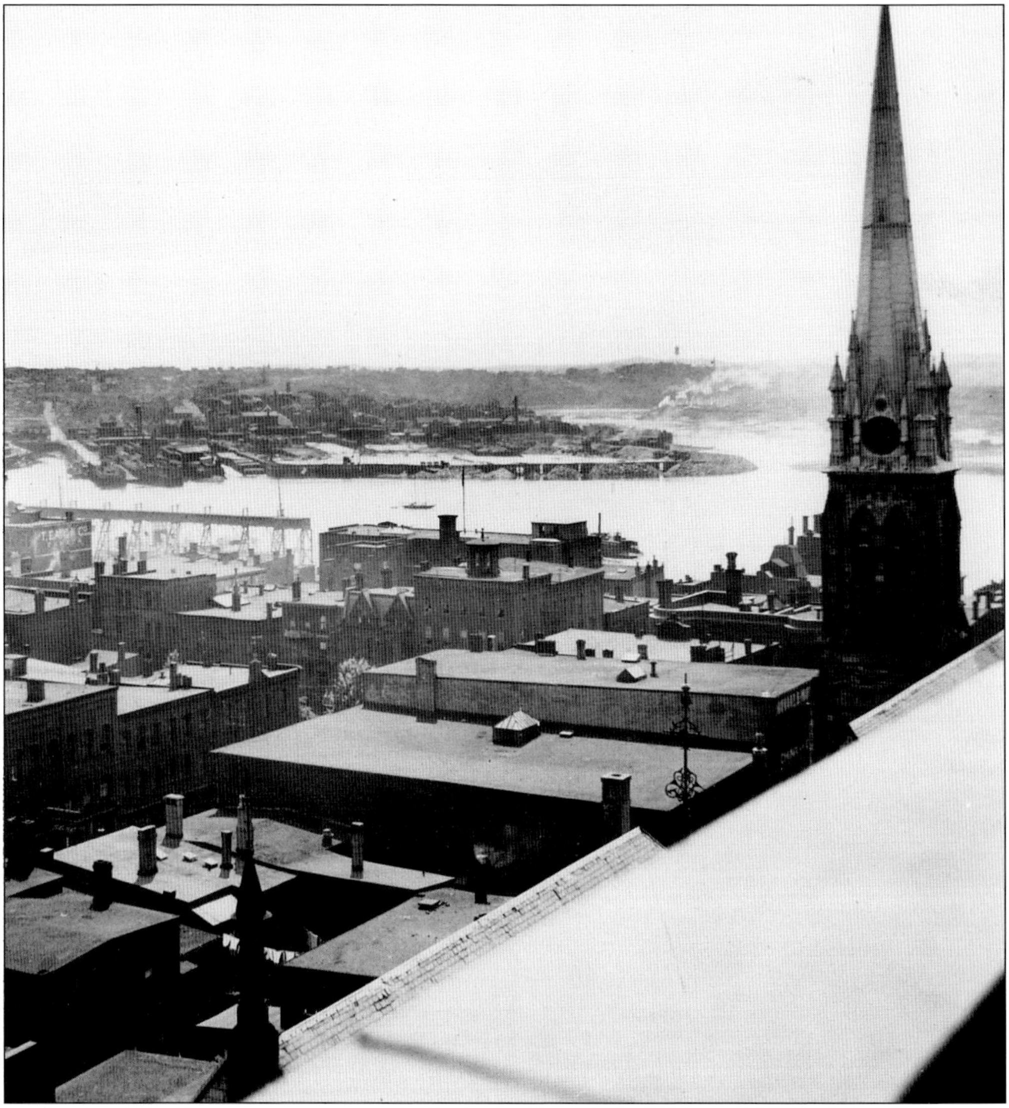

Our final view of Saint John West is a panorama from atop the Admiral Beatty Hotel and past the 210-foot spire of Trinity Church. The cofferdam which was built around what were then the Navy Island terminals can be seen across the harbour. This area is still in active use to this day as a forestry products terminal—but employs few men compared to years past.

We hope you've enjoyed this glimpse of Saint John West. Much has changed—but the spirit of the past is still a very real part of the fabric of the area. Each year, during the first weekend in June, "West Side Days" are celebrated with historic walks, church suppers, flea markets, ball games, boat tours, horse-drawn wagon rides, dances, and demonstrations that bring the community together to mark their common roots. Those who have read this book should consider themselves honorary West Siders, and come and join the fun!